MISSISSIPPI POETS

MISSISSIPPI POETS

A LITERARY GUIDE

Catharine Savage Brosman

with contributions by Olivia McNeely Pass

University Press of Mississippi / Jackson

The University Press of Mississippi is the scholarly publishing agency of
the Mississippi Institutions of Higher Learning: Alcorn State University,
Delta State University, Jackson State University, Mississippi State University,
Mississippi University for Women, Mississippi Valley State University,
University of Mississippi, and University of Southern Mississippi.

www.upress.state.ms.us

The University Press of Mississippi is a member
of the Association of University Presses.

First printing 2020
∞

Library of Congress Cataloging-in-Publication Data

Names: Brosman, Catharine Savage, 1934– author. | Pass, Olivia McNeely,
1946– contributor.
Title: Mississippi poets : a literary guide / Catharine Savage Brosman,
with contributions by Olivia McNeely Pass.
Description: Jackson : University Press of Mississippi, 2020. | Includes
bibliographical references and index.
Identifiers: LCCN 2020011832 (print) | LCCN 2020011833 (ebook) | ISBN
9781496829054 (hardback) | ISBN 9781496829061 (epub) | ISBN
9781496829078 (epub) | ISBN 9781496829085 (pdf) | ISBN 9781496829092 (pdf)
Subjects: LCSH: Poets, American—Mississippi—Biography. | Poets,
American—Mississippi—20th century. | BISAC: LITERARY CRITICISM / Poetry
Classification: LCC PS129 .B75 2020 (print) | LCC PS129 (ebook) | DDC
811.009/9762 [B]—dc23
LC record available at https://lccn.loc.gov/2020011832
LC ebook record available at https://lccn.loc.gov/2020011833

British Library Cataloging-in-Publication Data available

This book is dedicated to my daughter,
Katherine Brosman Deimling,
and her family,
and to the memory of my parents and Patric Savage

CONTENTS

Contents

PREFACE

The present investigation has as its purpose to introduce forty-seven poets associated with Mississippi in the twentieth and twenty-first centuries and assess their work with the aim of *appreciating* it, in the full sense of the word. Intended to be of broad interest and easy to consult, the study is thus a showcase as well as an *état présent* of Mississippi poetry. It introduces readers to the poets themselves, forms, collections of verse, and even individual poems particularly representative or striking.

The state has produced outstanding writers in numbers out of proportion to the population. David A. Davis is not alone in holding that Mississippi writers "made a disproportionate contribution to American literature" in the first half of the twentieth century (and, it must be added, since then) (in Watkins 102). In quality likewise, the body of writing coming from the state is exceptional, even for the South. In the preface to their 1979 anthology of Mississippi writers, Noel Polk and James Scafidel pronounced "incredible" the number of fine prose writers and poets connected, in one way or another, to the state. A promoter of Georgia literature was obliged to acknowledge that it fell short of the standards set by Mississippi (Watkins ix). The poetry of this rich literary heritage, acknowledged already nearly one hundred years ago in the anthology *Mississippi Poets* by Ernestine Clayton Deavours, has developed tremendously since. Among its most famous figures, from the present vantage point, are William Faulkner, Etheridge Knight, William Alexander Percy, Sterling D. Plumpp, Natasha Trethewey, Margaret Walker, and Richard Wright. Percy is less widely known presently than the others, but he is an important figure nonetheless, as a moralist in a new key.

The accomplishments and renown of those included vary widely. The grounds for selection may include connections between the poets (and their

poetry) and the state; the scope, excellence, and abundance of their work (usually two collections or more); its critical reception; and their local and national
standing. Natives of Mississippi and others who have resided there were equally
eligible for consideration. In *Lives of Mississippi Authors, 1817–1967*, James B.
Lloyd used the figure of fifteen years of residence as a general marker for
admission; the present standard is more generous. C. Liegh McInnis looked
at the matter more organically. "You do not have to be born in Mississippi to
be a Mississippi writer. . . . Some of your time and work must be invested in
discussing Mississippi from the standpoint of someone who has lived there. . . .
If what happens in Mississippi has an immediate and definite effect on your
work, you are a Mississippi writer" ("New African American Writers"). Illustrating the truth of that observation are poets such as Ann Fisher-Wirth, Derrick
Harriell, and Angela Ball, an Ohio native who became, as it were, native to Mississippi, and stated: "Every poem I write is Mississippian" (Zheng, "Interview
with Angela Ball," 17).

The poets' personalities and concerns range tremendously. Versatility marks
many of them. Some are fiction writers also, some performing musicians, some
painters, one a woodworker, and many, of course, teachers at various levels and,
for the women, "domestic engineers." Included in the number are a business-
man, a professor of medicine, a civil servant in the Department of the Navy,
important figures in the avant-garde of New York and Paris, and poets with
scientific backgrounds and careers. Their family backgrounds are diverse, as
are ethnic strains and beliefs they represent: African American, white, Native
American, Christian, Jewish. That men far outnumber women is a fact; commentators may wish to look for explanations.

Readers should note that though the Pulitzer Prize–winning novelist Eudora
Welty published verse, she has no entry in this book, because the genre was
a marginal one for her and she has no collected poems. Tennessee Williams,
likewise a native of the state, does not appear here, although he published
two collections of poetry; because of his close connection to New Orleans,
he is treated in the companion volume to this one, *Louisiana Poets*. Omitted
are certain famous figures such as Hodding Carter Jr., Stark Young, and Polk,
whose verse—a volume or so—is a minor part of their production and about
whom researchers may find information in numerous sources. Those authors
who wrote entirely or principally in the nineteenth century are not included.
(Many Mississippians of the period, men and women alike, whatever their
standing, published one or two volumes of verse.)

Since the 1960s there have been only five poets laureate of Mississippi.
(According to an authority, recent governors have not always followed the
recommendations of the Mississippi Arts Commission—a position that does

not invalidate, of course, the governors' choices.) Two of these poets laureate, Trethewey and Beth Ann Fennelly, are treated here. The others were Maude Willard Leet Prenshaw, who published under the name Leet, Louise Moss Montgomery, and Winifred Hamrick Farrar. They were active, variously, in teaching and promoting poetry through the Mississippi Poetry Society and other channels, and all published verse. Their book-length publications are almost impossible to obtain, however, and their careers do not bear comparison with those of Trethewey and Fennelly, both widely published professional poets of more than local fame. The perspective of time allows critics to exclude material too restricted in appeal, or too remote in style or attitudes, following outdated poetic usages. Thus the three just named, like earlier poets laureate, are not considered. As late as 1992, Elmo Howell wrote of such figures: "Mississippi lay poets write with Victorian clarity and fervor" (*Mississippi Scenes*, 53).

Dorothy Abbott's 1988 volume on poetry in her four-volume anthology *Mississippi Writers: Reflections of Childhood and Youth* includes work by 112 poets. While the subtitle of the series may explain the inclusion of some and the omission of others, the anthology provides a fair sampling of writing available at the time of publication; clearly, the poetic harvest was abundant. Not all these poets are examined below, however; the principles of anthologizing may differ considerably from those of literary history. For instance, certain poets chosen by Abbott are known chiefly for one or two poems, perhaps representative of Mississippi and often reprinted, but the poets occupy a marginal place in state literary history.

The methods of presentation and assessment here are those of conventional literary history, biography, and criticism. The author takes into account social and cultural contexts. Evaluation and interpretation of the poetry itself are based on close textual study and use of recognized aesthetic criteria, especially those concerning verse forms and taste applicable to the period. Although proposing no narrow model of what makes a "good poem," and understanding that aesthetic preferences inevitably enter into assessments, she eschews the extreme artistic latitudinarianism of today, deriving from postmodernism, which, denouncing hierarchy, places all art on the same plane. The word *art*, then, means simply what you want it to mean. That is senseless, and poems can truly fail. When and how, according to both critics' and poets' aims and criteria, is thus a pertinent part of the study. Given such criteria, which vary with the time and are never universally acknowledged anyhow—now less than previously—disagreements on evaluations are bound to arise; but the conclusions concerning any poet or work constitute a bona fide effort to provide balanced and judicious studies and avoid advocacy—except for the art of poetry itself and those who pursue it with success.

The alphabetical arrangement does not imply a cursory listing, and the author has endeavored to reduce the monotony invited by such a structure. Poets are identified and portrayed, with recognition of their connections to places where they were born or matured and plied their trade. Without intensive probing, the study suggests what makes poets and poetry, and how they work. That autobiography and other self-depictions, direct or indirect, receive attention frequently is to be expected. (Postmodern efforts by critics and poets to challenge the coherence of the text and challenge the authority of the voice do not dominate Mississippi poetry, even in the year 2020.) "However deep and obscure even to the writer," asked Robert Penn Warren, "isn't poetry always autobiography?" (quoted in Simpson 144). "Each book [of poetry] published is, however obliquely, an autobiography" (McFee 15). Or, as Benoîte Groult put it, "One writes with one's blood, ultimately, or one's viscera, or one's nerves. In any case, with one's unhappiness" (330).

Readers will note quotations from back-cover endorsements. These are not, obviously, intended as objective assessments; they emanate from friends and friendly critics and are promotional. Still, they are not valueless. They suggest ways of approaching the book, some of which reviewers follow. Additionally, they may indicate reception of a poet's previous books and public profile.

Quoted verse (limited to four sequential lines) is normally identified by poem title and, where needed, section number or name of collection, or by page number in cases where the poems are untitled or there is other justification. (Numerical citations within parentheses reference page numbers unless otherwise indicated.) Copyright law forbids quotation from very short poems without express permission (often difficult to obtain or expensive). Secondary sources utilized include, in addition to reviews, interviews, and literary studies (printed or online), e-mail exchanges and conversations with poets. Such exchanges, written or oral, with the present author are listed in the primary sources section of the bibliography as "Interviews," under the respective poets' names. In addition to the lists of primary and secondary sources, readers are referred to poets' individual web sites, state and institutional sites (notably the Mississippi Writers Page), and other materials easily located by a search engine. The index furnishes cross-references, identifying personal and aesthetic connections among poets.

The author is indebted to Olivia McNeely Pass, who contributed the entries on Ellen Gilchrist, Angela Jackson, Etheridge Knight, Natasha Trethewey, and Richard Wright. Thanks go likewise to staff at the Howard-Tilton Memorial Library of Tulane University and at the Fondren Library of Rice University, especially Lee Pecht, former director of Special Collections. Many poets provided information and copies of their publications; the author appreciates greatly their assistance. She thanks also Dr. David Middleton, who provided certain references, and Dr. Patricia J. Teed of Austin, Texas, friend of many decades, eager helper.

The author gratefully acknowledges permission from John P. Freeman to cite five consecutive lines of "The Sanitary Landfill" from *Illusion on the Louisiana Side.*

MISSISSIPPI POETS

INTRODUCTION

Poetry is central to human culture. Neither incidental, nor a mere decoration, it has an important function. Robert Penn Warren considered it as the "extreme resource of language-knowledge, of language being" (quoted in Bedient 3). William Faulkner wrote that the genre partook of the broad aim of all literature: "to uplift man's heart" (*Faulkner Reader* x). "The highest duty of art is to be uplifting," said Claude Wilkinson (DeFatta 47). Simon Armitage, appointed poet laureate of the United Kingdom in 2019 for a ten-year term, views poetry as especially meaningful to the present time. Putting the matter in stark contemporary terms, he said, as quoted in the *Independent* (May 10, 2019) that "in a hectic and sometimes frenetic age the combination of considered thought and crafted language is more relevant and vital than ever" ("Simon Armitage Named Poet Laureate"). Poetry makes readers slow down and savor each word as well as the rhythm of the whole.

The place of poetry in American artistic and civic culture presently is extensive; poetry is a profession. States, cities, and some counties, as well as the nation, have a poet laureate; as Billy Collins observed, the country is crawling with them. Poetry is cultivated in schools, universities, prisons, libraries. The Association of Writers and Writing Programs, the largest national conference of writers, which counts among its nearly 50,000 individual and institutional members a large number of poets, underwrites 125 writers' conferences and centers and itself puts on, according to Wikipedia, the largest literary conference in North America, where poetry plays a major role.

It is not only the poetry landscape in America that has changed; poets themselves, or their lives, have. With the advent of writing curricula in colleges and universities—not just the study of literature but a vocational track—lay or "Sunday" poets were succeeded by full-time dealers in words, paid by public or private institutions to teach their craft to the next generations and turn out their own work in abundance. While earning one's living as a poet, through publication and lectures, was not unknown in the late nineteenth and early twentieth centuries, the practices cannot be called widespread, and the term *professionalism* in poetry would not have been used routinely, if at all. Except for a few nationally known figures, to write poetry in Mississippi was an avocation, widely shared but generally confined to local scenes and genteel circles, where new twentieth-century styles had penetrated slowly, if at all. Now, small publishing houses welcoming verse have multiplied around the nation, even as most large trade houses have ceased issuing any. Public readings are no longer limited by an author's fame nor confined to poetry societies. Colleges sponsor presentations by their own staff and visiting poets, and slams and radio readings, along with poetry journals, online publications, and modest newsletters, provide much greater opportunity for the art to prosper—not in quantity alone, in fact, but in quality.

By now, virtually all American poets have been exposed to and been influenced by what Gary Davenport called "classical modernism" (although some may not recognize it); many have embraced its sequels, whether postmodernism or the formalist reaction to it (foreword to Shirley et al., *Rilke's Children*). Willy-nilly, modernism changed Anglo-American verse profoundly; the aesthetic criteria and preferences recognized in the Victorian and Georgian periods—including clarity and fervor but also sentimentality—were overturned in favor of irony. As Mark Royden Winchell observed, although modernism affected southern letters slowly, it was southern critics who promulgated most energetically the rule of irony, and their influence has not ceased (Rubin et al. 314). By 1950, the new standards of the avant-garde had penetrated generally into American poetic consciousness.

One consequence among many was the revolution in prosody (the move to free form) and the rejection of rhetoric and eloquence in favor of images. No more Tennyson. *Naked Poetry: Recent American Poetry in Open Forms* (1969), an anthology edited by Stephen Berg and Robert Mezey, showed how rejection of premodernist verse had triumphed almost entirely. A hundred years after the great modernists, the image (visual or as figure of speech, or both) still prevails as the touchstone of much poetry, and free verse outpaces formal verse, particularly among Mississippi poets, by a large margin. Yet skill with formal verse is not missing, frequently among authors who also write good free verse. Such see-sawing through literary modes was visible in earlier periods—the pursuit of the new in reaction to fixed forms and styles, the quasi triumph of the new, then reaction and a turn back toward classic styles. The results of such fashions are, however, unpredictable; novelty does not mimic the "new" styles of the past, nor do formal readjustments mean simply a reprise of earlier modes.

Against this backdrop of national trends, regional writing has not lost everywhere the prestige it had in earlier decades; it remains vigorous. Perhaps because of powerful homogenizing tendencies, fostered by television, movies, and near-instant communication by electronic devices, the need for a sense of place in the psyche of many Americans may even have increased; or they have become more conscious of place and their need to identify with it. Eudora Welty wrote, "Perhaps it is the sense of place that gives us the belief that passionate things, in some essence, endure" (128). Yet, as Brion McClanahan remarked, the label *regional poet* "often implies . . . a slight and academic classification as second-rate."

Whatever the reasons, although writing here generally postdates the civil rights movement—rejecting explicitly Jim Crow and colonialist attitudes—very little is postmodern. No matter how advanced the positions they take on social issues, Mississippi poets, with few exceptions, have not endeavored to overturn language and the rationality it has long reflected. Might this reflect pride in their heritage? And the conviction that they are not obliged to follow all trends? Nor, apparently, do these poets wish simply to adhere to what Anne Waldman called "the official verse literati culture academic mainstream"—that is, writing-workshop products without originality (quoted in Fried). To write as authorities from elsewhere propose, or dictate, would be to accept a new colonialism.

Aesthetic and practical questions arise. Is a writer impoverished today by rejecting poetic radicalism? Perhaps. Ezra Pound insisted, "Make it new!" From the advent, well over two hundred years ago, of the literary and cultural movement called Romanticism, with its emphasis on the idiosyncratic and its particular way of feeling, those who have opposed it have often been in the shadows, considered rigid, narrow, inhibited. Postmodernism of the late twentieth and early twenty-first centuries, a prolongation of the Romantic rebellion, may inspire similar scorn of established styles. The primitive and infantilist postmodernist aspiration toward, or demand for, formlessness appears to fit current manifestations of anarchy and thus be both true and suitable.

Yet, over the past hundred years and more, the supposition that verse is best when it is most obscure and directed only to select readers has harmed the art a great deal. Thus, might readers benefit by skepticism toward contemporary radicalism? More than one wave of poets and critics in the period has proclaimed what amounts to a new classicism. Poems in plain language remain appealing; the audience for Robert Frost's work includes true connoisseurs as well as less sophisticated readers. Numerous critics today agree with Yvor Winters, who deplored the stylistic affectation and willing obfuscation of much modernist verse and rejected Pound's understanding of the image ("that which presents an intellectual and emotional complex in an instant of time"). Winters argued instead for plain statement, or what he called the "post-symbolist" poem (*Forms of Discovery* 3–4): one with striking, dominant images, based on carefully controlled association, but utilizing traditional verse and governed by rationality. In such a poem, sensuous descriptive details carry meaning on both the literal and symbolic levels. Notwithstanding the effectiveness of "plain statement," it is certain that in today's poetry scene, achieving wide appeal and yet, by artfulness, not forfeiting standing entirely among the literary elite is a considerable challenge.

Mississippi has been home to dozens of accomplished poets, who have contributed to the phenomenon noted in the preface: the disproportionately large number of outstanding writers from the state. Readers will note time and again the facility displayed by many—not superficiality, but the effect of ease and simplicity in treating challenging forms and topics

Do the place, and its history, make the poet? But then the poet makes, that is, re-creates, the place. The state does seem to be generous with talent. Freeman reported that when he joined the MFA program at the University of Arkansas, a large one (some forty students in fiction and poetry), six were from Mississippi, and they were the stars; and their star poetry teacher, James Whitehead, was a Mississippian. Generous *to* talent likewise, and welcoming, both to natives and those who settle there. The privately funded Mississippi Institute of Arts and Letters, created in 1978 by Noel Polk, Aubrey Lucas, and others, has been instrumental in supporting poets by cash grants. Three cities and their universities have been significant poles of literary activity and achievement. They are Oxford in the north, with its historic university and rich literary heritage; Hattiesburg in the south, with the University of Southern Mississippi and its Center for Writers, founded more than thirty years ago; and Jackson, the capital and true cultural center of the state. It is home not only to Jackson State University, Millsaps College, and other four-year institutions in the immediate area, but also to the Mississippi Symphony Orchestra, a prestigious ballet company, and the Mississippi Museum of Art. Square Books in Oxford, an outstanding independent book shop, and Lemuria Books in Jackson, among other bookstores, are both sign and instrument of literary culture. The Yoknapatawpha Press in Oxford has supported poetry by issuing numerous collections.

A fourth literary hub, the home of many important literary figures, is Greenville. It is the chief river city of the state and the queen of the surrounding Delta, a large alluvial floodplain between the Mississippi River and the Yazoo. In his book title James C. Cobb called it "the most southern place on earth." Both Oxford and Greenville are tied, culturally, to Memphis, where according to David Cohn, "Mississippi begins" (quoted in Watkins 106). The southern part of the state, in contrast, has been connected historically and environmentally to the Gulf Coast and New Orleans. "Location," wrote Welty, "is the crossroads of circumstance . . . and that is the heart's field" (118).

Yet James B. Lloyd found little in common, beyond the facts of birth or residence, among those included in his compendium, *Lives of Mississippi Authors, 1817–1967*. "The fact is that a transient, melting pot society gives the lie to all arguments for environmental determination in culture" (xi). His conclusion was due, perhaps, to the huge corpus of figures and the breadth of genres he treated. Certainly one can identify in the present study many shared markers, enough to suggest influential, if not determining, factors, examined below.

While Mississippi has provided a stable foundation and firm centering to many of its authors, many others have been expatriates, constituting a centrifugal force. Some, such as Maxwell Bodenheim, Charles Henri Ford, and Turner Cassity, became entirely cosmopolitan, disconnecting themselves from their state; others have remained connected, even attributing to their move elsewhere the maturation of their art and perhaps their ability to draw on their background. Lewis Nordan, a fiction writer from Jackson, commented on the importance of exile in providing a point of view, an understanding. "We will always be Mississippians—we will return to its swamps and cross its bridges and hear the stories, its rhythms will be our ritual, people will know us by them. And yet we could not write of our sweet home until we were gone from it. . . . We ache for Mississippi, but to its rich images and good people we are blinded by its light. . . . Still, we carry it in us . . ." (Abbott, *Reflections* 404). Sterling D. Plumpp, who settled in Chicago, drew from its blues music much of his inspiration; but those blues originated in the Delta and were already in his mind and ears. Authors who chose to remain on their native soil, or returned there, have drawn from it not only their materials but the deep sympathy that allows a writer to depict and gloss on a place.

Lest readers suspect that, after all, most Mississippi writers, living there or elsewhere, have been parochial, unaware of the rest of the world, one should observe how frequently modern wars have furnished material for them. Starting with Faulkner's poems on aviation in World War I, one can follow the vein to the present time. It passes through Hubert Creekmore, who published *The Long Reprieve and Other Poems from New Caledonia* (1946), based on his experience with the Navy in the South Pacific during World War II; D. C. Berry, a medical corpsman in Vietnam, the author of *saigon cemetery* (1972); Brooks Haxton, who underlines that conflict in *Dead Reckoning* (1989); and Sibyl Pittman Estess and her poem "Texas Memorial" (on the Vietnam dead) in *Blue, Candled in January Sun* (2005); finally, George Drew and his poems on the American-Iraqi war in *The View from Jackass Hill* (2011). Etheridge

Knight's poem "At a VA Hospital in the Middle of the United States of America" is a dramatic homage to American wounded from three wars. The topic of war will repel certain readers of this study; others will find acquaintance with these war poems rewarding.

Whether in their state or elsewhere, Mississippi poets, like their novelist and dramatist kin, illustrate what may be designated, broadly, as the Mississippi imagination, or what Lloyd called "a particular Mississippi temper" (xi). Not all, but many of these figures have drawn deeply on local resources, observed and remembered, to create in their verse what amounts to an indigenous and unique expression of their land. Many could subscribe to the words of Freeman: "Mississippi *is* the subject of my poetry" (Interview). While this understanding of subject and subject matter may not be unique, it is noteworthy; along with social and political factors, which it embraces, it sheds light on the fascination Mississippi writing has exercised over readers elsewhere—as well as Mississippi over its writers. By placing themselves as voices within their communities, they have not given the lie to what Fred Hobson identified as the "rage to explain" (quoted in Watkins 247).

Of course such writing shares many features, historically and presently, with other products of the South. It is nevertheless particular enough to be recognizable to many connoisseurs of literature and has been cultivated for popular consumption. If questioned on what the term meant, readers might suggest "magnolias and magnolia-like young women," "slaves sold downriver and backs bent over cotton fields," "gunboats," "great floods and great hurricanes," "the flight north," "old families, high-class" or "old families, white trash," "sit-ins, riots," "the Klan," and even less favorable images; or a reader could simply say "Yoknapatawpha." Time and again poets writing even today demonstrate by their topics and metaphors how central these themes and motifs have been to Mississippi writing, erudite and popular. The recurring motif of blues (and sometimes jazz), belongs to numerous poets, furnishing aesthetic principles and a vision.

Why poetry should have flourished so well in the state ranked repeatedly last or near last in the United States for literacy and other measures of educational achievement, healthcare, and prosperity can be only a matter of speculation, never of fact. As Willie Morris put it, Mississippi, ironically, "remains at the bottom in the whole of the great American republic in social and educational and human services while perhaps being first in creativity and imagination and artistic accomplishment." According to Morris, the "remarkable literary tradition derives from the complexity of a society which still, despite the conflicts of technological change, retained well into the late twentieth century much of its communal origins and along with that a sense of continuity, of the abiding land and the enduring past and the flow of the generations. . . ." It has been suggested, he adds, that Mississippi has produced so many fine writers "because the state is such a complicated place that much interpretation is required" (95).

The history of Mississippi is complex. Although the Spanish—Álvar Núñez Cabeza de Vaca and Hernando de Soto—explored the territory tentatively in the first half of the sixteenth century, the French were the first European claimants. Robert Cavelier, Sieur de La Salle descended the Mississippi River to its mouth in 1682 and applied the name *la Louisiane* to the entire river basin. Pierre Le Moyne d'Iberville, a French Canadian, explored the Gulf Coast, and in 1699 landed with his men at Ship Island, in the Mississippi Sound, and then set foot on the mainland and founded the first permanent settlement, called (Old) Biloxi or Bilocci (or Fort Maurepas), now Ocean Springs. It briefly served as the capital. Subsequently Iberville learned, it is asserted, from an Indian the portage from the river to Bayou St. John, which leads to Lake Pontchartrain (Louisiana)—a crucial connection. In 1718 Iberville's brother, Jean-Baptiste Le Moyne de Bienville, established the city of New Orleans. Natchez preceded it, being founded in 1716.

Established thus as a French foothold on the Gulf Coast, the entire territory, quite vast, remained under French sovereignty until 1763, when, by the Treaty of Paris, England received nearly all French territory east of the Mississippi River and Spain received the lands to the west. The latter were ceded back to France in 1800, then transferred to the United States by the Louisiana Purchase in 1803. Most territory east of the river remained under Spanish occupation until, following new treaties and territorial disputes, American soldiers occupied Natchez in 1798. The cultural and ethnic influence of France and its language endured into statehood (1817) and long thereafter, especially in certain areas; the term *Creole* (in its sense of "whites born in the colony") applied to many in Mississippi as well as Louisiana. The Spanish likewise left their mark, long visible also in Florida. Under the French and Spanish, the principal, indeed nearly sole, religion was Roman Catholicism.

The characteristics of place likewise are destiny, shaping human time. "Geography is fate," in Natasha Trethewey's term (Turner, "Southern Crossings"). The state has always been rural, even with twentieth- and twenty-first-century industry; after population growth in the twenty-first century there are still only seven cities of more than 35,000 and none larger than 175,000. The fact that there are eighty-two counties has meant small, though numerous, centers and often thus rural standards of judgment. The additional fact that for decades the principal crop was cotton dictated attitudes, shaped rural arrangements, and discouraged the growth of industry. The topography varies from shore, riverbank, and field to swamp, lake, low hills, some not so low, and pine forest, to monumental Indian mounds. Rich soil and a generous growing season favor crops; pine and hardwood forests are both beautiful and revenue-producing; and among the numerous waterways, natural and manmade, is the majestic artery of the continent, "the great river, the shifting unappeasable god of the country, feared and loved, the Mississippi" (Percy, *Lanterns* 4).

Religion is another factor in the cultural landscape of Mississippi and of high importance for writers. John Shelton Reed identified religious belief and practice (along with localism and violence) as an enduring trait of the South: nine-tenths of southerners are Protestant, more than half Baptists (*Minding the South* 18). Flannery O'Connor remarked that most southern writers were haunted by Christianity and the figure of Christ; similarly, Paul Ruffin, a poet and fiction writer, titled a collection of his stories *Living in a Christ-Haunted Land*. After statehood, Protestants from other southern areas settled in Mississippi in numbers and founded churches, Baptist and Methodist—in both towns and the countryside, where they prevailed—and Presbyterian and Episcopalian in the cities. Some five thousand churches are scattered through Mississippi (for a present population of slightly less than three million). Many poets come from deeply pious Protestant families, often Baptist; historically, Southern Baptists made up 41 percent of all church members. The Baptist church of Woodville, established in 1798, is the oldest church in Mississippi. Christ Church at Church Hill, built in 1815, is the oldest Episcopal church there. Until the Civil War, the two principal races did not always maintain separate churches; many were biracial. With Reconstruction, African Americans began founding separate congregations.

The mark of Protestant Christianity remains deep and extensive; presently Mississippi (with Alabama) has, according to statisticians, the highest state percentage of Protestant Christians (77 percent). Throughout most of the twentieth century, it was even higher. Missionary Baptists and Southern Baptists are the largest groups, by far. The Pew Research Center gives the Roman Catholic population as, roughly, 4 percent.

The great cultural divide in the state, since antebellum times but particularly afterwards and following the Plessy-Ferguson decision (1896) establishing in law the "separate but equal" principle, has been race. Jim Crow is a powerful symbol as well as a fact. For decades, reaching well into the twentieth century, the majority of the population was black. Beginning in the second decade of the twentieth century, with what is known as the Great Migration, that proportion began to change. In 1940 still, slightly more than half were black, the only black-majority state remaining, but shortly thereafter the population became, and remains, predominantly white. But the state retains a higher percentage than any other of African American residents (more than one-third). As modern literature has demonstrated over and over, all those, residents and visitors, who have spent considerable time there remain scarred by its history of ethnic separation and terrible strife. "To me, growing up in Mississippi was like getting a doctorate in life as a black person in these United States," wrote Margaret Porter (Abbott, *Reflections* 408). Segregation was not alone in creating social divisions: for long years, what amounted to a caste system prevailed, by which "a person's social station was largely determined before birth and was unlikely to change" (Davis, in Watkins 109–10).

Countervailing forces were few; one was literature, in Welty's phrase "an attempt to part a curtain" (quoted in W. Morris 101). Historians have emphasized the social glue in southern culture. Yet Patti Carr Black proposed as an explanation for Mississippi literary achievement the very lack of community (commonweal with others) among the white population, despite the widely shared sense of place. Writing about the broader South, Reed observed that notwithstanding social and economic conflict and separation, "the tale of the cultural South . . . is one of blending, sharing, mutual influence, continuing unity and distinctiveness" (*Minding the South* 17). The figure of Emmett Till, murdered in 1955, has served as one focus of past indignation and present reconciliation, as illustrated in poems by Sterling D. Plumpp, Ann Fisher-Wirth, Philip Kolin, and Angela Jackson.

Those who reflect on the rich Mississippi literary heritage may see in the historical and social features just mentioned its chief wellspring. Not strictly deterministic in a nineteenth-century sense, these features are still salient enough to suggest more than a casual relationship between the place and its poetry. Additionally, one must not overlook local peculiarities. Berry spoke of the "root-canaled iconography" of the Delta, which has "its own rhythm section, a low-buzz humid vibe of catfish, fried bacon, prom queens, screeching crickets and dizzy June bugs, sexual frustration . . . roadside Bible verses, minimum wage . . . and a dogmatic certainty that everything is Baptist until proven otherwise" (Ryor interview). Mississippians' deeply rooted pride, their labors, regrets, struggles, and sufferings all have contributed to an extraordinary self-awareness, widely shared, instantly recognizable by natives and those who have adopted the ethos of the state.

JAMES A. AUTRY

The career and poetry of James A. Autry (born 1933) are atypical. He is both a poet and writer of inspirational prose, directed principally toward those in business and others in the urban world—an attempt to humanize the contemporary order from the Christian viewpoint. With poet and translator Stephen Mitchell he published *Real Power* (1998), which features in a modern connection the moral principles of *Tao Te Ching*. Born in Memphis, where his father, Ewart Arthur Autry, was pastor of the Southern Avenue Baptist Church, Autry spent his early years there. (Ewart had a modest literary career; he is listed in James B. Lloyd's *Lives of Mississippi Authors*.) When the boy was six, his parents were divorced; Ewart had fallen in love with his secretary, whom he later married and with whom he had children. The events, James wrote, had "an impact on two things in my life: religion and sex" ("How I Got Here"). In 1941, Ewart returned to Mississippi and in 1943 became pastor of the Pine Grove Church, Benton County; his father had served there likewise. The mother remained in Memphis, where she and James lived in public housing. The project was, however, close to prosperous suburbs, and he attended good schools.

Through summer visits, the boy became familiar with Mississippi country life, enough so that he could depict it later in poems, where the deeply nostalgic tone may spring from lifelong unfulfilled need for his father as well as memories of his extended family. He had friendly relationships, as a boy and later, with his father's second family. Willie Morris, in his laudatory introduction to *Life After Mississippi*, says even that Autry was reared in North Mississippi. Ewart's second wife, Lola Mae Lineberry Autry, became a photographer and contributed to that volume a portfolio of period photographs showing her children and husband, and occasionally her stepson. Certain scenes from local life are accompanied by captions connected to Autry's poetry.

Autry attended the University of Mississippi, supported by a music scholarship (he was a clarinetist) and by various jobs. He majored in journalism,
having resolved to make it his career. After receiving his bachelor's degree in
1955, he served four years with the US Air Force as a fighter pilot, stationed
in Europe, mostly France. He pursued a career as a journalist; one of his jobs
was in New Orleans. He moved into magazine publishing at the Meredith
Corporation, where he ultimately became a high-ranked executive. He is identified on the cover of *On Paying Attention: New and Selected Poems* (2015) as
a former Fortune 500 executive, whose work had "a significant influence on
leadership thinking." Retiring from Meredith in 1991, he became a consultant
and a popular speaker, traveling to numerous distant locations. His career
resembles somewhat that of the younger Dana Gioia, vice-president of market-
ing at General Foods, though Gioia left the corporation (1992) to devote all his
working time to literature.

The Autry holds four honorary degrees. He wed twice. One of his three sons,
Ronald, was born severely autistic; a number of Autry's poems treat the sad-
ness and difficulty of dealing with him. Sally Pederson, to whom the poet
has been married for some thirty-five years, was similarly an executive with
Meredith. She is also a Democratic politician and was lieutenant governor of
Iowa (1999–2007). The couple resides in Des Moines. He suffers now from
Parkinson's disease.

In 1989 Bill Moyers featured Autry on his PBS series *The Power of the
Word*; they appeared together again in 2012, when Autry spoke on *Moyers
and Company* about his home state and read his poem "Leaving Mississippi."
Moyers furnished an endorsement for *On Paying Attention*. The *Kentucky
Poetry Review* devoted a special issue to Autry's work (1991).

Autry wrote his first poem in college. Years later, having put poetry aside,
he heard James Dickey read and was inspired to start anew. In Oxford,
Mississippi, Willie Morris attended a reading by Autry. Morris suggested
that he speak with Lawrence Wells, the owner of Yoknapatawpha Press.
Favorably impressed by the evocations of Autry's boyhood, Wells published
Nights Under a Tin Roof: Recollections of a Southern Boyhood (1983). In 1989
he brought out *Life After Mississippi*. Marked by nostalgia, these early books
have the mark of authenticity, with genuine "down-home" tone and topics.
They are not, however, paeans to the dominant social order, segregation.
Autry said later that he was "ashamed" to be a white Mississippian ("How
I Got Here").

The poems reflect the conflict, central to Autry's poetry, between a rural
environment and order and the urban and mechanized order, including the
culture of big business, that displaced it. "What are you doing here / in this

conference room / out of the cotton fields and red dust ... ?" ("Dialogue with the Past" 58*). "Cousin El" (the title refers perhaps to a son of Autry's Uncle El, his father's brother, a song-leader at church) puts the matter even more plainly, contrasting hills and fields and sweet gum trees with "video stores and pizza shops / and straightened rivers /and thinned forests" (91). Autry's poetry thus belongs to a principal current in American literature since the nineteenth century—lamentation over the displacement of the wilderness and the frontier by towns and industry, and thus the death of the pastoral ideal—what Leo Marx called "the machine in the garden."

Autry uses only free verse, presenting, usually, unadorned narration, with simple syntax and few attempts to startle or amaze the reader. Some components constitute paragraphs, of two to ten lines, the first flushed left, the others indented. In "Of Corporations and Communion," the text, though labeled and printed as verse, is essentially cut-up prose. Generally, lines break at the end of a phrase or other word-group. Italics and indented left margins indicate quoted material. The poems often present multiple scenes, related by theme or narrative line; they are not, however, a collage. While Autry's poetic practice is not that of the Victorians and Georgians, he remains close to them in his choice of domestic and nostalgic topics, and he does not avoid sentimentalism and the tendency to moralize. (Inclusion in *On Paying Attention* of a poem by his wife and one by a son indicates sentimental indulgence.)

The poet provides an abundance of authentic features of life on farms, woods, and creeks as boys knew it: avoiding or killing snakes, fishing for catfish and bream, picking blackberries, devouring fresh biscuits at every meal, spying on girls through chinks in the walls. Boll weevils, slop jars, the outhouse all make their appearance. Women's work—never-ending, exhausting—gets attention in the course of things; the men likewise cease work very rarely. Autry's head is full of voices, often heard directly, which he has preserved from the past. The speech is familiar, even homely, like the surroundings, as in "You didn't neither" ("Nights Under a Tin Roof" 3). Even the third-person narrative voice uses familiar speech, as in the reference to "our most wore-out shoes" ("Grabblin'" 92). Characteristic pronunciations appear. "Now you chirrun / keep those coats buttoned" ("Seasons Came with Food" 15). Portraits of "Aunt Callie" and "Uncle Vee" have the ring of truth. "Communication" paints a charming picture of the early telephone, as "Aunt Callie" yells into the instrument the way people yelled across the fields. She "looks at the phone / holding it so her eyes can aim the words / through the instrument and across the hills / where they

---

* Page numbers for Autry's poems, though they may have appeared in earlier collections, reference *On Paying Attention: New and Selected Poems.*

are to go" (9). No particular effort at humor is needed; it belongs to the fabric of the stories, as in this comment in "Genealogy" from an acquaintance about a newborn whose "daddy was no count": "Might's well send that chile / to the penitentiary soons he's born / gonna end up there anyway" (53).

Autry's writing provides view on his Baptist background and the Protestant milieu. In poems of boyhood, revivals, baptisms, and religious prohibitions get their due. "It was a sin for a Baptist to dance / so we went with Methodist girls / who taught us to slow dance and jitterbug" ("Scenes of Courtship" 30). His relationship with Christianity, complicated by his father's history and position, evolved to include interest in New Age philosophy. He calls himself "a mystical Christian" ("How I Got Here"). "Taking Communion to the Shut-ins" is set during the speaker's adulthood.

Less marked by nostalgia, poems composed later in Autry's career display different tones and topics removed from his Mississippi youth. Among them are difficult moments and experiences (illness, death) in contemporary settings such as nursing homes and funeral establishments. In such scenes, he does not rise well above the incidental level, and there is little poetic virtuosity. Apart from writing in free verse, eschewing majuscules at the beginning of lines, and using little punctuation, he embraced little from modernism and following developments; and yet he did not turn to his advantage practices of the New Formalism. Even with its limitations, however, his writing will doubtless continue to attract readers in his home state and elsewhere.

ANGELA BALL

Angela Ball, who has published several collections of verse, was born in 1952 in Athens, Ohio. Her BA in English is from Ohio University, where she graduated first in her class. She then took degrees at the University of Iowa (MFA in poetry writing) and the University of Denver (PhD in creative writing and modern literature). Since 1979 she has taught at the University of Southern Mississippi, where she was named professor in 1993. In 2018 she received the university's Lifetime Achievement Award.

Ball won the Duncan Lawrie Award in Sotheby's International Poetry Competition 1982 and the Donald Hall Prize (2007). Twice she has won the Mississippi Institute of Arts and Letters Award in Poetry. She is the recipient of a National Endowment for the Arts grant. She represented the United States at the Poetry International Festival in Rotterdam and served as Writer in Residence at the University of Richmond and the Château Lavigny in Switzerland. Her poems have appeared in anthologies such as *Best American Poetry 2001* and in the *New Yorker*, *Atlantic Monthly*, *Denver Quarterly*, *Southern Quarterly*, and *Poetry*. She is interested in translation.

Tellingly, Ball wrote, "Since Mississippi has been around me for most of my life, every poem I write is Mississippian" (Zheng, "Interview with Angela Ball," 17). "Hattiesburg, with its community of writers, has made my poetry possible. It's a source of energy," she added. True to her southern Ohio roots, she began as a pastoral poet. Subsequently she was drawn by poets of the New York School—John Ashbery, John O'Hara, James Schuyler. An additional influence is that of William Blake, with his double understanding of humanity—innocent and ironic. David Lehman pronounced Ball's poetry to be "as intimate as a dream" (Zheng, *Valley Voices*). Jordan Sanderson praised her for enacting Keatsian negative capability to an extraordinary degree. "The poet overcomes loneliness—even if temporarily—by losing herself in the poem" (22). This loneliness, which Sanderson qualifies as "existential," does not preclude, indeed bespeaks, her desire for union with the world.

Kneeling Between Parked Cars, Ball's debut collection (1990), is in four parts. She uses free verse with short lines, generally, and, in "My Life" and "Grandfather, Granddaughter," prose. One endorser praised its "graceful" cadences, its "phrasing of ease and fluency." Her metaphors are fanciful, usually effective, occasionally beyond easy grasp. In "What," the persona speaks of "the oak that points in every direction, death," of "the star holding the center / of a tent" and "a lake churned into foam." These are all what "we were." "The Courtyard" describes a woman "who has a machine / for reading, who trips back the window to address / the oranges, faces of lifting angels." Objects may undergo alterations, even metamorphosis, quietly, without explanation. "Windows fleeing into heights. / I'm delivered into rain / and become a burden to stay / one edge" ("Rilke: A Time"). A submarine boring under continents grows "whiskers / and a long nose" ("Nautical"). In "Alpine," a multipart poem set in a European resort, the poet moves skillfully from one scene to another as the persona, alone, imagines "the mountains / swimming in the world" and, "at a signpost / in the angle /between two places," feels "the pull of each." (The collection title comes from section two.)

Love poems, often a touchstone of feeling in a collection, include such appealing notations as "Our bed a gentle crossroads" ("What"). "Sunday Baseball" has the light touch of a good fielder and a happy lover. In "Road," the metaphor allows the speaker to "think toward you"—"the shadow we pinned / on the grass, // the darkness and stars / over your bed." Yet the road, "now lifting / to dusk . . . // leads away / from you, from everything."* Mississippi is not often visible; but one wonders whether the city evoked in "Suspense"—"a town of uncertainties . . . / . . . no center, just an axle of highways"—might stand for Hattiesburg.

Possession, with a cover by Frederick Barthelme, then director of the Center for Writers, who furnished three other covers for Ball, appeared in 1995. It is divided into three parts, one with a subsection, "Poems for Anton Chekhov." Voices shift between first and third person. The tone is frequently wistful, the psychology subtle, the moral space uncertain, between shadowy possibilities. A feeling of transition as well as yearning rises from numerous poems. Possession, as the title poem shows, is less property than a condition, perhaps that of self-possession, but barely, tenuous at best; or perhaps being possessed. Living is risky. Bodies figure into the matter; but, rather than having integrity,

---

* These two groups, totaling five lines, are separated by six lines, including three in a mini-stanza.

reliability, they may fly off in parts—hands, eyes. Human contacts allow sharing of "our hearts' true loneliness," offsetting, by doubling it, as it were, the dread to be alone. Such contacts are, however, precarious. The "obsessed . . . / know that love is measured / by the strength of its detachment, / the deadlock of fear and desire" ("Elegy for Edgar Allan Poe").

In short, *Possession* is understated theater, depending upon a quiet, undramatic imagination, aslant, fanciful, slightly surrealistic, recalling the delicate uncertainties of Paul Éluard. Mental states need objects, however shifting, and "the world is much with" even a diffused psyche. One poem is called "Materials"; others concern an architect, houses, and a ship, that of Captain Cook, in the poem bearing his name. While he is "one body"—a curious observation—"he travels on impulse / like oceans, thinks nothing / of survival." What is apparently solid may not be so. His job is "to keep the ship whole. . . ." Death, he perceives, is "the hole, the nowhere I always suspected / everywhere inside the world." Everywhere, disappointment is inevitable, as in "The Kiss"; desire cannot be realized. Reveries may be "delicious"; everything else is tedious—or so says a voice that may be Chekov's ("The Lady with the Pet Dog"). "Many circle love, / never approaching," according to "Adjustments"; "Wild light unwinds / the trees, disheveled and surprised."

Quartet, which likewise appeared in 1995, presents long poems, in numbered or titled sections, on four women, all originally Anglophone, connected to literary Paris in the 1920s and 1930s: Sylvia Beach, Nora Barnacle Joyce, Nancy Cunard, and Jean Rhys. Paris, always fascinating to foreigners, is even more so as the backdrop for expatriate exotica. Each woman is the subject and speaker in one of the poems, based on biographies but giving to the facts Ball's own slant. Details, including linguistic idiosyncrasies, drawn from their lives and the period make the portraits vivid. What, besides language, they had in common—exile or at least long absences from their birthplace, personal and sexual boldness, devotion to writing (their own or others')—makes the grouping coherent. Ball again uses free verse, in short lines that can accommodate narrative, interior monologue, quotations, and the wit and insight that finish off the portraits well. She evinces enormous understanding of these women, willing addicts of the freedom that Paris offered. The book is of particular interest to teachers of women's poetry.

The monologues range, chronologically. Amidst World War II, as "wind scans the backs of leaves" (13), Beach looks backward at her meeting with Adrienne Monnier; the founding of Shakespeare and Company; her acquaintance with famous expatriates, such as T. S. Eliot, Gertrude Stein, and Ernest Hemingway; and the publication of *Ulysses*. "The American exiles had an air / of having become their own creations" (15). French figures appear likewise;

Gide speaks, in indirect discourse, of Stein's diving technique: "Pas fameux." Nora recalls her unhappy girlhood in Galway, her departure for Dublin, her work there in a hotel, acquaintance with "Jim" ("true miracle") (32), and their sexual play in a field. She stresses how a normal life was not possible with him. "Some of the places / we stayed! Unfit to wash a rat in" (34). Nancy Cunard, the heiress, starting, she says, with the *facts* (wishing to disguise nothing), acknowledges that she does not know which of two likely candidates her father is. She reports, in the third person, what people said of her. She then recalls the atmosphere of Montparnasse ("I collected loves / without bothering to discard") and her meeting and affair with jazz musician Henry Crowder (39). Ball quotes Aldous Huxley on Cunard: "The logical conclusion, of money and leisure" (43). In impressionistic stanzas, Rhys reminisces about her arrival in England, aged sixteen, from Dominica, her first love affair, and taking up writing; she then evokes Montparnasse, dresses and hats, aging.

Night Clerk at the Hotel of Both Worlds (2007) won the Donald Hall Prize. The Associated Writing Program committee that year clearly wanted to bestow laurels on imagination, not outrageous, but fanciful and mercurial. "I put on one leg of my pants and ran outside . . . // The factory whistle put its 'W' on the end . . ." ("Color Film"). Famous names mark several titles: Byron, Frank O'Hara, Baudelaire, and other French figures. "I had summer on the planet of distraction," says the poem of nearly that title. "I embraced Beethoven's comb, / Ready to fling its richest music / Into my teeth." A certain whimsy contributes to a sense of strangeness. Ball defines "acommania" as "the malady that causes people to leave out commas, / As in "That seems a lot of Pilaf Francis." Wariness about human relationships persists. In "Pup," "sex appeal gets no further than the front fence. / I've bitten off enough beds in my time."

The cover of *Talking Pillow* (2017), a collage by Ball, features scraps of words and pictures related to film. Movies are a motif in the collection. Reintroducing the topic of body parts, "To Lon Chaney, in *The Unknown*" evokes the actor playing an armless man. A poem whose lengthy title begins "Some Regrets That Will Attend You . . ." announces that at the movies "you are disappointed at your failure / to stop kicking the seat / of the person in front of you, / and take your leg outside . . ." "Elegy," among Ball's best poems, mentions another film, *Scandal Sheet*, pertinent not thematically but by the fact that as the movie plays on a DVD, the persona's partner (based, clearly, on Ball's real partner, Michael Helwick) suffers an attack, subsequently proven fatal. This unfortunate turn of events, recounted in stages, dominates the book by its seriousness and, to some degree, its implications. "Second Elegy" confirms the weight of the first on the book. Elsewhere, what the poet calls "the sense that thing / is not thing," or "cognitive dissonance"

("Lo Que Hay," "Boyfriend Story"), may arise from the unreality following death's intrusion. Such dissonance in the world, whether experienced as gravity or whimsy, invites dissonance in the self—or is the same. Denying reality, may one deny death?

CHARLES G. BELL

Charles Greenleaf Bell (1916–2010), a native of Greenville, was a versatile and highly educated man who had a long career as a writer, teacher, and lecturer. His intellectual position was secular humanism, or so it appears, largely; religion, at least for him, no longer seemed vital, at least in the earlier of the collections considered here. Alluding to the body as the seat of passion, caresses, and "lost regret of enfleshed memories"—although the body "burns" them—the poet writes, "When religion had also body it could wake such images" ("The Locus of Love," from *Songs for a New America*, 1953).

Bell was the son of a judge, a northerner, Percy Bell. The poet was acquainted with two local contemporaries who became well known in literature, Walker Percy and Shelby Foote. His poetry indicates that his Mississippi origin and connections were not unimportant to him, but once he left for college he did not return to the state to live. Still, the poems in *Delta Return* (1956), inspired by a visit to Greenville, reveal his sense of place and history.

Bell studied physics at the University of Virginia (BS, 1936). As a Rhodes Scholar, he went to Exeter College, Oxford, where he changed his field to English literature and took three degrees (BA and MA, 1938; LittB, 1939). During his time abroad, a brother studying at the University of the South committed suicide; the death affected Bell greatly.

Returning to America in 1939, he taught at Blackburn College (Illinois), Iowa State University—both English and physics—and the University of Chicago (1945–56). During World War II, when physicists were needed, he was on the research team at Princeton. In 1956–57 he was a Fulbright lecturer at the Technische Hochschule in Munich. Thereafter he was attached as a tutor to St. John's College, first in Annapolis, then in Santa Fe, starting in 1967. He became very fond of northern New Mexico, where he remained until, in 2006, a widower, he moved to Maine to live with a daughter. He received prestigious fellowships from the Rockefeller and Ford foundations and lectured at universities and libraries. In 1939, he married Mildred Winfree, from whom he was divorced in 1949. That year he wed Diana Mason, called Danny, who lived until 2004. From those unions he had five daughters. His collection *Five Chambered Heart* (1986) is dedicated to "wives, loves, mamas, daughters, granddaughters."

Bell took as his province much of human knowledge. He published novels and essays as well as poetry. His *Millennial Harvest: The Life and Collected Poems of Charles Greenleaf Bell* (2007) weaves among the poems an autobiography in prose. His undertakings included a wide-ranging series of slide-and-tape lectures, launched in the late 1930s, called "Symbolic History through Sight and Sound." His purpose was to investigate and illustrate history viewed holistically, without the reductionism accompanying many similar studies. He wished to show that all aspects of human culture and action belonged in such history, tied in with each other. The ambition calls to mind such projects, similarly begun in the 1930s, as Arnold Toynbee's multivolume *A Study of History* and Will and Ariel Durant's *The Story of Civilization*. Bell's lectures did not incorporate the work of a professional historian, but they were innovative in their mode of presentation. As audiovisual techniques changed, so did the format, the final one being DVDs.

Many poems in *Songs for a New America*, composed between 1944 and 1953, appeared in prominent magazines. The epigraph is reminiscent of biblical language, without any note of belief: "Between the dust and dust, / In a little moment of green." A note preceding the poems thanks Galway Kinnell, long a friend, for his counsel. The book shows the poet's classical tendencies by its topics (Roman history, for instance). The forms are conventional. Bell uses rhyme sometimes, or loose rhyme, as in "These Winter Dunes." The dominant tone is reflective.

The book is in three parts, each with a title drawn from the text. The initial poem, arranged in ten blocks of fourteen lines each, gives its title to the collection and introduces it. The whole collection evokes America, especially its waters, perceived in a modern fashion as the persona flies westward from New York. The Atlantic—its obvious role as the route for European immigrants unstated—appears as the plane rises and the Statue of Liberty comes into view. The Susquehanna and its forests appear next, and the persona reflects on a Quaker whom he knows there, who gathers sap for maple syrup and makes beautiful furniture but has turned his back on urban life and its encroachment. Then the Great Lakes and their "brute and butcher," that is, Chicago, attract the observer's attention. Images of the metropolis include its "miles of tenements" and the crowds "in the noontime canyons," then, "heaving in the winds," the "great pearl / Of rounding beauty" at evening (14–15).

The Mississippi River, the Missouri, the Platte have their place, leading toward the Laramie peaks and "the broken teeth of the Wasatch Range" (16). Deserts that look like moonscapes make the persona think of the difficult, sometimes heartbreaking treks of pioneers. California follows, with "its goblets of wheat and vine," by which one can "drink the god sun" (16). In the final poem of the series, "the fog comes rolling in from the long Pacific; / The redwoods tower in the mist where we go down." The poet addresses his country directly: "O land, / O cities; and down to the salt sea again" (17). While the series is shorter than previous epics synthesizing, through perception, American history and geography, one may see parallels with writing by Longfellow, Whitman, William Carlos Williams (*In the American Grain*), and Robert Penn Warren (*Audubon: A Vision*).

The following poems in part one pick up motifs and places. Nature acts as both setting and subject, as in "Chestnut Trees," where the poet evokes "the poor red hills" of Mississippi. In "These Winter Dunes," the speaker sits among sandhills on the shore of Lake Michigan, with the smoke of Gary, Indiana, in the distance. "Long Beach Island" reintroduces the seashore; "Vista-Dome" and "Another Flight 609" present perceptions of transformed understanding. The latter poem announces clearly what readers may have suspected from the outset: that these evocations of America in its geographic beauty, strength, and variety are also a warning. "From high above we saw America / The symbol of its own expanse and spirit, / This good earth Thoreau and Lincoln walked on." But failure of "hope and promise" is not impossible. Through atoms, cells, and rain (as Bell specifies), human beings were created and developed as they are now. (The poet mentions additionally such phenomena as stellar explosions and "nuclear pyres.") The present world is available, but vulnerable. "The property of spirit / Is transcendence. We have much to transcend." Not only do human interventions alter nature; the universe itself is unstable, with "perilous urge and instability / Fluctuating balance and chain reaction."

Part two comprises poems in various settings, including Italy, France, and Germany. The opening poem, "Bloodroot," in eight six-line stanzas, with variable arrangements of loose rhyme, describes woods and a character living there and his drama. A central image is that of morel mushrooms, cooked. Called "devil's fingers," they are nevertheless quite edible; and they are contrasted explicitly with the bloodroot, "the strange white flower with the bitter stem," lovely to look at but somewhat toxic, causing burning of the viscera. The two are compared implicitly with the man's first wife, a beautiful girl (too beautiful for him; she left) and the second wife, safely plain, but good. Bell's moralizing here is not excessive, unlike that in the unsuccessful poem "'License They Mean,'" which deals with drunken American soldiers in Frankfurt and the ideals of democracy, which the persona considers and attempts to rehabilitate.

Following "Bloodroot" comes a series of seven titled poems, mostly short, under the general title "An Interlude of Loss and Love." The fifth, "Woodbird," is a lovely lyric on autumn. A later poem, "Spring Interval," offers further reflections: "And we require some little time / To mend the shaken destinies of man."

The third part of *Songs for a New America* brings reinforcement by poems, for example, on Italy, a deceased friend, Heraclitus, and a flowering peach tree. The poems also offer qualifications to certain foregoing views. In "Fold of Friends," set in Philadelphia, the speaker, before going to the museum to see Botticelli paintings, meditates on the urban landscape and the river, a "sad spectacle." Nonetheless, the world is green. "We only blight by parts; the whole they form / Evades the withering of our ghastly charm. / When we have laid our last curse on the land, / That curse burns beauty in the everlasting hand." A forest fire, "the sudden suicide of nature," does not take everything; "one ray, / Blood-red of flame, like the last flash of sun, / Caught on the pool the imperilled swan / Mirrored the pluming breast . . ."; and the swan's song "melodized immortal wrong; / And this has wrung the heart of God forever" ("Fall of Troy"). Religious belief may have a place, after all. "The God has myriad forms," Bell writes. Faith appears rewarded by "the all-shaping / Lord" ("Balsamum"). In sixteen lines "The Wheel" reconciles implied and certain evils with the capacity to hope. "Life is a wave that moves by breaking. / . . . The wave advances. / . . . It is knowing the bulk and bond of all ocean, / Crest and calm, the rounding of the wheel, / That it turns in beauty, and its ways are good."

The ambitious reach that led to "Symbolic History" is on display in *Five Chambered Heart* and its complex structure. The poems tend toward the formal, often with rhyme or assonance, iambic pentameters, and frequent symmetry among lines and stanzas. Unbroken blocks of lines vary from couplets to a dozen, twenty, or more. A note preceding the table of contents explains that the poems constitute twenty numbered "waves," which "move recurrently through five archetypal states of love"—namely, Love, Lust, Earth, Waste, Soul. Each word bears a brief definition, or tag, although the reader may not grasp the puzzling order of these substantives nor the relationships among them and their connections to physical energy. A physicist may do better than a critic at grasping the complex structure and its meaning.

The volume is divided into five parts: "Five Chambered Heart," "Wave Plots in Space and Time," "Archetypes," "The Number of my Loves," and "Water-Fire-Air-Earth-Void." The first four parts comprise five short poems each, the twenty numbered "waves." Longer poems, "imaging the same states," as the note says, surround "each sequence of waves." The subtitle of "Archetypes"—"Hugo, Goethe, Petrarch, Catullus, San Juan de la Cruz"—refers to five poems, one by each of these poets, printed in the original language and, on the facing page, in Bell's translation. They precede the five poems constituting the section proper. The fifth and final part, "Water-Fire-Air-Earth-Void," is a single poem in five numbered sections.

The waves, or "archetypal states of love," constitute the matter of the title poem, "Five Chambered Heart," in five stanzas. It begins: "The first begins to beat like a drop of blood / On the egg-yolk of the world the fifth day / When vessels reach to guide the coded wave / Under brooding wings in the dark of LOVE." The third chamber, "of two and one, admits a space / Between self and other, EARTH-manifold, / Where love meanders the sensible. . . ." The following poems, "Rainbow," "Litany of Women," "Rainsong of Fish and Birds," "High Tension," and "The Voice of the Chambered Fire," which make up section one of this first part, do not display close connections with each other or with the surrounding structural material. The first-person voice may well be that of the author-in-the-text in "Rainsong of Fish and Birds," but in "Litany of Women" the voice takes on an epic tone, as in the lines "One [a woman] all flesh who beached from primal water / . . . / That lost empress who rode hard to the kill. . . ."

Here and in similar sections, what might initially appear familiar is off-key, traduced in some manner or another, presumably disclosing further aspects or layers of being. Occasionally, the poems invite comparison with work by the metaphysical poets, in which one image, developed, deepened, provides the entire meaning. Similarly, Bell's may be likened to writing by modern phenomenological poets. But his poems are frequently multifaceted, far-ranging or convoluted, and concentrate less on the object itself (a stone, a candle).

Among more approachable poems than "Five Chambered Heart" is "The White Room," which begins: "A high window, a white room. / Paper, pen, table, chair. / Of the longest life, half is gone. / Cars on the street below are a blur." Whether or not read as personal reflections, the stanza coheres. Similarly, "Resonance of Towers," spoken by a persona in a lighted tower who has "outwatched the Bear," introduces readily recognized figures: Dante, William Butler Yeats, Robinson Jeffers. It then moves to an effective concluding image with spiritual suggestions: "The night web of the soul in the world / Leans from tower to tower." Terminology from science—as in "Doctrine of Signatures" ("entropic December," "nebular immensity")—does not exclude allusions to God, perhaps not simply rhetorical. That a mother's "wits are with God" can be simply figurative ("The White Room"); but that all flesh is "grass / In the hands of the living God" (from the poem "A Fly Thrown into the Fire") may express an embrace of biblical text, not just its use.

Living through most of the twentieth century into the twenty-first, Bell witnessed tremendous developments in theoretical and applied science, as well as changes in poetic taste, illustrated in the plain language of Robert Frost, the modernist masterpieces of Williams and Wallace Stevens, the confessional school of midcentury, postmodernist writing, and New Formalism. His verse shows affinities with Frost and the New Formalist spirit as well as with the paradoxes of Stevens. Where it will be placed in a future assessment of twentieth-century American poetry is unclear. Even less clear is the reception such poetry can have among those committed to scientific principles to the complete exclusion of the unseen, the spiritual. Suspension of disbelief may be their approach.

D. C. BERRY

With *saigon cemetery* (1972), his first book, D. C. Berry (David Chapman Berry Jr.) became an important war poet in the vein of lamentations. He is also an important satirist, as following collections indicate. In *The Vietnam Ecclesiastes* (2007), he was both at once.

Berry was born in Vicksburg in 1942 and reared in Greenville, where he graduated from high school. He had a sister, born in 1946. His father, said to be a humorous man, managed gasoline stations. The poet's roots include territory near what is now Clark Creek Natural Area, in the Tunica Hills, where his grandfather Berry bought three thousand acres of land and operated a "peckerwood sawmill." David's religious background was "feverish fundamentalism," and among his college degrees is one from Bob Jones University. For decades, however, he identified himself as an Episcopalian (Interview). In "Stained Glass," from *Divorce Boxing*, the speaker says that he is not a believer. That statement does not reflect the poet's position, it would seem; he calls himself a theist, while expressing suspicion of dogmatic theology. God is "the great Why Not?" "God's got to be / a jester" ("Questions").

Berry began writing poetry out of boredom in church. He had formed his taste by reading and rereading his English textbooks, the only entertainment his mother would allow. He attended Delta State University, preparing for medical school, and working meanwhile in an ER unit in Greenville General Hospital. He was admitted to medical school but, after graduation (1965), he went to Flint, Michigan, to work in management at General Motors. He married that summer. The following summer he was drafted into the army, where he served for three years in the Medical Service Corps, attaining the rank of captain. Much of that time he was in Vietnam, at Cam Ranh Bay, which had a convalescent center. He experienced considerable boredom there. He spent time reading poetry by Ezra Pound and Williams Carlos Williams. Having been discharged, he enrolled at the University of Tennessee, where he earned his PhD, with a dissertation on James Dickey (1973).

From 1972 to 2002 Berry taught at the Center for Writers of the University of Southern Mississippi, where he received three teaching awards. The Mississippi Arts Council and the Mississippi Institute of Arts and Letters supported his writing by grants. He published widely in magazines and reviews. Since 2006 he has lived in Oxford. Among his retirement activities was fly-fishing in the Rockies (he tied his own flies); he also makes art from found objects. He is fond of trees and animals. In 2012 he created a fund to provide income each year to two students in the MFA program at the University of Mississippi. His first marriage ended in divorce; he remarried and was again divorced. From that marriage he has one son, David. From a third marriage (1985), which likewise ended in divorce, he has a son, Hays. For his marital failures, Berry blames himself and his overbearing stance and bipolarity.

Berry displays wit, often acerbic, relying on allusions, wordplay, including puns, and echoing sound effects. He cultivates aphorisms. "Poetry without prose can't walk; prose without poetry can't dance" ("Ars pugilistica"). While he writes in free verse, he understands it as crafted, not loose or unregulated. "Free verse," he observed, "is free *of* verse, not free *with*; is, rather, free prose" (Interview). In speaking with students, he characterized poetry as a way to "hotwire" reality. (He borrowed the term Jackson Browne's song "The Road and the Sky.")

Like Dickey and Dave Smith, Berry is a man's poet. It is not simply that he deals with war, or likes the outdoors, or writes in a strong, confident voice; chiefly, it is that he lacks romanticism. Throughout his verse he displays a male nature, with respect to himself, his family, and especially women, who are powerfully attractive but too different not to be exasperating; the effect is that they are sometimes reduced to their anatomy.

In his foreword to *saigon cemetery*, George Garrett recalled Wilfred Owen's statement about his war poems: "The subject . . . is War, and the pity of War. / The Poetry is in the pity." Berry, wrote Garrett, "honors that intention, not flinching from hard facts, mixed feelings, not deviating from the subject and the pity of it." Garrett acknowledged the fact that even as the book appeared the American war in Indochina continued apace. War, he observed, is fundamentally the same, always, however outwardly different in details and idiom; its substance changes little. What was new in Berry's book was "the poet's own voice." Berry is "traditional in his search for a form, one flexible enough to leave the language free to be itself, yet strict enough to permit the requisite self-control."

The viewpoint is that of the medic, close to the fighting, hearing, observing it and its results, but different, often fixed on the physiological or anatomical;

elsewhere simply human. The voice warns us: "A poem ought to be a salt lick / rather than sugar candy. A preservative." Something, that is, to give "the full flavor / of beauty and grief" (50). The poems, untitled, separated by only a printer's emblem, can be considered as discrete units or as one single poem, although without narrative line. The sequence owes something to William Carlos Williams, and e. e. cummings as well as journalism and popular culture. Capitalization is erratic, used chiefly for emphasis; punctuation is minimal; short lines, frequent interruptions, dropping down words to complete a phrase, and loose spacing provide the structure, or nonstructure, of the war experience. The semi-discontinuous composition, featuring incongruous juxtapositions, recalls early World War I novels and fictionalized diaries in France. One is reminded that modernism burst on the scene just before that great catastrophe. Even line placement points to an anti-logic. Modernist style has, however, its own reason, its own classicism. In Berry's book, always, the particular points to the general. Nor was the composition hasty. (Revisions of later poems attest to Berry's poetic labor.)

Words are fractured, or recomposed: "lungshot," "throw / ing," "Bang / ing the lung" (3). Repetition creates mental sound effects, some implying tedium, as in "rattle rattle / against your ear drumdrumdrumdrum / drum   machine gun / roar   gut gut gut gut gutgut" (6). The trope of the unsayable ("Language cannot express . . .") appears; a death is "too quick / for a dramatist to do" (10). The language is highly figurative. Metaphors are borrowed from animals (toads, spiders, a waterbug) and plant life (bulbs, flowers). Women, barely eroticized, are present: occasionally, a Vietnamese, a generic mother, or the speaker's wife, in a somewhat oneiric poem, "To Terri, For Easter." The speaker thinks of "the yellow slash of Forsythia [sic] / that must be blooming / where you are" (50).

Occidental cultural tradition is not absent, but is undermined; what did it do to prevent this war? There are references to Flannery O'Connor (49) and "blue guitar" and names such as "Sergeant Sublime," "Lt. Donne," "Captain Kepler," whose space is erased by "a 20 mm red-tailed tracer" (46, 47). Sublime's spinal chord [sic] is "knocked completely out of tune / by the whack of a 10,000/ pound bomb / from a B-52" (48). "Go catch a falling   burningstar / and give it to the Vietnamese Piers / Plowman peasant in the eternal / paddy kneedeep" (19). A helicopter, a "phantom" jet, four soldiers playing cards, a Timex Electric watch crushed from "timekeeper / to timekept" and "Time [closed] . . . Forever" (23–24) provide flashes of arrested action—a film repeated from the beginning of warfare. Men "love to kill / more than love" (34). The Fall is not forgotten. "What will we do / when we're done / with civilization" (33).

Relief, if it is such, comes only with mention of the "patient sleep," which "never becomes impatient" until resurrection discloses the bodies of the earth (29).

In 1978 Berry published a chapbook called *Jawbone: Portraits of Contemporary Poets.* Berry makes his titles work for him. The tone is challenging, even sarcastic, not laudatory; even pastiche is, however, an homage. Among the subjects are Dickey, Theodore Roethke, David Ignatov, Robert Bly, Mark Strand, William Stafford, Anne Sexton, John Berryman, and Sylvia Plath. Clearly, suicidal poets present special interest. Allusions fit the subjects' literary bents as well as their characters. "Allen Ginsberg Leaps Over the Aisle of Syllogism" is particularly effective.

Divorce Boxing, Berry's next collection, appeared in 1998. The cover, not custom-designed but fitting nonetheless, features a man, seated, glaring sideways under his eyelids, and a battle-axe woman, standing, weapon in hand, staring ahead—the picture of alienation. The verse is less disjointed than in the Vietnam poems. Quatrains are the most common form, and there are sonnets. Excepting occasional end-rhymes and interior sound effects, the lines are unrhymed. Stanzas may break off, whether in mid-sentence or not; in "Cigar," such breaks cascade down the page, emphasizing what is thus dropped.

Divorce Boxing demonstrates the versatility and quickness of Berry's imagination. The pugilistic image in the title poem fits the collection. "Marriage is a bullring," the poet writes ("After Adultery"); and there is shadow boxing, at least, with oneself, the perennial adversary. Sarcasm is the heart of many images. Along with narrative leaps, metaphoric reach is wide. He transforms characters and surroundings by figurative designations: "The Cactus, a Divorce Present"; "Snow Woman," a divorcee. Plausibility is not required: "Waves were slamming doors at no address" ("Shark"). Wordplay underlines unexpected similarities, as in the end-line consonance and half-rhyme of *clowns* and *clones* ("middle-agers" at a bar, looking for women) ("Cigarette"). Numerous titles—some incongruous, or playing off the poem in fanciful, mocking, or adversarial ways—illustrate an indulgent use of the real: "Frisbee Love Takes Biloxi Beach," "Hawk Formal, The Way to Go When God Is Deaf," "Your Shadow Is Death's Accountant."

The three parts of the book, "Divorced," "Married," and "Divorced," provide no strong narrative line, but markers show up, as in "First Birthday After Second Divorce." The speaker, with his father, watches a Marlon Brando film. "The black-and-white bomb of a TV / snowed on him a five-minute avalanche / just when the girl was discarding her clothes." That glimpse, along with frequent allusions elsewhere—"Miss Playboy"—presents one end of the feminine spectrum; the other is suggested by "Miss Coca Cola," in the poem of that title (a figure from an old calendar, smiling but not provocative). The erotic dimension of human life is, in the poem "Thorn," passion in both senses. Casual love weaves through dramas of marriage and its dissolution. Elsewhere, "Speed Love of the Swallow and the Shark" illustrates a tendency toward fabulation. Teaching, illness, old age, childhood memories are central to some poems, William Butler Yeats, fatherhood, and insomnia to others. A slightly jaundiced tone colors a maternal figure, "hard . . . / to live and let live" ("Ten-Pound Bible"). "Daddy," bearing the dates of the poet's father, is inspired by viewing the deceased in his casket and recalling his sartorial preferences and habit of making jokes. Like various others postdating Plath's famous piece, it contrasts greatly with hers, and to Berry's honor. Two especially noteworthy poems are "Eating a Fish After I'd Seen My Face in the Pond" and "Marina Lounge," displaying skill in combining scenes and impressions.

As the twentieth century waned, Berry, under the influence of Marshall McLuhan's contention that illiteracy would prevail, became more interested in formal verse, viewing rhyme and rhythm as ways of keeping poetry alive by making it easier to remember and recite. He judged, perhaps too severely, his own free verse; yet in fact he did not abandon it entirely.

Zen Cancer Saloon appeared in 2004 in an issue of *Black Warrior Review*. The manuscript, one of five hundred entries in a chapbook competition, won its "Anniversary Award." Composed as Berry was on his back recovering from spinal surgery to remove a multiple myeloma tumor (2002), the poems are, he stated, "the backbone of *Yes, Cancer French Kisses*" (2017), which adds writing connected to his second bout of the disease (2006) (Interview). Original, avoiding the trite, and written from the sufferer's viewpoint, not an observer's, the two works, considered here together, constitute an unusual contribution to contemporary literature of illness and body failure.

All the poems in *Zen Cancer Saloon*, often pithy, are centered haikus, or what Berry later called "telegrams from Cancerland." They follow the classic form. Both startling and quiet juxtapositions characterize the lines, leading to a modest conclusion or a question. Many are explicitly interrogative. Rather, however, than simply asking "Why me?" they take as a starting point the problem of embodiment, then range over points of metaphysics, epistemology, and especially theology. The subject is not reduced to his body—and he endeavors to leave to others its care; nonetheless, the body is a constant actor. The expression is spare, with grammatical elements elided. "Worried; out on limb, / can't curl tail for parachute, / too busy sawing" (118). Hospital features and physiological processes are designated only briefly. In contrast to the syntactical simplicity, the text is richly metaphoric and allusive; readers encounter chaos theory, Eliot, Lewis and Clark, and Chaucer along with Elvis and Superman. God is mentioned or evoked frequently (and Jesus and the Spirit); but He is the unknowable, a question mark, or an ace up a short sleeve. "God: absence of some / thing or presence of nothing . . .?" (114). Or is God the Joker? Buddha likewise appears. "Buddha Shadow says life is noon illusion" (110). The poems valorize laughter, which is "how we / swallow life's alligators" (116).

Yes, Cancer French Kisses is riotous. It too presents haikus, aligned at the left margin, but irregular. They alternate with tercets. The haiku form is blown away by the explosive style, featuring mixed typefaces (capitals, boldface, italics, and combinations thereof). Assonance, rhymes, alliteration, and wordplay add to the visual impact and disjointed sense. Again, the viewpoint is the patient's, distinctly male. He addresses his disease as "Miss Myeloma." The introduction, with wry or outrageous remarks and a hands-off stance, sheds light on what follows. Quotations on adversity and other matters from such as Epictetus, St. Paul, Shakespeare, Carlyle, Dickinson, Nietzsche, and Paul Simon illustrate the author's points. Both laughter and beauty are highlighted as ways of dealing with illness, as with life.

The Vietnam Ecclesiastes: 1945–1975 appears initially to be tongue-in-cheek. This prima facie impression arises from encomia facing the title page, purportedly from authorities, among whom are "Walter" Whitman, Dickinson, the Preacher, "Oinky Pink," and "Sgt. Death." Genuine quotations in the table of contents, from Ecclesiastes, Thucydides, Tacitus, Plutarch, Napoleon, proverbs, and modern sources, were originally poem epigraphs. They frequently contrast with the titles, farcical and hyperbolic, to which they are attached; they *may* apply to the respective poems (Interview). Berry has hedged his bets, a stance in chaos. The back cover contains purported blurbs by such figures as "Crazy Mouth," "Skinny Mama," and "Em Dick." "Nor porn and not comics. And not short," says one. Cartoonish sketches illustrate the book. Might this tone have been responsible for its complete neglect by critics? Or perhaps it was disdained, first by high-profile publishers, then reviewers, because the subject was no longer fashionable and, worse, Berry saw responsibility and evil among all participants, not uniquely America.

Pseudo-endorsements and sardonic tone notwithstanding, the undertaking is serious, and original. Historical ironies abound, not the least a sense of *déjà vu*, not just in the parallels between French and American errors. As phrases from Ecclesiastes indicate, man has not improved, and history remains oppressive, its evil exposed. (Lucifer himself is mentioned.) The authorial viewpoint is not, however, internationalist or pro-Viet Cong. Jane Fonda is no heroine, and the North Vietnamese display brutality, blowing up, for instance, a populous market in their own territory ("The Di Ann Market Dalmatian"). Yet the South Vietnamese and the Catholic regime are not much better. Agent Orange can scarcely be considered a benefit. American culture, as it was then and largely remained in 2007, comes off badly. Berry draws on the obvious conundrum of means and ends. "Why are we here? Why fight for rice? . . . // We won't even try / to win. We fight only for apple pie" ("Joker Reports Unpleasantness Overcome"). To what purpose did American soldiers die fighting the North Vietnamese? So that in Vietnam mom's apple pie, Coca-Cola, red Corvettes, and birth-control pills would still be available?

The poems, all short, in unrhymed tercets, are organized chronologically, with historical markers. Berry drew his scenes from a volume of photographs covering the events following World War II and the remnants of Japanese occupation, through the last years of the French presence and their defeat at Dien Bien Phu, to the American war and the fall of Saigon. He was never involved emotionally in the material; he wrote as an historian, not as a former participant, and the writing came easily (Interview). This apparent distance from the topic may attest to changes in him. In mocking, jaundiced tones and, often, crude language, yet with empathy, the poems depict events and human figures persuasively. If the overall theme is the saying of Ecclesiastes, "All is vanity," human lives matter nonetheless. "The Not Much Weasel Curse" evokes POWs as they leave the camp and its commander, "Weasel," who has fattened them up a bit for the show. "No more blinking / Morse code—T O R T U R E—/ when tap dancing // for Weasel's chickenshit cameras."

Matching the Preacher's admonitions, Berry's imagination tends toward the parabolic and aphoristic. Many poems are fables of a sort, as one title, "Grasshopper Ho Chi and Peacock Pierre," suggests. Pierre is the iconic Frenchman, Nguyen, the archetypical Indochinese. Neither comes off well. "When Pierre boards the ship, Nguyen smiles // as if he invented ice cream, / French Vanilla, and Pierre can / taste how sweetful it is to win" ("Viet Minh Cold Boys"). Realistic observations on human nature are set among outrageous humor, as in "Moi Deals With It." Both the North and South Vietnamese scorn the Mois, "goons" and "hillbilly trash." They also are men, nonetheless, and have problems, "such as this Moi's. Hanoi skinned his / father screaming, and Saigon tied his child / to a swinging gate for target practice. // This Moi is so human he plans to kill both sides."

The final poems, "Miss Ole Miss" and "Going Show Nguyen, April 1975," convey convincingly the sorrow, the pity, the irony and cruelty as Saigon falls and the covetous victors—Nguyens—stroll the streets of the former capital. A "Vietnamese beauty" dressed in red, white, and blue, stands by the US consulate. She is first hopeful, then forlorn, then frightened at the thought of the Commies; no helicopter appears for her. For his part, Nguyen stares "goggle-eyed" at American wealth displayed around him. How can he win it all? "Just fail longer, / that's it, outfail."

Hamlet Off Stage (2009) is a clever, sarcastic reworking of characters and motifs from the tragedy, reset in contemporary times. The cover shows a boxing ring, with the fighter and his trainers (two high-heeled, tightly wrapped girls) and a bill advertising "Tonight, 15 Rounds." All poems, some with end-rhymes, are printed as a single block; most are short. They constitute no narrative line, but motifs recur, suggesting monomania. The presumptive speaker is Hamlet; his tone is often outrageous, with echoes of the original, as in the first lines of "Three-Legged God": "The moment I punctured Polonius / God's sword began swinging over my head, / ticking: Vengeance Is Mine Saith The Lord." Hamlet's voice slides easily into another's. Berry introduces allusions to Rimbaud and T. S. Eliot as well as Shakespeare. Reductio ad absurdum is a principal technique. "Life's a piece / of cake, but wedding cakes are sugared urns" ("Pansy Icelandia and Panty Toast"). Mel Gibson, Elvis Presley, and Dr. Freud appear; the latter reappears as "Fraud"; Rambo becomes Hambo, Hambeau, then Hambone. Gertrude, Claudius, Ophelia (or "Oh"), the ghost, Laertes, "Polonius Viagrasaurus," and the Prince of Denmark himself—none is spared. As in Hamlet's imagination, the erotic is coarse ("Radish Me Mama"), and misogyny is prevalent. "All women are Gertrudes. . . . / Each female's Jezebel. . . . Even for God, women are too complex" ("Monty Brings Out the Mama in Them").

Hamlet's maladjustment, expressed by hostile, sarcastic absurdities with contemporary references, surely reflects aspects of the poet's discomfort in a time "out of joint"—an age, for him, of dubious warfare, repeated marital failure, and melanoma. Readers will remember his jaundiced question from *The Vietnam Ecclesiastes*, an essential question of life: How can one win? "Just fail longer, / that's it, outfail."

MAXWELL BODENHEIM

Maxwell Bodenheim, once a famous poet, dramatist, and fiction writer, is now neglected. That neglect is unwarranted; he was for years a leading literary figure, and his poems belong to the literary history of the period. He was born in Hermanville, in southwest Mississippi, in 1892 (not 1893, as some sources indicate). He died in 1954. He spent only the early years of his life in Mississippi; after his parents left the state, around 1900, he did not live there again. Yet he belongs to it. Mississippi furnished the family background against which his life and career unrolled and made him an exotic species in northern literary circles. Moreover, the rebel requires something to rebel against, even if he does so almost instinctively. Bodenheim (or someone writing in his name) wanted "to drum out the ghosts of my Southern upbringing" (*My Life and Loves in Greenwich Village* 30). His life, which discredits somewhat the image of glamour in the *vie de Bohème*, held achievements but also countless miseries and misfortunes, often of his own creation.

Born Bodenheimer, he discarded the last syllable of the surname, as part of his rejection of his roots. On both sides the family were Alsatian Jews. The family Bible was printed in French and Hebrew. Whereas his mother's brother, M. B. Herman, who had founded the little town, was a successful merchant and, later, a doctor, his father, Solomon, a sometime merchant and salesman, was consistently unsuccessful. Straitened circumstances, job changes, moves (Memphis before Chicago), quarrels, and his mother's prodding of both son (the only child) and husband to do better created an unpleasant family life. "It was a disaster he never recovered from," as Jack B. Moore wrote in his study of Bodenheim (14).

The future poet attended Hyde Park High School in Chicago until he was expelled for an unidentified offense. His formal education ended then, but he became a well-read man. At age sixteen or so, he joined the US Army, under an assumed name. Any discipline at all was too much; he deserted. Recaptured, he swallowed lye in a failed attempt to kill himself, perhaps, or simply to avoid barracks life. He was interned in Ft. Leavenworth. After his release, he wandered some, working in Texas and elsewhere. In 1912 he returned to Chicago, took unskilled jobs, and became part of the classy bohemians of Chicago's Renaissance, whose members, especially Ben Hecht, recognized his talent. Harriet Monroe of *Poetry* published verse of his in 1914; Margaret Anderson followed by printing his poems in the *Little Review*.

Bodenheim is most closely associated, however, with New York, where he had good connections in his early years with numerous poets of note, including such modernists as Alfred Kreymborg and William Carlos Williams, who wrote that his poetry was "colorful," with "sensitive and well observed images" (quoted in Moore 32). Bodenheim had a strong personality; he was described as "gently arrogant, quietly obtrusive and immensely self-possessed" (*My Life and Loves* 252). He became notorious in Greenwich Village and was one of its faithful portraitists. Poetry soirées were a staple there, and many aspiring writers kept the poetry mills going. He benefited from the vigor of these literary scenes, the glamour of artistic pursuits, the numbers of publishers and book-buyers, and the arrival of imagism and other strains of modernism. He was fortunate in some ways. Two plays of his were performed by the Provincetown Players in 1917. His friends were often generous and loyal; he was able to travel to England and also was a resident at the MacDowell Artists' Colony in New Hampshire.

Bodenheim published in distinguished magazines such as the *Dial*, the *Nation*, and *Harper's* when still young. New musical modes did not find him indifferent; his collection *Bringing Jazz!* appeared in 1930. He published nine additional collections of verse, including *Introducing Irony*, 1922, which he labeled "A Book of Poetic Short Stories and Poems." Among his novels is *Georgie May* (1928), with a southern setting. In 1925 legal action was instituted against him and his publisher for the novel *Replenishing Jessica*, called pornographic; he was acquitted. He also wrote plays and numerous critical articles.

Although attributed to him, the memoir *My Life and Loves in Greenwich Village*, published posthumously by friends, with illustrations, is considered, by more than one source, spurious. Yet its style, labeled uncharacteristic, is sustained throughout. Its first-person observations are persuasive; and the pseudo-author, who knows how to sketch characters, chose some who appear in Bodenheim's narrative verse. Only the final chapter, "The Last Phase of Maxwell Bodenheim," is explicitly in another voice, that of "S. R.," presumably the publisher Samuel Roth, owner of the imprint "Bridgehead Books," to whom the text alludes earlier as a Maecenas. The book may have been prepared from drafts Bodenheim left; the voice of "S.R." alludes to working on reminiscences under Roth's sponsorship, and Roth alludes to scenes in the book written by "Max" (254–55).

Whatever the case, Bodenheim's life in New York is well documented, especially the chief fact: that he was an alcoholic, driven finally to the gutter. In 1952 he was arrested for sleeping in a subway car. He called himself "a distinguished outcast" (Moore 92); to some, he appeared a miserable specimen of manhood. Friends, including Kreymborg, gave him handouts, and sometimes he lived on the proceeds of poems that he sold on the street corner in the Village. He was repelled by those who lived, as he saw it, for money. Joseph Wood Krutch called him an "absolute idealist" (quoted in Lloyd 44). He was sympathetic to Communism, though not to the puritanism and conformism it required. He included "Poems of Social Message" in his lengthy *Selected Poems* (1946).

Bodenheim's love life was turbulent. He was something of a libertine; women threw themselves at him. He was married three times. His first wife, Minna Schein, with whom he had a son, divorced him; his second, Grace Finan, died of cancer. From his third wife, Ruth Fagan, he reaped much misery—as did she; they quarreled, and each was unfaithful. Earlier misfortunes included the death of an early love, Feyda Ramsay, who was killed by falling from a horse in California. Bodenheim learned of the accident from a newspaper as he was about to board a train that would take him there. Ramsay remained for him a muse; his *Selected Poems* are dedicated to her ("the driving force behind my first eight books of verse") and to Grace. He died in his Third Avenue rooming house, shot by a psychotic drifter and hanger-on, who stabbed Ruth Fagan to death at the same time. The assailant was convicted and committed to a hospital for the criminally insane. The novelist Dawn Powell wrote that Bodenheim's murder proved that "violent deaths are the only thing that can give writers now any immortality" (52).

Selected Poems (to which page numbers below refer) has a generous selection of Bodenheim's verse. From the outset, he was attracted to free verse, the avant-garde form. Ezra Pound commended his attempts to "take more care of his actual writing than either [Edgar Lee] Masters or [Carl] Sandburg," but did not praise him highly (quoted in Moore 30). In a letter, Hart Crane wrote that Bodenheim was at "the top of American Poetry today" and a "first-class critic" (quoted in Lloyd 43). Yet the rhetoric accompanying Bodenheim's images seemed excessive to some. Not many years after publishing his first book, *Minna and Myself* (1918), which critics such as Louis Untermeyer and John Peale Bishop praised, he returned to rhyme and traditional metrics. Even the "Jazz Poems" in *Selected Poems*, written to be set to musical compositions, are in rhyme.

Bodenheim composed many short lyrics. In "Poet to His Love," his adoration for the beloved is "an old silver church in a forest. / ... / The trees around it / Are words that I have stolen from your heart" (13). "Sharpness of Death" begins with lovely images: "A fan of smoke in the long, green-white revery of the sky, / Slowly curls apart. / So shall I rise and widen out in the silence of air" (17). The series called "Poems to Minna" echoes the classical trope of enumerating a beloved's traits—eyes, cheeks, hair. Narrative and dramatic poems likewise occupy an important place in his work, and human figures populate his pages. Among them is "The Scrub-Woman," originally subtitled "A Sentimental Poem," which displays his sympathy for the downtrodden: "Time has placed his careful insult / Upon your body" (74). There are series called "People" and "Portraits." "Condensed Novel," "Candid Narrative," "Platonic Narrative," and numerous other poems are developed over more than one page. "Condensed Novel" advises readers to "shun the abundant paragraphs / With which a novelist interviews shades / Of physical appearance" (82) and, instead, get the character and plot in a few lines. The instruction to "shuffle the cards on which I have written / Alvin Spar's changes in physical appearance / And deal them out to the various players" is contemporary with surrealist writing emphasizing and using chance and also foreshadows postmodernist fiction that aims at the aleatory (21).

"Lynched Negro" and "Poem to Negroes and Whites" show that Bodenheim had not forgotten his southern homeland. His approach to "the race question" reflects southern racial understanding as he knew it, exemplified by the best representatives of both races, and the tensions he saw increasing around 1945. "A quiet, level spontaneity / Springs only where familiar burdens pile." The speaker blames the "men of venom," those who "spread old lies" and thus sow discord. "Without them, southern Negroes, Whites could meet / And plan sane compromise within one year. / The soldiers in the fox-holes, black and white, / ... / Will shoulder memories close and erect" (190).

Such impressionistic poems as "Steel Mills: South Chicago" and "South State Street: Chicago" demonstrate that the poet was sensitive to the twentieth-century urban and industrial milieu, which had become not only a setting but a topic. The latter poem evokes a busy street: "With driving majesty, the endless crowd / Pounds its searching chant of feet / Down this tawdrily resplendent street" (57). In "North Clark Street, Chicago" he depicts afternoon, which "has fallen on this street, / like an imbecilic organ-grinder / grinning over his discords" (118). (The organ-grinder is reminiscent of Baudelaire's urban poetry; Bodenheim was familiar with the French predecessor.) These Chicago poems, showing the influence of Sandburg, are, in David Perkins's words, "warmly sympathetic" (1: 533). "Summer Evening: New York Subway Station" provides a glimpse of Manhattan, sketching "two figures on a subway platform, / Pieced together by an old complaint" (63). "New York City" emphasizes the city's seedy side, "the flatly carnal beggar," "filthy brick," "New York, sardonic and alert" (87–88).

It is no great wonder that Bodenheim's poetry is ignored presently. Tastes have evolved in America in the century since he began publishing and even more since his death. A glance at *A Miscellany of American Poetry 1920* is illustrative. Only two names of eleven—Robert Frost and Carl Sandburg—remain so current that they would not, presumably, be omitted from any school anthology today. Edwin Arlington Robinson, Conrad Aiken, and Amy Lowell, the last as a woman poet, might easily appear in any broader collection. Most others, such as Vachel Lindsay, James Oppenheim, and Sara Teasdale, are known generally by specialists only or are considered poetic dinosaurs. Like them and others in the company of the excluded meritorious, Bodenheim deserves recognition again.

BESMILR BRIGHAM

Besmilr Brigham, originally Bess Miller Moore, was born, according to sources, in Pace, Mississippi, in 1913. One biographical note adds that she was reared in the Lower Rio Grande Valley of Texas; poems show her interest in Browns- ville (Turner and Wright). One grandfather was a Choctaw. While she did not reside in Mississippi as an adult, she considered herself a Mississippian. She died in 2000 from complications of Alzheimer's disease, in New Mexico, near her daughter, according to the same source. An eccentric in some ways, she adapted her given names to reflect "how people spoke" (Bledsoe)—that is, in Mississippi. Following the example of e. e. cummings, moreover, she used no capital letters in her names and often omitted majuscules from her poems. In 1970 she received a "Discovery Award" from the NEA to work on what became *Heaved from the Earth* (1971).

Her other poetry books are *Agony Dance: death of the (Dancing Dolls*, punc- tuated thusly by Brigham (1969); *Death of the Wild* (1984); and the posthumous *Run Through Rock: Selected Short Poems* (2000), edited by C. (Carolyn) D. Wright. Wright, an Arkansas native, read the title poem from "Heaved from the Earth" on recordings in the "Poetry of America Readings and Commentary" series. Wright likewise introduced her and her son-in-law, Keith Wilson, a poet, in the 1993 PBS documentary *United States of Poetry*. Wright described Brigham and her husband as "the last free people," explaining that they had not been broken by the life they had chosen, "itinerant and subsistent" (Bledsoe).

Little information is available on Brigham's early years. She graduated from Mary Hardin Baylor College in Belton, Texas, then went to study at the New School for Social Research in New York. There she married Roy Brigham. They had one daughter, Heloise Wilson, who remarked how her mother did not seek to publish her poetry unless fellow poets urged her to do so and assisted her

(Bledsoe). Roy worked in the newspaper business, sometimes as a linotype operator. Once, at least, he owned a small newspaper in Texas but sold it when the couple decided that "they did not want to live that way" (Bledsoe). Besmilr taught school. They lived in various foreign countries as well as Alaska, Oklahoma, New Mexico, and especially, during their later years, the town of Horatio, in southwest Arkansas. She corresponded with John Gould Fletcher and perhaps was influenced by his verse. Her poems, some of which reflect their various locations, appeared in both small magazines and high-profile publications such as the *Atlantic Monthly*, *Harper's Bazaar*, and the *New York Times*, and in prestigious anthologies. Among her publications were short stories.

A pamphlet (so classified in the University of California, Berkeley, library) by Brigham shows her poetic tendencies. The title page displays the word *Spring* and the imprint, "IS. four / designed and printed by Victor Coleman." In the poem, one page only, the words, some related to the season, such as *jonquils*, are loosely scattered on the page, without punctuation or capitalization. (The library record gives the place of publication as Horatio, Arkansas? [sic], and the date as 1967, the postmark date of an envelope in which Brigham apparently mailed the pamphlet to one James Koller at *Coyote's Journal* in San Francisco.) Her following poems are similarly in the modernist vein. While they have received praise for their "innovative structure, sound, and rhythm" (Bledsoe), they are not, in fact, particularly avant-garde; cummings, and Marianne Moore, sometimes, had already dropped majuscules, and dispersion of words across the page and images through the poem was far from new. Meaning achieved through images and particularly their juxtaposition is fundamental to modernist writing. As for the neglect, if not abandon, of rationality and ordinary syntax in poetry, it had been established as a mode by major figures in the early twentieth century. These uses had, in fact, become new conventions, with their own "grammars," that is, means of structuring language and lines. Thus Brigham's work could even be viewed as retrograde, since by the last third of the twentieth century a new formalism had spread widely and had acquired enough prestige to seem, to some observers, the true vanguard of American poetry.

Agony Dance: death of the (Dancing Dolls is a series of fifteen numbered poems, mostly short. They illustrate various practices, central to modernist literature and graphic art, that can be called *breakup*. Daniel Cross Turner remarks, nevertheless, that Brigham's work "concerns itself chiefly with structure—verbal and psychological coherence," even as the poems point toward "a chaotic, incoherent world, inside and out" (in Watkins 235). There is little punctuation except for an occasional comma, slash, and opening parenthesis mark. Parentheses are rarely closed. A third-person anonymous voice is usually the invisible narrator, but the poet does introduce also first-person speakers, women. Brigham puts capitals only on "Satan," "Christ," and a few other words. Alliteration creates coherence in lines such as these from poem xiii: "you who went will-wise down your own ways / of fulfillment // the surface is / calm, look at the suspended wing." Short groups of lines have syntactical coherence, sometimes, but sense is often dislocated. The poems depend partly on motifs and figures, such as angels, a sword, a son, a dead baby. The chief structural and hermeneutic resource is, however, juxtaposition of disparate images and notations.

Mentions of Christmas celebrations, "Christ mass," Mary, blood, and thorns carry the weight of the Christian drama from its beginning to its end, both suggested by "manger bier" (xv). A Christmas tree is a motif in the first and last poems and elsewhere. The epigraph mentions "doleful women" in houses; they might suggest mourners, although "satyrs shall dance there." By the final poem a "giddy madonna" is hanging on the cross, "little drunk angel her hysterical / voice runs the morning a bird / in the bush its feathers burn // struck on the thorn." The accumulated effect of such notations gets attention. Moreover, by rearrangement of elements, clear sense can sometimes be reestablished, as at the conclusion to poem v, where the shadowy allusions to a manger scene—barn calves and mules flicking their tails—are followed by: "we ran— red cranberries! / we sat by the fire that winter / and strings and strings of // do you love me." Blank pages follow the final lines of poem xv, which mention "our so distant and strange / ideas of god // (the holy day." Far down on a third page, nearly blank, one finds the sentence, in bold face, "who shall tell us where lies joy." These poems offer evidence of Brigham's interest in spiritual matters; she corresponded with Thomas Merton.

Her time in New Mexico may have suggested elements in poem iv: "ranges of living wild dead-house where / women go women in child birth / cry over gorge rivers, brush lloronas." Mentions of a water gourd, dancing, and weaving contribute to the southwestern atmosphere. Poem v may allude to the great flood of 1927: "her first was born / Mississippi flood river negro / women water on the fire hearth / alienated from time."

Heaved from the Earth, published by Knopf, is divided into "Poems of Warmth" and "Poems of Cold." In the table of contents, the titles, or most words in them, begin with the conventional majuscules; but the poems themselves (aligned at the right margin) have no capital letters and no punctuation. The titles sometimes belong to the syntax of the first sentence. Thus, the title "Caught / in the Car's Lights, / the white owl" leads into the first line, "wings / before the racing wind- / shield [sic] / glass. . . ." Imagination has full rein, as in the poem called "In the Month / of the Jaguar / of Sweet Laughter." The first line mentions "the whale and little fishes"; after ellipsis points, the line adds "he hides the young in his mouth." Then comes "the blue cat, scale-less / fish. . . ."

These lines convey further the unstructured, unsettled quality of Brigham's writing in this collection, which depends largely on images. Relying on quick touches of observation, short lines, relatively few finite verbs, and occasionally uncertain syntax, poems offer impressions but not always a sense of a whole. They are as if suspended, not moving distinctly to new insight or other clear conclusion. Yet her characteristic topics may benefit from this discretion. Although her language is not vulgar, she does not always reject bold moves, such as using *sperm* as a verb ("Painter Crayon 2").

In *Heaved from the Earth*, nature is the principal setting and subject. Brigham evokes the Arctic tundra and other topography, botanical topics, horses, birds, and rocks. "Hunters in the Snow," a three-part poem, offers beautiful details, from "a covey of quail, frost-feeding," to pines and yellow-breasted larks. The season invites reflection: "i dream of wild ways / and there is / something about the 'wild ways' that comes to us / the strangeness. . . ." Despite the snow, the cold, and the wolves, the figure whom the Indians call "the Old Woman Who Never Dies," who makes the crops grow, is there, quietly. The poem "Your Hands" sketches delicately a gardener at work among saplings, pruning a fruit tree; the poem then foresees the future harvesting of "big gold plums" and imagines a hand "in the heavy fig growth." Evocations of birds suggest airiness. Mythical creatures, even archetypes, appear. "The sun eyed fire-macaw sits in a white tree // at the corner of the universe," according to "A Dream in the Cold."

"From the Chamberino House: New Mexico," a disturbing poem, shows how vulnerable nature is when human action impinges on it. The first-person voice evokes an unidentified sensation at night, which is followed by noise of screaming birds, "the steady high-air sound that a rocket makes." Strange shapes against the skyline inspire anxiety in the observers; then the odor of gas "seeping down / you smelled it full in the road" confirms some awful occurrence (a scientific experiment). ". . . we sat until morning, still in the house again / waiting for the strange sun to come up; even the animals came inside with us." Lines that end with *the* and *a* contribute to a disturbed syntax, which supports the sensations. What may be memories of Mississippi appear in "To My Father, in the New House." From the epigraph line, one concludes that the house in question is a nursing home. "he missed / the back screen porch his old place / the pump the well his cows his chickens / filling the water trough." Hackberry limbs, roosting poles, a minnow pond, and other details fill out the scene, which the narrator sketches from the father's memories. This poem suggests that Brigham's home state remained important to her and nourished her poetry.

JACK BUTLER

Jack Armand Butler Jr., a versatile creative artist, has published novels, short stories, for which he has won awards, and cooking books. *Living in Little Rock with Miss Little Rock* (1993) was nominated for the Pulitzer Prize in Fiction and the PEN/Faulkner Award. It would be wrong, however, to assume that poetry has been a sidelight to him. "Poetry," he wrote, "has been the main instrument for my life, the main way of appreciating and remembering." He finds writing in general to be "a continuous way of being—a way of life, not merely a career or an avocation" (Interview). He is the author of three collections. "Not Quite Like Son" was included in *Best Poems* of 1976, edited by Joyce Carol Oates. His verse has appeared in the *New Yorker, Atlantic Monthly, New Orleans Review, Southern Poetry Review*, and *Poetry*. His fellow Mississippi poet, Larry Johnson, places him among the greatest living poets in America (Johnson Interview).

Butler was born in Alligator, Mississippi, in 1944. He spent his early childhood in New Orleans, where his father was studying at the Baptist Theological Seminary. Following his ordination, the family returned to Mississippi but moved, mostly within the Delta region, each time he took a new position. The poet claims the King James Bible as a major influence on his writing; another is science fiction (Abbott, *Reflections* 387). He graduated from high school in Clinton. He was ordained a Baptist minister (even as a boy he spoke some from the pulpit) and briefly had a church. His family having moved to Missouri, he enrolled at Central Missouri State College, then spent a year at Mississippi College, where he ran on the track team, was active in dramatics, and wrote for the college magazine. Returning to Central Missouri, he took a BA in English and a BS in mathematics. He has expressed surprise that poets generally view science and literature as opposed and incompatible.

In 1968 Butler enrolled in the University of Arkansas creative writing program, but did not receive his MFA until 1979. In the interim he lived in Arkadelphia, where he was poet in residence for the Arkansas Arts Council, and Fayetteville. He held various jobs and positions, working in public relations and actuarial analysis for an insurance company. Subsequently he held the position of assistant dean of Hendrix College (1988–93), then moved to the College of Santa Fe as associate professor of creative writing and codirector of the program (1993–2004). After his retirement, he resided briefly in Oklahoma, then settled in Eureka, California, where he writes, paints, sculpts, and practices Zen Buddhism and yoga. He has been married three times; he has two daughters. Women figure prominently in his poetry.

Butler's poems are often in conventional forms, and he considers himself a formal poet. This is despite the fact that he frequently writes what he himself calls free verse. In his understanding, it is not really so; it is strongly affected by the sense of rhythm and other sound values that he acquired by studying traditional forms (Interview). He cites William Butler Yeats and Robert Frost as influences.

The title of *West of Hollywood: Poems from a Hermitage* (1980) alludes to Hollywood, Arkansas, a small community west of Arkadelphia, where Butler created the "hermitage" of the title. Forms vary. One part, "Jingle-Jangle," consists of wordplay (and thus thought-play) poems. The collection is replete with markers of the rural South—pickups, blackberries and briars, snakes, Baptists, the "long Delta highways" ("Withdrawal"). Poetry, he says, must "follow a man" into a world of brambles and stink-bugs ("Blackberries" pt. 3).*

The opening poem, "The Ant-Hill," is marked by rhymes, sometimes strict, sometimes slant, all well handled, distributed loosely. Butler does not fear modifiers, which do not seem excessive even when abundant. Thus "each tiny lunar silhouette" commingles "with wilder shadow yet." Building a house, the speaker shovels earth on a hillside. "In its flank I frame slowly our great hope, / the oldest, most banal, deepest, most sweet" ("Apology for Hope"). He is not entirely solitary, as the little poem "Bois d'Arc" shows; the speaker cuts the "bo-dark," known for its toughness and durability, to furnish wood for a neighbor's fenceposts. In "Waiting for Kohoutec: Binocular," dedicated to Johnson, the speaker, gazing at the moon, realizes that he cannot share his reflections with "metropolitan / poets who feel nature has had a good run / ... but what's the new show?"; so he talks to Johnson, though he "of all men" needs no explanation "of men's eyes struggling to widen and stay linked, / of the tired brain struggling to understand, / the heart to reach the breaking-point and not

---

* Parts of multipart poems are designated throughout this discussion by Arabic numbers, whatever the poet may have used. Poets are not consistent always.

break." The depiction of rural Baptists in "A Peculiar People: For My Nephew in Church"—their character, speech, mores, and religion—is a fine study. In "Blackberries" part 4, the poet contrasts churchgoing and its significance with poetry. "Not much difference—you roll your own, that's all." He writes, "It has been hard to lose those meanings / and keep my own."

Frost's influence may be visible in the lovely lyric "The Way Through the Woods," in rhymed stanzas. "I sang a song as wild and sweet / as any I've written anywhere. / A tithe to nothingness, I thought—let it be written on the air." The persona follows a dark creek that pulls him, like a tide, "to go down where it went, and prove / (if I could keep from getting lost) / it ended where I thought it did / and crossed the road I thought it crossed." The beauty and cruelty of nature meet in "The Rabbit on the Highway." However its dead body and the "stupid, battering vehicle" that killed it are to be remembered, "I will not have it made a mere anecdote, a joke. / Whatever is to be made of it, / it must have the gravity of poetry at least." Elsewhere, nature blends, quite properly, with family love, as the persona imagines a woman and a little girl "dancing / and slowly changing from foot to foot," coming through trees or moonlight "toward me in low bronze light / in my mind forever" ("Ways of Loving" pt. 4).

Among the forms used in *The Kid Who Wanted to Be a Spaceman* (1984) are tercets, sonnets, a villanelle, rhymed quatrains and quintains, free verse, and prose poems. These forms and others serve what Butler identifies in a preface as his aims: setting scenes, telling stories, provoking laughter and surprise, including incongruity, and avoiding excessive seriousness—hence a bit of irony. As in his first collection, the world to which he points is the real one, recognizable. Yet epistemological questions and other challenges to thought are everywhere. "What do I know of geese in the high wind?" ("Geese"). Within poems, imagery and meditations range widely. Rhyme words generate images, it would seem. Times and spaces rub elbows: Thales, Einstein, "a memory of some extinct volcanic cone" ("Parameters"), and "the canyon of the thunder of time" ("Morning in Zion" [Zion National Park, Utah]). A representative poem is "The Mooncalf," where the speaker, who has felt sick, nevertheless accompanies his wife and little child out at night to see a newborn calf, "a little shadow-calf under its mother." He adds, "That was not reality less color, / but a glimpse of something flowering past attention, / past all of attention's possibilities."

In "A Prayer for Jehovah's Witnesses" (perhaps two who visit the speaker, perhaps anyone who has borne witness for faith), the voice admits that God "is only a story in me, / a story out of which I make stories." "The Binomial Theory of Hope" declares: "Hope feeds on hope like compound interest: / time's tiniest opening, the infinitesimal / pasturage after the stopped and stony decimal...." "Homage to the First Geometer" contrasts water and fire, its syntax carried over from one free-wheeling stanza (though with assonance and consonance) to the next. In the title poem, the speaker recalls how he became a Christian at age six, "coming forward" by accident, but he remembers more keenly his fascination with space travel and his determination to go to the moon. "Science fiction and Scripture, / . . . day-dreams in the red-dirt hills and the Delta" led to the study of science, its wonder and its "poetry." Another poem announces that "there are no seas or stars wilder than those / imagination offers" ("The Theory of the Rose").

In his foreword to *Broken Hallelujah* (2013), William Wright identified "keen intelligence, formal grace, verbal play, and a musicality lacking in most contemporary poetry." The title is borrowed from Leonard Cohen. The inclusion of poems from previous collections underlines authorial concerns. Stylistic and formal characteristics follow generally those used earlier, though one poem, "Solomon in His Wisdom," of more than seven pages, departs significantly from the norm, and "Youth Is a Passage, Aging's the Play" uses centered lines. In "The Kid Who Wanted to Be a Spaceman," short paragraphs, some very short, replace the separate lines of the first version of the poem. The second version may be better. In a copy of the book corrected in Butler's hand, two poems, "So I Went to the Ant" and "The Mantis," he replaced *his* by *its* repeatedly and deleted occurrences of *he*—a revealing nod to changed views on gendered pronouns and adjectives.

Philosophy and science reappear, with notes of appreciation and reverence. The initial poem, "Gyroscope," stresses the laws of science and their utilization by ingenious man. In "Mr. Entropy Meets the Weak Antropic Principle," the first line announces that "we're born into a dying universe." Furthermore, "nothing is getting better that won't be worse." Yet "the ruin of novae made this heavy earth. / We die, and something novel comes to birth." In the charming sonnet "The Interstellar Tourist Shows His Slides," a cosmic traveler, reporting on his visit to earth, describes the seasons, which offer "the purest praise." Two poems among the last, "The Spider at the Bottom of the Bottle"—a poem of "splitting up" as well as nature—and "The Practice" are particularly effective.

Butler has a new collection in progress; his admirers will welcome it. One poem surely to be included is "Lost Road Blues," which the editor of the *Southwest Review* solicited after learning of it. A short lyric, it is in tercets rhymed aab, ccb, dde, and so on. "Lost Roads" is the name of a small press in Arkansas founded by the poet Frank Stanford, whose catalogue included collections by Ellen Gilchrist and C. D. Wright. Stanford committed suicide when he was twenty-nine. Butler addresses Stanford directly, clearly admiring him but distancing himself: "Im [sic] just trying / to keep on breathing here."

TURNER CASSITY

(Allen) Turner Cassity (1929–2009), who was born in Jackson, grew up there and in Forest. He was reared as a Presbyterian. Readers may see the influence of this denominational background not only in his explicit references to Calvin and predestination but also in the pall that hangs over much of his writing, pointing to the ubiquity of sin and evil and the sense of doom. On both sides his family was in the sawmill business. His father died when the boy was four; at sixteen he began managing his own inheritance. His mother, Dorothy Turner Cassity, a violinist (to whose memory he dedicated *No Second Eden*, 2002), was a charter member of the Jackson Symphony and at one time concertmaster; she also performed in silent movie houses. He began writing poetry as an adolescent. He did not consider himself a southern writer, and he lived in his home state only briefly after 1951. His focus and tastes are cosmopolitan, not local. Occasionally, however, he draws on his early experiences in the South. The three sections of "In the land of great aunts," from *Steeplejacks in Babel* (1973), present homely scenes: putting together costumes for the Christmas pageant; visiting the cemetery, "a genealogy in stone"; and making blackberry jelly, by which "the whole of sense is gathered on the tongue."

After finishing secondary school, Cassity took a BA at Millsaps College (1951). He then enrolled at Stanford University, where he studied very profitably with Yvor Winters, who stressed both form and moral importance in poetry. Keith Tuma observed that Cassity "never obscured his allegiance to Winters" (19); indeed, he was faithful to both the moral tone and the poetics of his master, described by Francis Murphy as "an extraordinary combination of passion and detachment" (quoted in Lloyd 81). But in calling himself "perhaps the wildest" of Winters's students, Cassity distinguished himself from both the teacher and other disciples (Tuma 19). This "wildness" includes bold poetical choices as well a vein of the grotesque, or southern Gothic, and emphasis on human foolishness. What Tuma calls his "arch posturing and camp sensibility" amount to "a departure from Wintersian earnestness" (19).

Drafted into the US Army after receiving his degree at Stanford (1952), Cassity was stationed for nineteen months in Puerto Rico, a period he viewed as an education of a different sort. Afterwards, benefitting from the GI bill, he enrolled at Columbia University and earned a degree in library science. He accepted a position at the public library in Jackson, then was recruited by the Transvaal Provincial Library in South Africa, where he worked from 1958 through 1960. Returning to America, he spent another year at the library in Jackson, then traveled in Europe for four months. In 1962 he became a librarian at Emory University, a post from which he retired in 1991. Following his retirement, he divided his time between Georgia and California. He died in Atlanta.

Erudite, with a tremendous imagination, Cassity was a poet of keen wit, both humor and sense. He published more than ten collections as well as verse plays, and his poems appeared widely in literary magazines. *The Airship Boys in Africa* constituted an entire number of *Poetry* magazine (July 1970). At 247 pages, *The Destructive Element: New and Selected Poems* (1998) presents a generous and judicious choice of his work to that date, to which one must add a substantial output subsequently. Ray Olson, of *Booklist*, called him "a national treasure" (review of *No Second Eden*). Cassity's poetics are traditional, and, as Olson put it, he disciplines himself to form. He favors the couplet, although he employs also quatrains and blocks of lines. The iambic pentameter is his preferred line, but he does not exclude shorter meters, even dimeters, and uses blank verse widely and alexandrines occasionally. The vocabulary is rich, the language carefully wrought, the rhymes deft; many are polysyllabic. J. D. McClatchy called his language "at once clear and mysterious" (quoted in "Turner Cassity"). Cassity can develop an image to the point of turning it into a full conceit; readers may catch resemblances between his imagination and that displayed by various English metaphysicals. Like them, he can make his mannerisms, in form and matter, serve his material.

His subject matter ranges over the globe and vast swaths of time. Not permanence, but history—human action in the world, as carried out by fallen mankind—marks his writing as a whole. Numerous poems have as their setting British colonial territories or what replaced them. *Yellow for Peril, Black for Beautiful* (1975) features a verse drama imagining the death of Cecil Rhodes. Among additional backdrops are South America and the Far East. The poet applied the term "colonial pastorals" to these poems (Tuma 20), but they are scarcely Arcadian. Cassity was a historical pessimist; his work is Swiftian. Backward looks that, for another, might be rose-tinged yield to the poet's realism, not to say cynicism and misanthropy. He "regards everything with a cool, dissecting eye.... He brooks no pretension and no romanticizing," wrote Olson. The tone may be farcical, noir, or deadly serious (as in his glimpses of apartheid). Such notes indicate resemblances between Cassity and Baudelaire, another poet of the noir, where farce, melancholy, and violence (as in "The Poor Glazier") burst into the serenity of beauty and the ideal. (Donald Davie likewise observed the similarity between the two poets.)

A few titles alone suggest Cassity's drollery and range of interests: "Eva [Perón] Beatified," "The Entrance of Winifred into Valhalla," "The Shropshire Lad in Limehouse" (all from *Steeplejacks in Babel*). Consider also "Cities of the Plain and Fancy" and "Let My People Go, but not Without Severance Pay" (from *No Second Eden*). His technique and expression seem effortless. Not facile, however; his poems carry considerable human baggage, historical and psychological. He excels at setting scenes economically and at drawing human portraits. The pervasive allusions, many unlabeled, such as references to Keats, Baudelaire, Henry James, and Wallace Stevens, demand erudition on readers' part. From James, for instance, comes the phrase "the distinguished thing" (meaning death), which Cassity turns on its head, to make it mean *time*, the *undistinguished* thing.

Watchboy, What of the Night? (1966), Cassity's first collection, displayed his poetic maturity, in style and material. He was right to reprint numerous poems from it in *The Destructive Element*; he pursued strains of that first collection throughout his career, particularly the intertwining of past and present. In "Teatro Amazonas," the speaker visits the nineteenth-century opera house of Manaus, seeing from a modern perspective "its awkward, beaux-arts force unworn by years, / ... / Its belle époque of rubber millionaires." He asks, "Is it illusion that to caned seat-bottoms, / A sweating Bernhardt droned the chill Racine? / Illusion too, that ferried here as totems, / European singers, un-divine ... ?"—their mortality proven when, unvaccinated, they died of yellow fever. "Calvin in the Casino" is more philosophical. Anachronistically, the poem places the great theologian before a roulette ball, "sphere of pure chance," from which vantage point he observes "the limits where predestination ends." (That the invention of the roulette wheel and ball is attributed to Pascal, whose Jansenist creed similarly emphasized predestination, adds an additional dimension to the references.) Yet "divine election," though obscured, is also rejustified, as it "stands fulfilled in being here denied," and, paradoxically, caprice of ball marks the verity of "that one same Will which chooses the elect."

The cover of *Steeplejacks in Babel* is a reproduction of M. C. Escher's "Tower of Babel." The collection begins with the charming poem in rhymed couplets "What the sirens sang." (Generally here, Cassity capitalizes only the first word in titles preceding the poems.) "Who seals the ear sets free the eye," they announce, warning Odysseus that he "will not regain, / unmarked, the certain course. One chain / will rankle always on your wrist, / Along your spine be scored the mast." In "The procurator is aware that palms sweat," the poet reimagines the handwashing scene, and thinks of Judas, the betrayer, who may find "in dampened silver, truth I lost / In salvered water. Yes; but what is truth?" "Purdah in Pretoria" depicts deftly the hot, dusty atmosphere and a middle-aged flower seller in the market, with her caste mark and her disappointments. The title motif recurs in the poem "By the waters of Lexington Avenue," where men are at work high on the Chrysler Building. As an epigraph to that poem, Cassity quotes lines from Oswald Spengler, author of *The Decline of the West* (1918, 1922). Evoking the elevator shafts and cables to come, he thinks of how their sound is that of time, "the long captivity they strum." Meanwhile, "lightning waits for thunder, will to power / Then conquers the quotidian. Pure tower // Stands." That the rhyme is obvious does not keep it from being perfect.

The opening lines from "U-24 Anchors Off New Orleans" (from *Hurricane Lamp*, 1986)—set in 1939 and in the first-person voice of a German officer going ashore from his submarine—evoke the city in its perennial features: "The only major city, one would hope, / below the level of a periscope. / An air so wet, a sewer-damp so ill, / One had as well be under water still." The miasmal Louisiana atmosphere contains other notes, though. The officer seeks out a German restaurant—many fish but "no herring"—while the sailors go to "lower Bourbonstrasse." "Where they are / Becomes a high Weimar Republic bar." If he returns, thinking "to pack libido," then "for symbolism there will be torpedo." The poem—and there are many such—shows how Cassity blends a character, man or woman, and voice with setting and historical references to intimate a great deal. "The Aswan Rowing Club," for instance (same collection), describes the Nile at the Aswan Dam and the skilled rowers of a local crew—an incongruous picture, but not more so "than stereo on minarets." In their shell, they move out, with "congruity of stroke, of time, / Of place, for all their hint of Cam." Yet "oars are oars, and in their beat, / In little, are the galley, slave, / The distant sweats of Actium." Such historical re-creations may seem too remote, or simply elaborate chronological jokes, clever but pointless. Readers may prefer Cassity's poems set in the present time. In "High Fashion," among the new poems in *The Destructive Element*, his topic is the space shuttle, which is viewed as a "mode of transport" and, following its name, is expected to return. If it fails, "How name it? Probe? Projectile? Feint? / The triple rocket and the gross // Papoose it carries twist themselves / Out of the fire and into space." It maneuvers awkwardly; its shell is ugly; it seems "out of place" in "the nothingness of space." It is a "mode," that is, a fashion. "The burn that lifts was fossil laid."

The Defense of the Sugar Islands (1979) is not what its subtitle (surely meant tongue-in-cheek) proclaims: "A Recruiting Poster." It is a limited-edition chapbook on fine paper presenting a sequence of ten poems on military motifs, in a tropical setting. A few poems appeared previously in *Poetry* and the *Southern Review*. Phrasing in "The Twenty-Year Man" suggests retrospective composition; but most evocations use present-tense verbs. Cassity's command of prosody is well displayed. One poem, "Military Funeral," is in alexandrines. Rhymes may be strict or loose; some poems are unrhymed. Titles indicate topics clearly: "The New Suit" (blue serge), "Lights Out," "Off Duty." Beyond the picturesqueness (or boredom) of the island—"the genius of place," as "Lorelei of the Lighthouse" puts it—and the military routines, the real subject is, of course, the self, and the lesson of all exoticism: "For us, all footsteps lead back to themselves" ("The Sand Diviner").

In *No Second Eden* Cassity returns to the tower motif, in "WTC," composed after the 2001 destruction of the Twin Towers. "Against the best advice, / We put up Babel twice." In his continuing iconoclastic project, the poet probes the surface of things to get to their underside. In "Stylization and Its Failures," he considers the striking distance between the eagle and the buzzard by observing that the latter bears no symbolic value, as far as he knows, whereas the former serves to symbolize a wide range of features, undertakings, and achievements, from the Roman Empire and its successors to a rank of the Boy Scouts. A success for the eagle, thus. But, in the story of the Good Samaritan, Cassity points out, there *is* a place for a vulture; if the charitable Samaritan had not, by chance, happened by, "the body by the roadside nonetheless / would have received attention in due time."

Similarly, between the heroic and the mock-heroic the line is thin, "once an epoch and its codes are well behind" ("Transpositions"). In that line and elsewhere, the poet tries to identify even the narrowest slice of reality between surface and substance, because the matter has an aesthetic dimension. Truth in art is not mere transcription via recording. Thus cross-dressing is not necessarily a travesty, nor is "cross-voicing," as in the case of castrati and women with alto voices taking men's roles. Even androgyny might have a role, "somewhere between the sexes and between the staves." The speaker in "The Second-Guesser" similarly looks for the obverse of the usual. Calling on historical examples—Caesar, Pilate, Alger Hiss, Pol Pot—and an ordinary physician, he turns events inside out, thus highlighting, again, the place of chance in human decisions and their consequences. "A sort of retro-oracle, I drone / My might have been. An armchair is my throne." The poem "Enola Gay Rights" reintroduces the motif of crossover, although the illustrations of ambiguity touch less on the twentieth-century concern with individual rights than with popular representations of wide-scale destruction, such as a fallen Statue of Liberty.

Cassity's last collection, *Devils & Islands* (2007), bears a suggestive epigraph from Ivy Compton-Burnett: "I wonder who began this treating of people as fellow creatures. . . . It is never a success." Cassity uses again his favored rhymed couplets but also tercets, quatrains, blocks, and free verse. Curious titles, some with contemporary notes, awaken interest: "Fantasia on Dummy Keys" (concerning a soundless piano keyboard, for practice), "Amazonas.com" (set in Manaus), "Robinson Crusoe to Capt. Dreyfus," "A Course in Sax Education." But the wit is often sardonic, and the book is painful with the pain of being human and, in this case, being a disabused, ironic modern man.

The range is wide and not disappointing. Cassity revisits Soweto, in 1987, which he had seen thirty years before, and reflects on the Isthmus of Panama, its two oceans, its volcanic threat, and what a title identifies as "Opposing Colonizations." In "Free Trade in Mitteleuropa," the voice reflects on Vienna, Trieste, and the Adriatic, as well as famous figures, nations (so-called), and empires (including Yugoslavia). "Tourism shows decline can be an industry / Like any other. Venice does not live on glass, / Vienna on the OPEC meetings." History weighs heavily in such poems. "The Passion of 1934," concerning the drama performed that year at Oberammergau, examines the play, the actors and their biblical roles, the terrible contemporary circumstances, and the inevitability of the Passion and its consequences, both in the first century and the twentieth. Barabbas will be freed, Thomas will continue to doubt, and Peter to deny, in Rome, and "later, in the dock at Nuremburg."

These examples illustrate the poet's tremendous understanding of human beings and their circumstances, as well as his wit. His achievement has been recognized, but perhaps not sufficiently. In 1993 he received the Michael Braude Award of the American Academy of Arts and Letters, and the state of Georgia named him Author of the Year in Poetry for 2007. In addition, he won an NEA grant, the Levinson Prize for Poetry, and an Ingram Merrill Foundation Award. Yet it is still not clear whether his standing is what he deserves. Tuma observed that Cassity's long narrative poems, an unfashionable genre, may have alienated readers, who might not have seen that much of his later verse was terse, while dense. Nor was he progressive in any sense; his pessimism goes against the utopian project of his age. The odd subject matter cannot have helped him. Fashionable topics arise only obliquely in his verse, if at all, and he made no concessions to trends. The layers of erudition and the allusiveness—along with wry, sometimes sarcastic wit—could not appeal to all. He was, in short, a classical poet, dealing with what he viewed as enduring verities of humankind. Additionally, his profession as a librarian—often an invisible post—and his location in the South may have contributed to keeping him out of the limelight.

ADAM CLAY

Adam Clay teaches writing at the University of Southern Mississippi. Previously, he held posts at Georgetown College in Kentucky, the University of Illinois Springfield, and in northwest Arkansas, where he codirected the state's Poets in the Schools program and edited *Typo Magazine*. He has four collections of poetry in print; many poems have appeared in periodicals, and he has given numerous readings. In 2019 he was awarded a grant by the Mississippi Arts Commission. He was born in 1978 in Hattiesburg and grew up in the Jackson area. His degrees are in creative writing and English. He received a BA and MA at the University of Southern Mississippi (1999, 2001), where he was a student of Angela Ball's at both levels. He then took an MFA at Arkansas (2004). His PhD (2009) is from the University of Western Michigan. He serves as book review editor of the *Kenyon Review*. He lives in Hattiesburg and has a daughter.

Clay writes with confidence and authority. This is paradoxical; his view of language rules out authority. He is a modernist in his technique, a postmodernist in his assumptions and aspirations. His poems, in free verse, built on bizarre, often stand-alone images, have a deliberate vagueness as well as boldness, calling on extremes, pushing limits, transgressing. They are, presumably, to reflect reality as he sees it today. He uses normal syntax and spelling but forgoes other aspects of poetic rationality—strophic structure, consistency, and connections. Surreal association is his principal resource. He sets himself apart, thus, from most Mississippi poets, who generally ground their poems in common experience and, in many cases, local scenes. His stance is what Yvor Winters called "the fallacy of imitative form" (*In Defense of Reason*)—the expression of disintegration (social, historical, natural) through linguistic disintegration. (To be sure, "imitative form" need not be that of disintegration; the hierarchical and relatively stable social order of seventeenth-century France is reflected in the insistence upon literary order.) One poet in the state whose work offers parallels with his and the assumptions behind it is Melissa Ginsburg.

Clay's untitled poem beginning *"Caught No Fish Last night"* (2004) illustrates his approach. Most nouns are capitalized, as are selected other words, but the tone is contemporary. Apparent randomness and incongruity point to dreams or what is otherwise unreal ("I was in My Dream"). Is there mystical identification with nature? Having "shot an Autumnal Warbler," the speaker found it filled with seeds and "Wrapped them in The Paper in my Sock. The Page / Has a Line on it, the Length of My Wife's / Foot for a New pair of Shoes." He perceives his own face, as seen through the bird's, "Filled with the Glow / Of A Church Bell ringing."

A Hotel Lobby at the Edge of the World (2012) illustrates these tendencies further. The collection, which constituted his doctoral dissertation, is in four parts. While in part 2 the poems are printed generally as blocks and all have even left-hand margins, many elsewhere have staggered lines arranged in very short stanzas; they break, moreover, on the verso pages and continue lowerdown on the rectos. One cover endorsement notes that the poems "hover in and out of dreams." Another places Clay's "poetic realm at the very limit of what is known . . . teetering on the flat world's precipice." The judgment that the poems are "brilliantly anchored to the physicality of all things earthbound" seems off the mark; earthly things are present for lack of other referents, but they are less moorings than isolated uncertainties. (The word *anchored* is found, but qualified, in the poem "For Your Eyelash Anchored in the Sky," referring to an eyelash "sculpted from a thousand tiny feathers.") Although a third endorsement asserts that "each poem shimmers with physical and metaphysical insight," such insight does not reach far beyond the simple sense of strangeness.

Myth and memory are motifs, perhaps distant sources of material, but scarcely themes. Perceptions and generalizations, notational, touch on extremes, often alien. Phrases from "Natural History" emphasize lack of delimitation: "Unrecorded boundaries . . . concept of remoteness . . . something more than distance." While "the tree is a metaphor for something" (a repeated phrase), this "metaphor" has no referent. Finally, "nothing here has a name." Words such as "fragment" and "blur" point to both substance and form. Even fragments are unstable; the repeated line "In anticipation of a fragment breaking down" furnishes half of a twelve-line section (sec. 19) in the series "As Complete As a Thought Can Be." In "Song," the poet writes, "Let me think category without meaning anything / Let me think noise   without meaning camera angle."

A suggestion of older American romanticism may linger, however. Does the phrase "I am a line from Whitman knotted in itself" pay homage to Whitman's verse, in all its detail and sweep, or suggest something unfortunate about contemporary America and its culture? ("Song"). "Untie the sky," adds the poet. There are mentions of mustard gas and the dates 2003–2007, an "unheroic time" ("Gathered"). "When every thought of a situation / is plagiarized from Audubon, unintentionally, / a dream on the edge of a field // in the mind of America"—perhaps an allusion to Robert Penn Warren's poem "Audubon: A Vision."

Although poems point sometimes to myth or recognizable reality—Jonah, the South Shore Line, swans on a lake—objects, like those in surrealist art, may not remain themselves. Identity and completeness are false goals; everything is subject to breaking down, and, Clay insists, a fragment is "as complete as a thought can be," with or without capital letters. "I am certainly tired / of certainty," the voice repeats in that series (sec. 15). As in the Cretan liar's paradox and the linguistic theories of Ferdinand de Saussure and Jacques Derrida, any statement is open to contradiction; even to approach assertion is to risk error. Language is not only imperfect; it is arbitrary, as numerous images suggest. ". . . A hay bale rings on the nightstand / and you answer it" ("For the Earnest Days Before Summer"). Can one reduce that arbitrariness, capture the powers of language by any means? Mallarmé's 1897 poem (sometimes called *prose*) announced, "A roll of the dice never will abolish chance"; words scattered on the page are still just ink marks. Language, according to Warren's phrase, the epigraph to part one, is a "delirious illusion." To interrogate it gets one nowhere.

The epistemological implications of Clay's apparent position are unsettling, the ontological ones more so. If "we are only the language / we speak, nothing more" ("As Complete As a Thought Can Be," 16), and this language has no real being and objects no delimitations, then things are shaky indeed. Perhaps a new man is called for; the surrealists likewise wanted to change not just the world (as Communists set out to do) but life itself. Meanwhile, what can be the ground of poetry, a language-based art? Perhaps it should simply point to, then brush lightly past, any assertion, metaphysical or otherwise.

Stranger (2016) pursues the lines of the previous book. The cover image is a house in a bottle. The style is often aphoristic, in an abstract way. Wordplay furnishes lines of thought, departures or conclusions. A few poems have uneven left margins and stair-stepped lines. Numerous poems are long, some multipart; the poet seems to circle around problems, seeing them from different angles, like a phenomenologist. In a cover endorsement, Ada Limón calls the book "a heartbreakingly stunning collection dedicated to the unsung suspension of time that occurs when life suddenly goes awry." The poems, writes Kazim Ali in another endorsement, stake a claim "in the space between a phenomenon and a human reaching after an understanding." Inevitably, the title suggests the estrangement central to Albert Camus's *L'Etranger*; the sense of alienation is strong. Clay writes that "with the trees falling off the leaves, / the unworldliness // of the moment means less and less // until it means more and more" ("Elegant Comparison").

It is unclear, however, *what* has "gone awry." Is it in the world or conscious beings? Something has changed—*gone*. The speaking voice directs its words often to a *you*, and everyday settings are frequent: trees, a newspaper, a furnished house, an unfurnished one. The poet's wife at the time is named in "East Jackson Drive" and elsewhere; the little daughter appears also. The opening poem, an unrhymed sonnet, "To Take Note of Where We Are," speaks of the "insistence" of the world, proof of its "existence." But these elements of setting are often vague, unrooted, and there is almost no drama.

This mode of being partakes of Martin Heidegger's *Geworfenheit*, "thrownness"—being "thrown" into the world, already there. The identity of objects is questionable, as before; and there is no ground for supposing it should be otherwise. Again, various techniques convey uncertainty. Objects may metamorphose into others or disappear. "An ashtray wasn't anymore"; "There's / nothing. It's afternoon all of a sudden" ("Along the Edge of a Season"). Human beings themselves fear dissolution; they may "disappear into someone // completely different" ("Upper Peninsula"). "Tell Me Now, Again, Who I Am" is one title, "Occupied Elsewhere" another. Wordplay shows the unreliability of denotation: "Colors have run elsewhere" ("Along the Edge of a Season"). Space may be "filled and emptied / again" ("Disruption Without Shrapnel"). Common assumptions collapse. A week may have a Tuesday with no Wednesday; a hallway (an obsessive image) may be "hidden between the rooms, / the Iowa of a house." The speaker calls his worldview "palindromic." "There are no middles / anywhere" ("Along the Edge of a Season").

In short, the abyss between language and what it is to designate cannot be bridged. Is that good? "A sentence can fall apart in your hands," writes Clay, but such is "a wonderful thing" ("This is a Frame" 81). Language is "never transparent enough for me" (75). At the same time, in contrast to the distance between phenomena and human grasp (and consequent indeterminability) that Ali's endorsement identifies, Clay again provides enough standard linguistic rationality to tease readers even as images and odd statements disorient them, proclaiming in fact that there is no orient. Logic appears to be a hindrance to understanding, as its demands cannot be met. As major pre-existential texts demonstrated, the uncertain condition between understanding and mystification, like alternating hope and despair, may be the most exasperating, the most desperate. Language can convey this, at least.

CAROL COX

Carol (Moore) Cox, born in Washington, DC, in 1946, is the author of two collections of verse, *Woodworking and Places NearBy* (1979), a Small Press Book Club Selection, and *The Water in the Pearl* (1982). She selected the verse and prose excerpts to accompany the photographs in *Mississippi Observed*. Her poems have appeared in *Ploughshares* and various anthologies. William Matthews, Dave Smith, and Eudora Welty have praised her writing.

Cox was fourteen when her parents, after living in Alabama and Tennessee, settled in Mississippi. Indications of her affection for her adopted state appear in "The Territory Ahead" and "Listening to James 'Son' Thomas Sing Delta Blues" *(Woodworking and Places NearBy)*. She studied for two years at Millsaps College, where she was a member of Chi Delta, a women's honorary literary society. She transferred to the University of North Carolina at Chapel Hill, where she earned a BA. She went to New York City and became secretary of the English department at Columbia University. There she met Fletcher Cox, a student. They married, and after his graduation, drove west, intending to reach Seattle. Instead, they stopped in Wyoming, where both took teachers' jobs. In the early 1970s, the Coxes moved to Tougaloo, Mississippi.

Visiting the Renwick Gallery, part of the Smithsonian Institution, in 1972, they were dazzled by examples of fine woodworking by famous artisans. Both took up the craft. Fletcher Cox, now nationally known, is a founding member of the Craftsmen's Guild of Mississippi and adjunct professor in the Mississippi State University School of Architecture. Work of his is held at Millsaps College, the Smithsonian Institution, the Mississippi Museum of Art, the Fine Arts Museum of Mobile, and the Arkansas Art Center. He has done interior wood designs for numerous churches and government buildings in Jackson. Despite differences between poetry and woodworking—the one an aesthetic undertaking, the other initially utilitarian, a craft—the parallels are considerable. Fine objects of wood, made for beauty as well as function, become art objects; good poetry depends on verbal craftsmanship. Both may make use of ancient skills and tools as well as modern ones. Cox's poem "Finishing Mirrors" (*The Water in the Pearl*) sketches a moment in a woodworking task that turns into an artist's interrogation: "I wonder whether I've finished the work / or have missed the essential middle, skidding on." The persona stares at the framed mirrors, "parts of them, and whole ones, / and whole ones that have come apart."

The title *Woodworking and Places NearBy* is a composite of the titles of its two parts, in reverse order. The focus is on the familiar, in activity and place. A quotation from Wendell Berry precedes part one: "Each thing is carried / beyond itself." The initial poem, "After the Tornado, the Weather Turned Very Cold," in free verse, and, like numerous others, with no capitalization, evokes by disparate images a scene of destruction, the remnants of made and natural objects, and a few human figures, "their heads tipped down." In "Watching You Draw," an old lamp "sends you smoking colors / you do not need but use, / folding them into / your shadowed corner." A cedar tree outside a window, the heat of August, moonlight on a floor—such mundane encounters with objects and sensations become pretexts for musing. Cox's impressionistic metaphors are not, unfortunately, always effective; the mirror poem is not the only one that suggests fragmentation or goes off uncertainly. "The hours wind around my legs / and give me fresh strength, a link, the will to knock off numbers. . . ." ("Several Have Started"). The image of wood, however, is repeatedly put to good effect, as in the brief lyric "Night: 2": "Splinters of walnut / scrape across the sheet / . . . // The sun this morning is a thin edge of oak, / golden and knot-hard."

Nature—"the huge maple block / waiting to become a bowl"—is matter for human art as well as itself ("Waking"). In "Burls," "knotty grain," where the tree was injured, will become "priceless bowls." Work, domestic or artisanal, recurs in the poems as a daily routine (see "Mistake" and "Resumption"). The workshop receives its due as the place of creation and, not incidentally, a source of still-life scenes. "I keep a hand-blown glass near, / heavy and filled with water, / and a clay bowl full of dried fruit" ("In the Workshop"). A pleasing lyric is "Vases," in which the small, curved vessels the speaker makes, yielding up their "grain / and strength," show the paradox of destruction becoming creation, and "how one's breath / can be closed up inside a solid block, / turned into the gift of loss, / a solemn nourishment."

The Water in the Pearl offers sketches of nature, especially the seasons, and reflections on the human condition. "Red Mountain is full of dogwood blooms, / their heart-stopping beauty / reason enough for turning to music" ("When

Bryan Bowers Plays the Autoharp"). Again, Cox uses free verse; some poems have no capitals. Allusions to Mississippi features and places, such as the Pearl River (identified explicitly), remind readers where she lives. Various arts and handicrafts have their place—weavings, bowls, music, including the blues, and dance. Poetry arises, she explained, as "you feel something moving up and you try to throw a net of words over it" (Schaefer). The net is loose, impressionistic, notational: "I'll think of scraping up the wasted particles / of glass and bone from years of accidents / ... / (I'll float in circles past the windows, / checking from outside") ("Ragged Habits"). "An Hour in the Smokies" evokes autumn obliquely, using red and white as motifs. (Red appears frequently throughout the book, and yellow and orange even more.) Images carry the weight of the poems. "The swamps tip away from the road .... The smoky water / takes a song, / gives it back in lower voice ..." ("Driving Back from New Orleans"). Human figures are not absent: "Down on Congress Street, a few boys left to themselves / toss the whole afternoon around" ("The Empty Elevator"). Such images suggest why Cox's poems have admirers with taste.

HUBERT CREEKMORE

(Hiram) Hubert Creekmore (1907–66), an accomplished and erudite man of letters, was born in Water Valley, Mississippi, to an old and prominent family, which settled in Jackson some twenty years later. His father practiced law. Creekmore became a friend of Eudora Welty (his sister married her brother). Creekmore published four collections of poetry, in addition to novels, anthologies of verse, and literary criticism. He translated many poems and songs from Latin, French, Spanish, Provençal, and German; some, such as his Juvenal translations, appeared in books, while others accompanied sheet music. A devoted gardener, he wrote a book on daffodils and similar poisonous but attractive plants; he also played the piano. For many years he reviewed books for the *New York Times*.

Creekmore graduated from the University of Mississippi in 1927. For a while he worked for the state highway department. He wrote scripts for local theatrical productions. To pursue his interest in dramaturgy, he studied first at the University of Colorado, then at Yale University, with George Pierce Baker. When the Federal Writers' Project was created, Creekmore became part of the Mississippi team. In the late 1930s he enrolled at Columbia University and he took an MA in 1940, with a thesis on the poetics of Ezra Pound, to whose poems his have sometimes been compared. From 1942 until the end of World War II he served in the US Navy, which sent him to the South Pacific. After the war, he returned to Mississippi, but he felt out of place, and ultimately settled in New York, where he pursued his literary career energetically. In 1947 he taught fiction at the University of Iowa. He died in a New York taxi from a massive heart attack.

Creekmore's attitude toward his home state and the South in general was critical. His disapproval appears in his verse. He was sensitive to and condemned the class system and its effects. His novel *The Fingers of Night* (1946), about poor whites, did not find favor with local readers; the *Jackson Daily News* wrote that it was "nasty drivel," fit for the garbage can *(Mississippi Encyclopedia*, 303). Through its depiction of three generations of an African American family, *The Chain in the Heart* (1953) depicted unfavorably the historical institution of slavery, its legacy, and the treatment of blacks in his own time. The reviewer of that novel in *Jet* called Creekmore's criticism of the North "self-satisfied" and reproached professional and other blacks with status for leaving the region rather than staying to help mend matters ("Book of the Week").

Moreover, as a homosexual, Creekmore felt ill at ease in the proper, tradition-bound society around him, where departures from norms had to be veiled. His novel *The Welcome* (1948) treated the topic but only obliquely. His cautious depiction of underground, transgressive behavior corresponds to and "exemplifies the lived experiences of queer men in midcentury Mississippi" (J. Howard 192).

Creekmore's first collection of poems, *Personal Sun*, came out in 1940, with the subtitle "The Early Poems of Hubert Creekmore." Some had appeared in magazines such as *Poetry*, the *North American Review*, and *Prairie Schooner*. The poems are short and in conventional forms; many are sonnets. Rhyme prevails, strict or, more often, loose; but some poems have none or are marked by consonance or assonance. Among the best are "Encounter with a Dog" ("Foolish dog to waste such good on man") and "Tyrant," not political but, rather, a "found-object" poem (a pebble). The tone of the collection is pessimistic. Themes include murder and self-destruction, as in "Note After Suicide" and "The Decision," depicting a woman walking to the water's edge and, presumably, entering the "foam," Ophelia-like. Love appears likewise, called, as a title puts it, "The Wound."

The poetry tends strongly to the abstract; that feature, along with terms such as *darksome* (deemed "poetic") and inversions ("Lax would fall your fingers from my heart," from "Lullaby"), made the diction somewhat dated even for the period. Creekmore was forward-looking, however, for insisting upon human brotherhood, whatever the skin tone ("Genus Homo"). "To the Very Late Mourners of the Old South" dismisses those seduced by "feudal charms." "Boxcar 388146" speaks for the hungry tramps riding the rails.

The Stone Ants (1943), a slim collection, consists of six multipage poems. It is partly in free verse, with strange images joined to somewhat heavy rhetoric. Forms change within the poems; lines may be quite short, or drawn-out. The atmosphere is dreamlike on occasion. Meditations can be effective. "The timelessness of this premeditates / its death, and all such intervals / resolve into the conscious dying minutes / of an empty sea" ("Intersection"). The South is present in "Southern Night," which begins: "In a shy distillation / over trees and houses / the darkness hangs / while the sunset hesitates. ..." The poet imagines together "the Venices of Turner" and "the clouds of Mississippi." Part IV of that poem ends as "the great tree bodies shudder. / ... / Oh love, oh love, oh love." A pointed poem is "New Year's Eve by Radio," dated 1938: "Mid fraction of the wave-lengths / speeches interlock the New Year's cry / like a cannon's fugal / counterpoint, announcing 'thousands die.'" Similarly rooted in history is "Genealogy," concerning Jews, notably section IV, set in Ukraine, 1900.

The Long Reprieve and Other Poems from New Caledonia (1946), based on Creekmore's Navy experience, is his most ambitious collection. In an introduction, Selden Rodman assessed it severely, speaking of "arid objectivism" (ix). Creekmore's intellect may work "on a level closer to the dictionary than finished poetry permits"; elsewhere, lines turn into plain "statements of fact" (x–xi). But Rodman praises Creekmore's sympathy for the dispossessed and his experiments with off-rhyme—cross-rhyming vowels and final consonants, a procedure used in earlier books but developed further by having all syllables of cross-rhymed words correspond to each other. Rodman reports that the poet did not consider strict meter to be musical at all; it is, rather, "monotonous"— hence the use of a syncopated beat (xi). The critic notes that the poems and their titles resemble those of Hart Crane but do not appear to stem from that model.

Dealing with two historically conditioned topics, war and exoticism, *The Long Reprieve* may lend itself to criticism on cultural grounds; today the Pacific war of 1941–45 is unpopular in some quarters, and exoticism strikes certain cultural critics as inadmissible at any time. The verse cannot, however, displease pacifists; the poet does not veil his disapproval of warfare, its rationalizations, and the military-industrial complex. "Fear Is Why" condemns alike armed conflict and those who carry it out: "Drop the pose, Gold Braid." "Dividends" illustrates the cost of war on a personal scale: an arm lost here, a leg there, a face gone; and all for stockholders, investments, coupons to clip. Both poems, especially the latter, are suitably didactic and obviously sincere. Exoticism, similarly, is criticized, as in "Conducted, All-Expense Tour." In that poem, along with a further indictment of war, the author takes to task those who worship change, who "travel only to buy the picturesque," who "grab the souvenir / And not the understanding." There is no curio of the Coral Sea, only "waves washing the light from a sailor's eyes."

Published in 1947, *formula*, a very short book, has clear connections to its predecessors. "Stone ants" appear, as do natural features that suggest New Caledonia. Yet the prosody is a new departure. Each of the twenty-four poems bears the title "formula," with a number. Nearly all in free verse, they vary in spacing, stanza arrangement, and capitalization. The final poem is loosely rhymed but otherwise free and, like several others, enigmatic. It does offer, however, a clue to the title *formula* by mentioning "the conjurer's pot." The poems have a metaphysical quality as well as dreaminess. Motifs and themes, scattered irregularly and not pursued, include chemical processes (a modern magic), light, loneliness in a city, and atheism. Number 9 evokes a rough landscape where a cow has wandered, "and a boy in wordless wonder / To and from the pasture." Number 10 concludes a description of surf, rocks, and bits of shell by declaring, "The flower blooms unlike a man / in the stones and the sea, / philosopher." Number 15 reveals Creekmore as a sometime phenomenologist musing on the being of things. "In their smallness, pebbles / show a wise adjustment. / . . . / Their insignificance is protection."

Creekmore's choice to leave poetry is unexplained. He may have expressed to his satisfaction what he wished to put into verse; or he may have found prose more rewarding. He remains important among Mississippi poets for his craftsmanship, his criticism of his state, and his war poems. Moreover, his novel *The Welcome* and its burden may have inspired other writers and many readers.

GEORGE DREW

Despite years living elsewhere, George Drew (born 1943) has something of a southerner's voice. His southern literary heritage is a source of pride to him (Interview). His medium is colloquial language, in free verse, printed as blocks or stanzas. In an endorsement for *The View from Jackass Hill* (2011), Robert Phillips writes of his "postmodernism," as attested by allusions to Visa cards and motion pictures. This is an inappropriate characterization, however, unless one defines postmodernism, as David Perkins did in 1976, as simply what followed after high modernism was established and flowered, or after the Second World War (II, 331–33). Drew's material is contemporary but not postmodern in the very different sense now given to the term; nor is his style. It is simply of the twentieth century, kept up-to-date. Both the construction and diction of his poems lend themselves to oral presentation. Nothing is dislocated. Line breaks tend to follow syntax; second-person pronouns, used for addressees within the poems, add a sense of familiarity; and the tones are generally conversational. The voice, usually first-person, is an observer's (the author-in-the-text) or a character's.

Drew was born in Greenville and reared there until he was fifteen. His mother was a native Mississippian, his father a New Yorker from Highland Falls, near West Point. He had a brother and a sister. Drew calls himself an itinerant in his youth. After Mississippi, he lived in New York and the Northwest; he graduated from high school in Corvalis, Oregon. He holds a BA from SUNY, Albany, and an MA from Western Washington State University. For thirty years he taught in the SUNY system; he also held visiting positions, one in Bucks County, Pennsylvania, another in Norwich (UK). He has spent time in Maine also. He married Lyla Bates and had one son, Christopher. After her premature death, he wed Enid Keeler and had twins. He has published nine collections and chapbooks. *American Cool* (2009) won the 2010 Adirondack

Literary Award for poetry, and *Pastoral Habits* (2016) was cowinner of the 2017 award; *The View from Jackass Hill* won the X. J. Kennedy Award, given by the publisher. Drew has given countless readings, and his work has appeared widely in periodicals and anthologies.

The title of *Toads in a Poisoned Tank* (1986), his first collection, is borrowed from Browning; toads and frogs are motifs. A poem on a boy's drowning in an icy pond opens the collection. The drowning motif recurs, and numerous other poems record small fatalities. Water serves often as a metaphor. The voice is strong, the poems well crafted. The writing is basically plain style, as Yvor Winters defined it in *Forms of Discovery*, that is, direct. Images, whether word-paintings or figures of speech, are numerous and effective. Form varies considerably but within standard boundaries. "High Tea with Mrs. Rosie O'Shea," for instance, is in quatrains; many other poems are stanzaic; some are blocks. Generally, the lines are of medium length. The poems in "Southern Roots" have little capitalization—to fit, perhaps, the downhome familiarity and unlettered speakers. Geographic locations vary; Maine, New York, and Cajun Louisiana are visible. Drew includes autobiographical elements, some connected to his mother and men in her life.

Drew's ability to see as others see serves him well. Rosie O'Shea, on the West Coast of Ireland, has grown old; husband and children are gone. "Can we imagine it?" asks the poet. "For forty years the same prospect / of water-bludgeoned shore, the sea, / the sky, and at their backs always / green Ireland rising like the sun." Anchored there in her widowhood, "what could she do but carry on / and count the blessings of each wave. . . ." Serving tea and cakes to tourists, she who as a girl "climbed the tall mast of a life, / and from the top the prospect is / more of the same: more sky, more sea, / and more of Ireland, green and bleak." In that poem as others, Drew is particularly skilled at treating the ocean. Hearing a gull shrieking over the dunes, he imagines the Ark grinding apart at the base of Ararat and the animals coming ashore ("Walking with the Logans at Montauk"). Of the poems the speaker reads at the funeral of a friend killed in an air crash, others say, "Oh how they flow, like a river, a sea. / All I can think of is a pair of eyes / stormingly gray, awash and depressingly free" ("The Service").

The Hand That Rounded Peter's Dome (2010), an outstanding work, is concerned with Michelangelo and his art. Endorsing the book and calling Drew "a brave master poet," Darrell Bourque stressed the way imaginative writing can go beyond ordinary biography. Drew utilized published studies and spent time in Italy to research the artist and his period. While the milieu and most characters are historically based, the poems are imaginative. Each of three parts lists a cast of characters, who then speak in the first person (the poem titles are their names). They are not limited to famous Italians of the time, such as popes and other artists. Even sculpted figures have a voice. Dürer and Erasmus discuss Michelangelo's virtues as a painter. While eschewing sonnets, which the artist adopted for his poetry, Drew uses certain forms of the time (letters and dialogues) as well as one modern form, the interview. The diction is today's. The effect is not incongruous. Drew's control of his lines—not of regular beat always, but smoothly rhythmic, often close to pentameters or alexandrines—and the easy flow of the syntax are persuasive.

The following examples, all from part one, suggest the richness of the whole. Pico della Mirandola concludes, in an epistle dated 1490: "Trust me: this young boy's going to be a god / creating gods. The spark he carries in / his fingertips bespeaks a greater fire within." He adds, "I almost pity him the torment he will know." Torrigiano, a fellow student of sculpture, boasts of having, in a fit of envy, broken his rival's nose. David, the statue, remarks, "It was himself he carved, not me." In a letter, Lodovico, the artist's father, remonstrates with him for his way of life. He could have had children, a good trade, perhaps a literary career. "But, no, you'd rather chisel stone / into these mad perversions—naked men. . . ." Asking, "Why do you never chisel girls?" Lodovico confesses that he was too indulgent with his son. He ends by giving advice. "Oh, / and if you must carve stone, my boy, / then carve—carve *girls*!" Julius II, reviewing his papacy, understands that the "haunted Florentine" was "the masterpiece of my studio." "The Pietà," a beautiful unrhymed sonnet, is in the voice of Jesus. "Here joy has been / exiled, and sorrow set upon the throne." The concluding lines describe his "horror-ridden shape," the "fingers splayed like broken wings." "Here, mother, piety and pity are the same."

The title poem of *The View from Jackass Hill*, a meditation on a lovely landscape with snow-capped Rockies, mentions Milton, damnation, paradise lost, and settlers' failed visions of a new Eden, all composing a great cosmic joke, which the speaker acknowledges but rejects; he chooses instead a "rosy vista" and Elysian Fields, "imagined or not." Diction in the multipart collection varies between standard and popular, as do cultural references. "This Truly Crappy Pastoral Ode" illustrates how the modes can be combined.

The opening part presents poems on death. They are not formal elegies, but the mood is elegiac. "The Older I Get The More I Think of Keats" is constructed cleverly, using real and imagined details of his parting with Fanny to foreshadow "the disembodied, the loitering ghost of Keats," and thus his death. Fittingly, the language is not colloquial. "Three for Jack Wiler," addressed to a friend, ill, then dying and dead, is, in contrast, very familiar. "Hey, Jack," dated 2002, evokes the friend's wracked body and sufferings. A painting of sky, ocean, and birches seen in Maine, described at the conclusion, serves as a correlative for the memorial lines, or the rationale of writing them. "Jive for Jack," 2009, with a caption from Larry Johnson, is a grieving poem couched as an accusation against the deceased for deceiving his friends. "How could you? / How con us with such a lousy hand?" He had been on "designer drugs" and looked healthy; he had given a splendid poetry reading. "We absolutely ate it up, / adored you and your throat-cutting metaphors, / your demonic hipster, shaman hootenanny // elocution, your drawn and quartered syntax...." Now "we're so down even Jersey muck looks up." "Go Away, Jack," dated 2010, instructs the deceased writer to "go walk your Elysian Fields / and talk the livelong day / with other poets, poets like you...."

"Apology to Liam" concerns two wives, deceased, that of the title figure and the speaker's, called Lyla, thus identifying persona and author. (Later Drew dedicated to Lyla "The Dark Up Here," superior to countless run-of-the-mill last-days, last-hour poems.) There follow poems directed toward two dead poets, one Russian and one British (Drew spent time in Tula, Russia), and an American versifier. "Montpelier" demonstrates his skill at shaping lines. The final poem of part one, inquiring "Why me?" recalls the poets just memorialized, adding to their names those of (John) Berryman, (Sylvia) Plath, and (Randall) Jarrell, all self-immolated. The elegiac tone and theme of death and decay reappear in the subsequent parts. "The Angel of Death Comes to Saratoga" introduces religious myth into a Borders bookstore, connected to the trope of achieving immortality through poetry. The collection ends with two views of the American-Iraqi war. In "Swaggart's Candy," "basically he was blown to hell, / along with a whole lot of shoppers." "Winding Down the War" foresees fratricide when the Americans depart, "brother on brother, butchery in the streets," with bombings "each more improved than the one / before, legs and arms and other body parts / scattered...."

Down & Dirty (2015) is in two unequal parts. The first consists of twenty-one poems with titles beginning "The Down and Dirty Redneck...." The second comprises poems (some, at least, autobiographical) set in Memphis and Mississippi. They are reminiscences, artless, rather than artful, not striking in verbal values but well paced. Cars, liquor, candy bars, stepfathers, and a traveling Baptist Bible salesman afford local color, in nostalgic tones. After scenes of injuries, drunkenness, cuckolding, and ungraceful aging, the book ends with a little lyric, "Mississippi Idyll," a homage to homely sensations and the staying power of old attachments.

The Dirty Redneck poems of part one, in the first person, have considerable vulgarity, anticipated by some coarseness in previous books. Folk wisdom blends easily with incidents and musings. The tones are right, and the pace is good. Much of the language is nonstandard—slang, incorrect grammar ("you was"), "I come from original redneck stock," says the speaker of "The Down and Dirty Redneck Gets Down and Dirty," "and like them, / I love loving women looser than gravel in a shoe, / slapping cards . . . / gorging on chitlins and country music, and / swiggin' 'shine. . . ." The poem ends on a threat, directed to someone too big for his britches, to "kick ass." Sex, a recurrent theme, is complemented by death, sometimes in the same poem, and drugs. The world, as the speaker sees it, is in bad condition, "gone stone / cold"—the wars, the thieving politicians. "Lord, help me. I don't know where to / turn first, which evil to take on. / You're all I have left, and sometimes, / sinner that I am, I'm not so sure about you" ("The Down and Dirty Redneck's Last-Ditch Prayer").

Like much other contemporary poetry in America, Drew's 2020 collection, *Drumming Armageddon*, denounces, in *fin-de-siècle* tones, certain ills of modern civilization, represented in both idiosyncratic and generalized phenomena. They are suggestive of the Armageddon announced in the title. Drugs (as in the title poem), alcohol, highway deaths and other violent ends, and the author's intimations of his own disappearance mark the poems. Yet they are cheek-by-jowl with celebratory moments.

One line of these is musical. The collection is built around, but does not attempt to imitate by language, music that the narrator recalls from his youth and still seeks out—blues, rock, and country-and-western styles. As Jack Butler wrote in his cover comment, the book is a "celebration of the blues"—indeed, it is "the blues itself." Though in blues, lamentation is the major vein, the genre still speaks of and to individual and collective strength (see "The Blues Are Like a Shoelace"). Similarly, rock and country songs, expressing so often heartache, loss, ruin—often borrowed directly from musicians' disastrous lives—include nonetheless a dimension of what Drew identifies, in the opening poem, "The Word *Swagger*," as "a bray without a mule." The figures of Janis Joplin, James Brown, Jerry Lee Lewis, and Emmylou Harris are among many other singers to whom he alludes. Others are Elvis Presley, Chuck Berry, Eric Clapton, and the Beatles. The poems "render these characters much better than any history book could" (endorsement by Jack B. Bedell).

Throughout his writing, Drew uses very colloquial language and the tone is familiar, "down home." Mentions of Mississippi towns (such as what he calls "Greenweed," that is, Greenwood), recollections of a grandmother's cooking, her religion, and a mother dancing evoke surroundings of his early years and tie the speaker to the poet's home state. Although some readers will object to certain poems, for instance "Funk," in which extremely coarse speech destroys what could otherwise be pleasing local color at a Dunkin' Donuts shop, Drew, as X. J. Kennedy wrote in his endorsement of *Fancy's Orphan*, "holds a high place among today's lyric poets and is a masterful storyteller besides."

SYBIL PITTMAN ESTESS

Sybil Pittman Estess was born in Hattiesburg in 1942. She was an only child for four years. Her arrival followed family sadness: earlier, a brother had died shortly after birth. A sister was born later. She witnessed family depression and alcoholism and racism around her. She grew up in Poplarville. She took a BA at Baylor University, an MA in English at the University of Kentucky, and a PhD in English at Syracuse University, where she pursued English literature and poetry, studying with W. D. Snodgrass and Philip Booth. She is married to Ted Lynn Estess, a Mississippian, who likewise studied at Baylor before taking an MA in divinity at Southern Baptist Theological Seminary in Louisville and a PhD in English at Syracuse. They have lived for some forty years in Houston; Ted is on the faculty of the University of Houston and, for thirty years, was with the Honors College (founder, director, dean.) He has published a collection of family stories. They have one son. Estess's website states that her early milieu was "strictly Christian"; her mother was originally of a Pentecostal denomination. The metaphors and archetypes in many of Estess's poems reflect familiarity with the Bible and other ancient sources. She evokes what she calls Mystery. She wants to offer readers, using James Joyce's term, "epiphanies"— "moments that seemingly are out of time and [have] significant intensity" ("On the Path to Poetry," 16–17).

Estess began by using free verse only, adding formal verse later. A cover commentator for *Seeing the Desert Green* (1987), a modest first book, identifies "quiet, conversational texts that uncover themselves in the emotions of familial ties." Small-scale human dramas include a father's dying and a girl's cancer; the recollection, in a Christian context, of someone murdered; and, in the first poem, an unusual Christmas Eve scene where a daughter, having learned traditional French massage techniques, offers her aging mother oils and gestures of healing (moral and physical). The feminine motif recurs in poems with a mother and baby. Wider nets pull in scenes from Greece, Montana, a Houston bayou at sunset, the Olympic Peninsula coast, and Mississippi during hurricane Camille. "River Trail Ride," evoking "a slow Sunday in Mississippi," describes the banks of the Bogue Chitto. "For Mirinda" deals with racial matters. Using both plain description and subtle allusions, Estess evokes these scenes well.

Blue, Candled in January Sun (2005), pursuing her characteristic veins, presents numerous small stories of couples and families as well as city and travel scenes. As before, biblical figures furnish drama, emotion, lessons. Figures speaking or observed are often autobiographical, as clues indicate. Death and illness haunt the book. A quotation from Rita Dove is the engine for "You Start with One Thing"; Dickinson appears in a poem bearing her name; "The Wide Net" summarizes skillfully a story by Eudora Welty; Isak Dinesen inhabits "Every Sorrow Can Be Borne." "Scars" and "Library Sestina" are in conventional forms. New Orleans appears as the poet's father saw it—foreign, generally unpleasant. Poems set in Houston and nearby bring out features such as the Rothko Chapel, a Mexican café, a shrimp fleet at Galveston Bay. The sentimental poem "Texas Memorial" (to Vietnam war dead) expresses regret concerning the war. "Search for Perfect Blue" is a rhymed sonnet.

Labyrinth (2007) and *Maneuvers* (2010) display various forms. In the former, which was favorably reviewed in *Louisiana Literature* by Elise Elliott, couplets and tercets dominate. "Sonnet on Conjunctio" is rhymed. *Maneuvers* has prose poems. In both collections, illness and death preside on many pages. In *Labyrinth*, Space Shuttle Columbia and the Twin Towers offer dramatic instances of destruction and terror. Small-scale but real sufferings include difficulties between wives and husbands, fathers and daughters ("Remembering Colors of the First Hit"). Emily Brontë's Catherine and Heathcliff appear in a series of poems, one called "Withering Script." "What the Citizens of Texas Need," concerned with poor, half-abandoned towns and a pedophilia victim, must be intended as sympathetic but is not without condescension. *Maneuvers* contains poems on Poplarville; Bogalusa, Louisiana; riding the train from New Orleans to California; and evocations of youth in Mississippi.

Like That: New and Selected Poems (2014) contains some two dozen new poems. The new work is not strong. Certain family poems are reminders of the role sentiment plays here and in earlier books. "Parting," on the death of Ted Estess's brother, is infelicitous, prosy, and overextended. "Edge," evoking Big Sur, California, is similarly declarative. "Up," on a granddaughter, has sentimental but not poetic worth. In contrast, "Returning: High Place on Lake" expresses well how goals may lose their value, soon or later. In this case, a disabused speaker sees that a vacation house and its mountain view no longer kindle appreciation; even if the forest burns to ash, what can that matter? "Houston: How We Pass Through" opens with a fault in syntax. The short meditation "Emily's House," another Dickinson poem, is more polished than other pieces.

WILLIAM FAULKNER

William Faulkner (1897–1962) is known throughout the English-speaking world and elsewhere as a master fiction writer. He won two National Book Awards and two Pulitzer Prizes for fiction as well as the Nobel Prize for Literature (1949). He also published two collections of poetry, however. It is ill known and occupies a secondary position in his canon but is not insignificant. He once called himself "a failed poet." He labored over details—the order of poems in his books and the titles (which he replaced generally by numbers). Poetry was, he believed, the most demanding literary genre. His is difficult, sometimes abstruse. The genre partook, he wrote, of the broad aim of all literature: "to uplift man's heart" (*Faulkner Reader* x). He retained an exalted view of the art, which, in the 1950s he defined as "some moving, passionate moment of the human condition distilled in its absolute essence." On more than one occasion, using varying wording, he asserted that any writer, or novelist, "wants first to be a poet" (Adams 21). When he finds that he cannot write first-rate poetry—and "poetry of all must be first-rate"—he tries short stories (Blotner 91). Finally comes the novel. Many pages of Faulkner's fiction are indeed poetic, and certain novels are, in essence, long poems

Faulkner's biography and literary career, extensively researched by others, need only brief summary here. He was at once highly romantic and conservative; he has been called a reactionary (Skei 17). Yet influential fellow citizens pronounced his views to be unsuitably "liberal" (W. Morris 25). His connection to his home state is as strong, as organic, as an artist's can be. This does not mean parochialism; always, he strove, by means of local truths, to impart understanding of human life as a whole.

Faulkner (who, as part of his personal mythmaking, abandoned the family spelling "Falkner") was born in New Albany. He came from a family established in Mississippi in the 1840s. His great-grandfather William Clark Falkner was a significant public figure, involved in disputes, feuds, the Civil War, politics, and railroading. He was also a man of letters; among his publications was *The Siege of Monterey*, an epic poem. When Faulkner was five, his family moved to Oxford. He began writing verse as an adolescent and continued during his twenties and thirties. After dropping out of high school in his senior year, he managed to attend the University of Mississippi as a special student in 1919–20, thanks to having served meanwhile in the Royal Air Force (as it was then known) in Canada. He read widely in poetry, from Shakespeare, whose poetic achievements he admired, through the British *fin-de-siècle* figures Housman, a source of modernism, and Swinburne, who had used the figures of Faun and Pan and had cultivated attractive rhythms. Edward Arlington Robinson, Robert Frost, and Conrad Aiken similarly influenced him, along with the symbolists, especially Verlaine. Faulkner benefited greatly from informal tutorials by his friend Philip Stone, a literary-minded law student, who recognized his talent. Faulkner contributed poems, prose, and drawings to the university literary magazine and published verse in the New Orleans magazine the *Double Dealer: A National Magazine for the South*, including "Verse, Old and Nascent: A Pilgrimage."

The 1920s were what Lewis P. Simpson calls Faulkner's "poetic period." In 1921, he was employed briefly in New York by Elizabeth Prall, a bookseller (who became Sherwood Anderson's third wife). The Andersons settled in New Orleans, where Faulkner later called on them. Visiting again, in January 1925, he stayed in their flat for some weeks, moving then to William Spratling's apartment in what is now Pirates Alley. Carl Sandburg, Carl Van Doren, Oliver La Farge, Lyle Saxon, and other writers, as well as New York publishers and local intellectuals, appeared at Spratling's parties. These months were crucial for the young Mississippian; he courted various women, published his poetry, and wrote fiction. New Orleans was not merely a place but a state of mind; its attraction was erotic. "New Orleans [is] a courtesan whose hold is strong upon the mature, to whose charm the young must respond" (Spratling, in Faulkner and Spratling 12, 14). With Spratling, Faulkner sailed in July to Genoa, and he continued to write poetry in Europe.

The Marble Faun, his first collection, had already appeared in 1924. Stone paid Edmund Brown $400 for publication and distribution of the book. The key poem, "L'Après-midi d'un faune"—the title was borrowed from Mallarmé and Debussy—had come out earlier in the *New Republic*. By 1925 Faulkner had new poems; he gave to a former classmate, Myrtle Ramey, a sheaf of a dozen (published posthumously as *Mississippi Poems*). Then he copied out sixteen poems, mostly sonnets, for Helen Baird, whom he met in New Orleans and to whom he proposed marriage, without success ("Proposal"). The sequence contains some of his best verse, focused often on death, love, and sexuality. In fact, most of the poems from Faulkner's second book, *A Green Bough* (1933), which contains a dozen of those written for Baird and eight given to Ramey, were composed in the 1920s. He was maturing rapidly as an artist; in 1925 he had even told a correspondent that he could no longer write verse, having passed the required emotional stage. Yet poetry remained on his mind even as he brought out major novels; he continued to revise published poems. Such labor demonstrates his dedication to style and to his enduring personal image as a poet.

Despite "the defects of youth," *The Marble Faun* gave evidence of what Stone's introduction called "promise." The title echoes that of Nathaniel Hawthorne's last romance. (Faulkner claimed he was unaware of it [Blotner 379].) The reference is to the statue of Praxiteles, in the Capitoline Museum in Rome. Faulkner's collection shares with Hawthorne's novel features of the pastoral, as well as Greek mythological references. Each work is infected with a sense of melancholy, even error. The Faun, condemned to be alone, is Faulkner's earliest persona, both revealing and concealing moods and erotic impulses; it is almost a personal myth, another indication of his mythmaking. While critics have written of its "pastoral posturings," James G. Watson (21) calls it an "imaginative autobiographical sequence."

The collection is not a miscellany; tones and style are even throughout. Generally, the lines are iambic tetrameter, some irregular, in rhyming couplets, often in stanzas. It is structured around the seasonal cycle, from "the first chill spring winds" to ice and snow; May returns at the end. Except for "Prologue" and "Epilogue," the poems lack titles. Bits of dialogue are heard, as Piping Pan and a Faun call to each other, singing. The Faun is "marble-bound," a "prisoner" (Epilogue)—whence the sadness. Natural features are readily animated—poplars, cawing rooks, the moon, nightingales. These scenes often lack particularism. Yet Stone, in his preface, stressed, accurately, that Faulkner was "steeped in the soil of his native land," which was part of his "very being." In October 1924 Faulkner wrote out a poem entitled "Mississippi Hills: My Epitaph."

The poems of *A Green Bough* are identified by Roman numerals, suggesting a sequence, even if loose, but with varied tones. The forms vary from sonnets and rhymed quatrains to free verse with even left margins (some with irregular end-rhymes) to unpunctuated, uncapitalized lines and irregular indentations. There are mythological and literary allusions—to the Faun, Cynthia or the moon, a frequent motif, and Thomas Gray's plowman who "slowly wends" (29). Also present is Pierre Abélard, whose fate represents, presumably, frustrated love. These figures are imbedded into a modernist discourse, with notes of irony and urbanity.

By the 1920s Faulkner had become acquainted with the writing of Ezra Pound, whom he "admired tremendously." He learned how quick images, often synthetic, may constitute the heart of the poem. He also knew the early verse of T. S. Eliot, another important influence, as illustrated in "The Lilacs": "We sit drinking tea / Beneath the lilacs on a summer afternoon / ... // There are women here: / Smooth-shouldered creatures in sheer scarves, that pass / ... / To us they are like figures in a masque." Yet in the same poem flashes from the Great War—a flyer's fall (and probable death) after a raid over Mannheim, "the bullet-tortured air"—counter the modernist irony and oblique perspective. The shadowy aviator is another poetic persona, derived from Faulkner's wishful self-image as a flyer. (There are intertextual connections between *A Green Bough*, with its aviator figure, and *Soldier's Pay*, which he finished in New Orleans.) The fact that he was without combat experience—he was not sent abroad—was no obstacle to his imagination.

With similar tones, poem II introduces someone—presumably the aviator, perhaps in dream—who watches and listens while a woman plays the piano before a fire. His "sees his brain / Whirl to infinite fragments, like brittle sparks, / Vortex together again, and whirl again." A pewter bowl of lilies, firelight and shadows, and music serve as correlatives for uncertain references. Elsewhere, a wide range of juxtapositions—Roland in battle, Eve and the serpent, erotic suggestions (connected to Eve), sleep and death—create modernist uneasiness along with verbal interest. More traditional uses of images appear in poem VIII, where a word-painting, with plowman, blackbird, and flashing rabbit, gives way, ambiguously, to philosophy, as the blackbird "inscribes the answer to all life / Upon the white page of the sky: / The furious emptiness of strife / For him to read that passes by." In number XVII appear "the eagle / sharp in the sunlight and cleaning / his long blue ecstasy" and "wind on hilltops blond with the wings of the morning. . . ." The aviator is connected loosely to a boy "who watched amid / the piled and silver shapes of aircarved cumulae / A lone uncleaving eagle and the still / Serenely blue dissolving of desire" (XVII). Watson calls this "a dream reconstructed from memory at the moment of the aviator's death" (173–74).

The question arises whether Faulkner's verse, and the man, would be known presently had he not made himself famous through fiction. The answer is yes. The originality of his two collections is considerable, by tone, topics, imagination, and overall vision. Remarking first that the English language holds probably not a dozen good long poems, John McClure wrote apropos of *The Marble Faun* (which he treated as one) that it had failed, "but with real honor." Faulkner possessed "to an exceptional degree imagination, emotion, a creative impulse in diction and a keen sense of rhythm and form." This is not small praise. Clearly, Faulkner had acquired his own modernist and disabused tone; he left poems of lasting interest.

BETH ANN FENNELLY

Poet laureate of Mississippi for 2016–20, Beth Ann Fennelly lives in Oxford. She is professor of English at the University of Mississippi and teaches poetry and nonfiction writing. From 2006 until 2016 she directed the MFA program. She is married to the writer Tom Franklin; they have three children. She was born (1971) into an Irish Catholic family in Chicago, where she attended parochial schools. Section II of "From *L'Hôtel Terminus* Notebooks" (*Open House*) affords glimpses of unhappiness in childhood. To use her term, she has "recovered" from organized religion (sec. III). After receiving a BA magna cum laude from the University of Notre Dame (1993), she taught in the Czech Republic for a year. Following that experience, she studied at the University of Arkansas (MFA), held a one-year fellowship at the University of Wisconsin, and for two years taught poetry at Knox College.

In addition to poetry, Fennelly has published flash fiction and a novel done with her husband, *The Tilted World* (2013), set during the great Mississippi River flood of 1927. Among her other books are *Kudzu* (2005), *Great with Child: Letters to a Young Mother* (2006), and *Heating and Cooling: 52 Micro-Memoirs* (2017). Her poems, which have been widely reviewed and anthologized often in the United States, have attracted attention also in Asia and the United Kingdom. She has received numerous grants, fellowships, and awards. They include teaching prizes, a Fulbright Fellowship in Brazil, an NEA award (2003), a United States Artist Grant, invitations to the Bread Loaf Writers' Conference, the Sewanee Writers' Conference, the Poetry Center at the University of Arizona, and the MacDowell Colony, and grants from her university and the Mississippi Arts Commission. She is a contributing editor to the *Oxford American*. As a member of the Poetry Out Loud initiative (NEA), which encourages recitation of verse, Fennelly stresses the power of the spoken as well as the written word.

Fennelly's chapbook *A Different Kind of Hunger* (1998) received the *Texas Review* Breakthrough Prize. It is in free verse, the lines ranging from average to long, the poems often multipage; some are centered. There are prose poems also. "Mary Speaks to the Visitor at the Laying Out"—which sets the scene of Milton's wake and recounts his last month and death—displays skillful use of iambic pentameter. Fennelly is adept at construction and often good with endings. European history furnishes material for many poems: the Defenestration of Prague, on which she elaborates; the Paris Commune and horrible winter of 1871; Poland, "where things are not buffered / by habit or ease" ("Return to Krakow"). She includes also an effective love poem ("The Snake Charmer") and a letter in the voice of Gauguin's daughter.

The very personal opening and final poems in *Tender Hooks* (2004), long, multipage or multipart, with portions in prose, were inspired by Fennelly's first year of maternity. They are women's writing; they could serve as a handbook for new mothers and instructors in such matters. The physical details are graphic and abundant, valorizing the feminine body and its processes. The uninhibited embrace of maternity has a parallel in Fennelly's adoration of language and its potentialities. "Having Words with Claire" offers wordplay as it underlines the role of words in building the human being.

Other topics include the flat prairies of Illinois ("Land Where My Father Died") and a landscape in Arkansas ("When I Tire of Houses and People in Houses"). There is humor in "A Study of Writing Habits": the speaker alludes to "recked" spelling and "old wise tales"; a student mentions the "Bullet Surprise"; and Marianne Moore's revisions are considered, the "toads" missing. One poem of special interest, "On Collaboration: Downward Dog, Happy Baby, Cobra," features a woman poet and yoga teacher addressed as "Ann," that is, Ann Fisher-Wirth, Fennelly's fellow poet and University of Mississippi colleague. The title words signify yoga poses. Dating from before Fisher-Wirth's Fulbright year in Sweden, the poem depicts well a scene of friendship between the two women and its expression in discussions of writing and yoga. Contributing to the context of this poem and others is an admission in section III of "Telling the Gospel Truth" that the speaker no longer attends Catholic services. In another poem, "The Presentation," likewise addressed to Fisher-Wirth, she and Fennelly's first-person speaker are conflated, their lives, despite an age difference, paralleling each other, including, for each, the loss of a child to death or miscarriage (see *Unmentionables* 72).

Open House, first published in 2002, was reissued in 2009. Robert Hass, US poet laureate 1995–97, wrote in his endorsement of "a lively performance." In an introduction, David Baker, poetry editor of the *Kenyon Review*, called it "a brilliant blueprint of the imagination," praising its "inclusiveness, the intellectual size," and the "extraordinary range." The work and its republication signal important trends in American literary taste. While many poems, including several from *A Different Kind of Hunger*, do deserve their generic identification *poem*, others barely fit the term, even as usually understood presently. Taking advantage of her wide reading and experience, Fennelly creates patchwork quilts, or collages, some lengthy, of anecdotes, musings, recollections, quotations, and conversations. The tendency is centrifugal. Her interest in language as such is on display. The Irish examples of James Joyce and Samuel Beckett come to mind. In *Open House* she includes neologisms, puns, and other verbal jokes, and muses on the limits of language following the examples of Ferdinand de Saussure and Jacques Derrida. "We speak barest when we barely / speak" (5). Nothingness may be at the heart of naming, as Mallarmé saw. "The irony of metaphor: / you are closest to something / when naming what it's not" (3).

"From *L'Hôtel Terminus* Notebooks," a twenty-eight-page compendium of mostly unstructured ramblings (some marked by printer's bullets), is the most striking example of tendencies identified above. The presence of an addressee, "Mr. Daylater," to whom questions are addressed by a speaker and who volunteers sarcastic comments, furnishes an organizing, though insufficient, thread. The prose paragraphs are often unpoetic. One reason is the absence of beat. As Donald Stanford wrote, "Powerful yet sensitive rhythm is the heartbeat of good poetry. Without rhythm the poem is dead" (181). The "found poem" (55), clipped from a news sheet (a plausible item, real or invented), is printed as lines, but they are not poetically crafted. A report on Madrid bullfights (54) is strictly expository. Certain shorter elements resemble brief feature or news items in a local paper or present, at best, an amusing malapropism or misprint reproduced in the *New Yorker*. The poem the long title of which begins "I Would Like to Go Back" is, in contrast, an effective expression of love.

In *Unmentionables* (2008), numerous poems show how Fennelly can apply effectively her sense of composition to various themes, among them, again, motherhood and children. Occasionally, as in "Elegy for the Footie Pajamas" and "The Mommy at the Zoo," treatment of maternity is needlessly sentimental. The collection includes a very loose sestina and a rhymed poem, somewhat vulgar. The opening poem, in tercets with staggered left margins, directs its focus on aging: past (speaker's girlhood), present, and future, stretching into the distance. The multipart "Berthe Morisot: Retrospective," is in the voice of the French artist. Unspoken but not unfelt are the parallels between her, painting with one hand as she holds her baby by the other, and the poet, likewise a young mother, for whom working time is short. "The Kudzu Chronicles," another multipart poem, examines from many angles the Japanese vine, an invited guest that "aped the vernacular" and became an invader (63). The speaker considers herself likewise "an invited guest" to the state; she also has taken root. She poses the question of what makes a "southern writer," a fact that suggests both reflection and insecurity—especially given the enduring presence in Oxford of the Faulkners, whose graves she visits (sec. 11). Southern or otherwise, Fennelly evokes effectively homely features of the state—a county fair and the moist, heavy atmosphere (sec. 5, 8) "I love Mississippi," says the persona (71).

Fennelly is a very able writer, whose tendencies toward informality and dispersal in form and content may fit the present well. The classical Mississippi, both its strengths and its flaws, seems, however, distant in many pages of hers. The phrase "The whole landscape is psychology" (*Unmentionables* 55) is not necessarily what natives wish to hear.

ANN FISHER-WIRTH

The University of Mississippi is the academic home of Ann Fisher-Wirth, one of the finest poets now writing in the state. She joined the faculty there in 1988 and is now professor of English. Previously she taught at Pomona College, Scripps College, the University of La Verne, and the University of Virginia (1981–88). She has had considerable experience abroad, as an instructor at the International School of Liège, Belgium (1968–71) and, as a Fulbright scholar, at Fribourg, Switzerland (1994–95) and Uppsala, Sweden (2002–3). She was a finalist for the state poet laureateship in 2012.

Fisher-Wirth was born in 1947 in Washington, DC, to John and Irma Elizabeth Randall Welpton, both of Omaha, Nebraska. She has a younger sister; an older half-sister is now deceased. Her father, a military man, saw three years of service during World War II, then was assigned to bases in Germany, Pennsylvania, and finally Japan (1955–57), to all of which his family followed him. He retired in Berkeley, California, where Ann attended junior high and high school. The title poem of *Blue Window* (2003) gives glimpses of how she remembers those years. They cannot have been easy. From a brief liaison, she had a stillborn daughter. (The complicated drama furnishes one thread of *Carta Marina*.) Following graduation with an English major from Pomona (magna cum laude, Phi Beta Kappa, 1968), she went to Liège, along with her husband, John Fisher, with whom she had three children; they were married for fourteen years. Since 1983 she has been married to Peter Wirth; they are the parents of one son. (Wirth has a daughter also.) Reared as a Christian Scientist, she studied religions at Pomona and became particularly interested in Buddhism. During her marriage to Fisher, she was baptized as a Catholic but no longer practices. An environmentalist, she directs the program in environmental studies at Mississippi. She considers herself "well to the left of center" politically (Interview).

After her years in Liège, she returned to the Claremont Graduate School, where she took an MA in English and American literature (1972) and, in 1981, a PhD, with a dissertation on William Carlos Williams. Among her interests is dance, though she no longer is active; "Butoh: 'Bird'" (*Five Terraces*) describes a dance form, "born of the dying." Another pursuit is yoga, which, following her Buddhist studies, she considers as a spiritual discipline; she has practiced it for forty years and she now teaches it. (Yoga terms appear in poems and titles.) As a child and college student, she was an actress; she has appeared on the stage at the University of Mississippi. Her honors include the Rita Dove Poetry Award, two Mississippi Arts Commission Poetry Fellowships, and the Mississippi Institute of Arts and Letters Poetry Award. She was Poet in Residence at Randolph College, Lynchburg, Virginia (April 2017).

Blue Window, Fisher-Wirth's strong debut collection, is directly, sometimes brutally personal, though far from artlessly so. It is dedicated to her family. Appearing when she was fully in middle age, it is founded on unsparing examination of her past. Its raw, almost shocking details must spring not from her wish to *épater le bourgeois* but from determination to tell the truth. The effectiveness of the collection illustrates how poetry can carry out that aim. The poet's self, or persona, is not the only subject. Mississippi figures and topics likewise hold her attention; they include her husband, animals, paintings, photographs, and, in "Letter from Oxford, Mississippi," a black man tortured and murdered. She uses free verse generally, with irregular stanzas, substantial blocks, centered or scattered lines and fragments, but also includes couplets and tercets. Spacing is important; generous use of white spaces sets off lines and words. Many lines break partway and drop down one by one in a stair-step arrangement. "You Know This" is a prose poem.

The early poems in *Blue Window* depict, it appears, members of her family and the Christian Science beliefs that prevailed in the household. The poems likewise give the very feel of growing up in Berkeley in the 1960s. Surrounded by radical changes in the immediate neighborhoods and waves of dissent throughout the nation over Vietnam, she reacted bodily as well as intellectually. An enduring concern with embodiment is visible in her writing, whether connected causally to her girlhood and marriages, connected to her multiple pregnancies, or springing from some more remote cause.

Five Terraces (2005), Fisher-Wirth's second full-length collection, is similarly impressive. The title poem, in prose, belongs to part IV, of seven, and is thus central. The book has multiple thrusts and concerns. It begins with a multipart ekphrastic poem, "Walking Wu Wei's Scroll" (subtitled "Le Grand Fleuve à perte de vue," after the French labeling of the Chinese title), published separately as a chapbook. It refers to a room-length fifteenth-century silk scroll, displayed in Paris in 2004. The scroll conveys, as often in Chinese art, quiet, repetition, durability, agelessness. The poems are addressed to a "you," perhaps a man. The first-person voice is, presumptively, that of the poet who "walks" the huge representational work. "Where would I be in this? I would be anywhere. // Each thing singular, each thing perfect, / fog and water / and tree and rocks, the fish that swims in its bowl. . . ."

An endnote explains the connection of the following sequence, "The Trinket Poems," to a Tennessee Williams play, *The Mutilated*, part of a double bill called *The Slapstick Tragedy*. The original production closed after seven performances; the play received little notice subsequently. It was presented at the University of Mississippi in 2002, directed by Michele Cuomo, with Fisher-Wirth in the role of Trinket, one of two prostitutes in *The Mutilated*. Sexual matters are often at the forefront. The poems concern, variously, the performances, very graphic; the attitudes and reflections of the speaker and other actors in their roles; and the characters Trinket and Celeste as professionals and as women—along with the male characters who frequent them (sailors particularly) and actors taking their roles. The two planes often intersect, as in "Of Trinket, of Mary," where the persona (quasi-identical to the poet) boasts that she has had Mary's experience of motherhood, whereas Trinket, whom she addresses, has not and is, moreover, mutilated (she has had a breast removed). Similarly, the short poem "There Is a Diary Open to the Words" depicts the persona assuming her role: "Trinket, / you've become my dance, today I cannot go forward, last night when Arlene wanted / to do my makeup I just stood there weeping. . . ." In contrast, "'These Our Actors, As I Foretold You . . .'" (from *The Tempest*) emphasizes separation between players and their roles: "Actors / break our hearts, they rejoice in the bright / world in their hands then watch it vanish."

The remaining parts of the book, save the last, frequently display women's tones and concerns. Suffering and mortality seem endemic to the human condition. Fisher-Wirth is particularly good at conveying mourning. The title poem, depicting the terracing of an overgrown hillside in summer, sketches also the man doing the work and his subsequent illness and death—apparently the poet's father, whose presence, like the poem, must be presumed central, if in shade. The following series, "October," appears to concern her deceased mother, her husband's mother, and a cat fatally ill, visible elsewhere, as well as a stillbirth. In a neat bookend arrangement, the final poem bears the same title as the first. Moreover, the contents of each—untitled sections—are identical but arranged palindromically, so that the book ends with its beginning. This symmetrical structure provides a sense of permanence, even timelessness.

Slide Shows (2009), a chapbook dedicated to the poet's sister, Jennifer, and their parents, consists of nineteen ten-line unrhymed poems reflecting the girls' life in Japan. The cover photo shows them and a friend, in kimonos, prepared to dance on daytime television (Interview). Insofar as memory can retrieve, after more than fifty years, children's reactions, the poems do so, with freshness. The family is not alone in its reappearance; the Japan of the 1950s, with "Yankee, go home" street demonstrations and people dwelling in caves, likewise must be recollected or imagined. Whether the adult writer still has fascination, as well as distaste, for an old, bent beggar; "honeybuckets"; a boy with a skinned weasel, its head intact; and cormorant fishing (the birds are forced to choke up fish)—or feels pity—is unclear. Various rites, such as rubbing the Buddha's stomach for good fortune and releasing fireflies at nightfall, have strange charm.

Also published in 2009 was *Carta Marina: A Poem in Three Parts*, inspired by Fisher-Wirth's stay in Sweden and study of a 1539 map (reproduced). History, places, and dates, from October to April, provide structure to disparate elements, couched in a variety of forms. The effect is somewhat diary-like; but the whole does not simply record a stay abroad, bathed in local color; it is, rather, a philosophical poem, with aging and death at its center. Extensive quotations (translated) from Latin enrich the text. The poet's skills at description and evocation are evident when, for example, the borealis appears ("December 3"). The drama of the stillbirth, a gesture of fate, is threaded among glimpses of pagan rituals, modern Swedish customs, wisps of history, long nights, an engraving of an anatomy lesson, love's yearnings—all pointing to the tyranny of the body, which poetry can barely contain, and its frightening metaphysical aura. "Goodbye to the most beautiful roof in the world," says the penultimate poem, before the final one ends in "love and anguish."

Dream Cabinet (2012) concerns partly the poet's first marriage and divorce. Whether the grammatical person is first or third, the poems are intimate, confessional, not exculpatory but, rather, lamentations, even self-accusation ("Answers I Did Not Give to the Annulment Questionnaire"). Fisher-Wirth proves herself, again, a poet of domesticity, but in a minor key and often in the mode of dream, following the volume title, which is also that of a multipart central poem. A father, stricken by a tumor, a mother, an adolescent speaker in Berkeley rehearse family matters again, extended in time by thoughts of a grandchild ("What Boat"), then the child as she appears ("Of a Photograph"). In a Zen monastery garden, the persona meditates on a daughter's bitterness toward her ("Thirty Years After I Left Your Father"). The blessings of four generations, the curse of age and weakness, run through the collection ("Oh body body," writes the poet in "Family Gatherings"). Another running theme is the environment, from the mushroom clouds of nuclear detonation to climate warming. The Deepwater Horizon (BP) disaster of 2010 inspires a three-poem polyphonic set (left-hand, right-hand poems in different fonts, interacting).

The figure of Emmett Till presides over "Three for Mr. Keys," which recounts the enlightening talks given at a Liège school by the title figure, a black Mississippian studying for a master's degree there, since he could not obtain one at home. Sweden reappears as a setting, half-familiar, half-exotic. Much verbal beauty characterizes these poems.

Fisher-Wirth's volume *Mississippi*, with photographs by Maude Schuyler Clay (2018), can be classed as a coffee-table book. But unlike such in which photographs or paintings have been paired simply with miscellaneous poems or fragments, this volume constitutes a serious poetic undertaking, which gives literary images the same status as visual ones. There are forty-seven poems and the same number of images. The poems, all in free verse, appear casual—though not in an arbitrary, postmodern way. Punctuation is absent; occasional gaps within lines as well as spaces between them separate phrases. The directness and simplicity of expression, often in the vernacular, are, of course, strategic. Juxtaposition of images, spatial and temporal planes (including simultaneity), motifs, themes, and voices carries much of the meaning.

The voice is not the poet's but, through direct or indirect discourse, that of sundry Mississippians, or, if one prefers, Mississippi embodied, polyphonically, in a kind of chorus. The first lines serve as titles for the poems—and for the photographs, if one wishes. Fisher-Wirth was the instigator of the project; certain poems appeared in print previously. In February 2017 twenty-four of them were presented in performance by six actors at the Ford Center of the university. A statement preceding the endnotes indicates that the figures described or quoted are fictional. Two poems, however, concern Till ("He ain't done right to whistle" and "Well you know back then" [60, 62]). Like the three poems for Mr. Keys, these illustrate the truth of Natasha Trethewey's observation that Till's story "belongs to all of us and should be sung by many different voices" (Hearne 208)

In her foreword, the poet notes that the state "suffers from severe environmental degradation that cannot be separated from its history of poverty and racial oppression." Yet it has many beauties and a rich culture. She writes of the "rich orality of Mississippi culture" and "honors" the voices that express it. The diction is authentic; with neither apology nor condescension, she uses colloquial language, including lexical and syntactic features of white country speech ("Had me a dog once") and those of blacks ("The heron he come from beyond. . . . / I wonder what he be thinking"). The photographs are not all landscapes, waterscapes, or skyscapes. Still lifes of interiors are numerous; architecture, along with urban features (a derelict barber shop, for instance) furnishes other materials; a Confederate flag, a dog, a poster showing a blues musician, a high school girl on a blanket laid on the grass provide motifs.

While the book is a single art work, it incorporates distinct elements—words and images—each "a different way of seeing," as Degas said about sculpture and painting. One poem describes a painting by Robert Malone, a Mississippi artist—thus providing a third genre. Certain poems, such as "These August afternoons even the candles," fit nearly perfectly the accompanying images, in substance, as well as tone; others diverge somewhat, though never in an unaesthetic or puzzling fashion. At times the verbal and graphic texts are at odds, strategically so. The poem beginning "When it commenced it come on fast"—the lament of a man whose wife and infant died in childbirth and now lie "in a single coffin / in among the trees"—is paired with a serene skyscape above trees and a plain house in the middle ground.

The Bones of Winter Birds, Fisher-Wirth's 2019 collection, with a cover comment from T. R. Hummer, displays once more her command of style and material. She shows skillful handling of poetic forms she favors (prose, couplets and tercets, block stanzas). The range of topics and tones is wide, the images are effective, and she conveys characters and human drama well. Bird motifs recur. Features recurring from her previous books indicate the unity of her writing and vision. Yet the work is not simply a rerun. Settings include California, New Mexico (one of Georgia O'Keeffe's properties), the banks of the Seine and those of the Meuse in Belgium, and her state, introduced in a "Mississippi Invocation" and poems on Vicksburg National Military Park and Parchman State Penitentiary, where the poet and others present their work.

The cover is a reproduction of Monet's *The Magpie*—very much alive, perched on a fence or stile in snow. ("We Came Home . . ." mentions a magpie on a stile.) But in the prose poem "In That Kitchen (She Speaks to Herself)," "bones of winter birds" are boiled in soup and "mothers cooked the death of things" (yet that death nourishes human life). As before, the poems are often autobiographical and highly personal. Other voices and faces, as the poet hears and sees them, have their place also: Emma Bovary, Alberto Giacometti, the poet Guillaume Apollinaire by a quotation. The theme of separation, a watermark to the book, is underscored by formal technique: spacing between lines and stanzas, indentations, staggered lines, even unusual spaces within lines. Alternatively, these interruptions may be poetic parallels to the breathing discipline of yoga, a topic introduced directly in "Yoga Nidra," which describes a session with a class of hapless millennials, living lives of disorder, some nearly sleepless, others victims of violence. Silence, that of meditation, even within a poem, has its place. "Whatever is said is small, compared to silence," reads the last line of the last poem, "Ascending *les Gorges du Chassezac*."

To be noted is section 3, "For Joan," labeled "1933–2017." The central figure is, apparently, the poet's older half-sister, Joan Shepard, who, half-grown, fatherless, acquired a second father upon her mother's marriage to John Welpton. Described in her advanced years, the figure is a sad one, living alone in a double-wide, hoarding neurotically, tending to little, suffering pain, then dying in a care home. Whether she mulls over the past is unknown; but the poet-persona does so, trying to know her sister as a girl, sharing with the reader the woman's secret. This figure introduces a new dimension to the family sketched in Fisher-Wirth's previous volumes.

Fisher-Wirth's commitment to combating and remedying environmental damage is a poet's as well as an activist's. Writing can offer catharsis as well as raise consciousness. While beauty must never be forgotten (in "Sunlight, Sunlight," light strokes the birds' throats "so it comes out as song"), lamentations over the "toxic" features of America are prominent and insistent—sludge-filled rivers, forests falling, poisonous smoke. References to werewolves and the Beast of Gévaudan (a man-eating creature who roamed the French countryside) place the toxic vision in the past also. The beast is reported dead, says a voice, but "nothing ever changes" ("We Came Home over the Snowy Fields for Christmas"). Such pronouncements on the apparent persistence of evil, that of human nature, perhaps, are borne out in strident echoes of war, wrenching private dramas, the destruction of one's own past, aging, and death. They give the sense that, notwithstanding what would appear to be persistent and irremediable ills, human and natural, this book is a desperate appeal for understanding and change. The stakes, the poet suggests, are high.

CHARLES HENRI FORD

Despite leaving his state, where he had felt isolated and out of place, the avant-garde poet and artist Charles Henri Ford (1908–2002), born in Hazlehurst, deserves consideration as a Mississippian. From young manhood on, he lived a cosmopolitan and aesthete's life, chiefly in Paris and New York. In an act of self-mythologizing, he gave his birthdate sometimes as 1913. Additionally, he changed the spelling of his middle name to distinguish himself from industrialist Henry Ford (A. Howard 7, 171). Over his long career, in which he was propelled constantly by Ezra Pound's principle—"Make it new!"—Ford published novels and many collections of verse, often with art work by friends; additionally, he did collages, painted, drew, took artistic photographs, and made films. Photographs of his were exhibited in London in 1955. The following year, a Paris gallery showed his paintings and drawings; Jean Cocteau did the preface for the catalogue.

His maternal grandparents lived in Union Church, a Scottish settlement. His paternal grandfather had settled on a plantation near Hazlehurst and operated a sawmill. His parents, Charles and Gertrude Cato Ford, were hoteliers; they owned and operated hotels in four southern cities, including Clarksville. The model and actress Ruth Ford, who married Zachary Scott, was his sister. His family was Baptist. He was precocious in more than one way. His education was erratic; for a time he attended Webb School in Bell Buckle, Tennessee, and then St. Mary's University in San Antonio. He showed early literary aptitude and ambition; he published a poem, "Interlude," in the *New Yorker* in 1927. With $100 he borrowed (and did not return) and further assistance later, he created and edited (1929–30) *Blues: A Magazine of New Rhythms*, which Alexander Howard calls "non-normative" (21, 71). It counted among its contributors Pound, H. D., James T. Farrell, Gertrude Stein, William Carlos Williams, and Louis Zukovsky.

In January 1929 Ford went to New York for the launch of *Blues* 8. Among those he met there was Parker Tyler, from Louisiana, who became a film critic. In May 1931 he moved to the Left Bank in Paris. His acquaintances there, many of whom were expatriates, included Stein, Yves Tanguy, Peggy Guggenheim, Man Ray, Natalie Clifford Barney, Djuna Barnes, and André Breton, the pope of surrealism. Despite his early homosexual inclinations, he and Barnes had an affair and traveled to Morocco to visit Paul Bowles. Tyler and Ford collaborated on a formally experimental novel, *The Young and Evil* (1933), set in homosexual circles of Greenwich Village. It appeared in Paris, with Stein's endorsement, under the Obelisk imprint; copies were banned in the United States and Great Britain.

Despite, at one time, calling America a "penitentiary" (A. Howard 154), Ford returned to New York in the 1930s with his friend and longtime companion, Pavel Tchelitchew, who did a portrait of Ruth. Ford brought out *A Pamphlet of Sonnets* in 1936, then a collection, *The Garden of Disorder*, in 1938, with an introduction by Williams. More than a half-dozen volumes followed. In 1940 he created *View*, another arts magazine, which lasted for seven years. Its list of contributors from Europe and America is stellar. It stood out among such publications by being pacifist. Under the View Editions imprint, Breton's poetry appeared for the first time in America. At the end of the 1950s, Ford went back to France, but returned to New York in 1962. In the 1970s he divided his time among New York, Greek islands, and Nepal, where he cultivated an interest in Buddhism.

Ford has been called the first "full-fledged surrealist" poet in America; he "introduced surrealism into the bloodstream of American popular culture" (A. Howard 8). The movement dated from the early 1920s and flourished in America especially in the early 1940s, when Breton and other European avant-garde figures settled in New York. Ford published what Edward Germain considers his first surrealist poem in 1929—an early date for Americans (introduction to Ford, *Flag of Ecstasy* 7). Like Breton and Paul Éluard, he was devoted to the unconscious as a source for literature. Symbols, often erotic, flow and change, creating dreamlike atmospheres and yielding, perhaps, psychological meanings. The title alone of *The Overturned Lake* (1941) suggests the unreal or the suprareal. He dedicated poems to Breton and Eluard, whose simile "Earth is blue like an orange" affords a key to reading many surrealistic texts by its synthetic imagery (the unstated commonality of roundness). Ford likewise wrote lines in homage to Rimbaud (acknowledged by surrealists as a forerunner). Moreover, *Blues* and *View* played a role in spreading surrealism.

Ford's poetics were distinctive, however. The resemblances between his writing and that of French surrealists are partial only, and his poems do not look or sound like theirs. Like other American surrealists or quasi-surrealists, he did not write about World War II—a departure from models offered by Éluard, René Char, and Louis Aragon. Often he used rhyme, iambic pentameters, and even the sonnet form. One of his idols was Cocteau, who, under the guise of an *outré* aesthete, was, as his plays and fiction show, a classic in terms of form and language. Ford's controlled verse is within many readers' tolerance; fluid images that undergo metamorphosis and arresting statements may have their own rationality. Not everyone's tolerance, of course: John Crowe Ransom rejected "The Overturned Lake" for the *Kenyon Review* on grounds of its inadequate "strategy" and called Ford "the logical end to which modern tendencies come" (quoted in introduction to *Flag of Ecstasy* 7).

The album *Poems for Painters* (1945) includes illustrations, mostly photographed paintings, by the painters concerned, Marcel Duchamp, Leonor Fini, Esteban Francés, Tanguy, and Tchelitchew. The copy belonging to the Fondren Library (Rice University) bears the dedication "For Bébé [Christian Bérard, the famous stage decorator], Darling of the Muses, from Charlie." "Flag of Ecstasy," the first poem, stresses by the etymology of *ecstasy* artists' creative estrangement; they are "put out of place, in a 'trance.'" It begins: "Over the towers of autoerotic honey / Over the dungeons of homicidal drives / Over the pleasures of invading sleep / Over the sorrows of invading a woman." Following twelve more couplets, the last of which speaks of the end of the world, the beginning of the world, the poet writes, "Like one of those tender strips of flesh / On either side of the vertebral column / Marcel, wave!" "Marcel," as a later printing of the poem indicates, is Duchamp, who rejected "retinal" art in favor of art that impacted the mind. In the poem "Of," dedicated to Francés, the first letters of the lines, read vertically, compose the phrase "Of magic and the sense of grandeur." The poem "There's no place to sleep in this bed, Tanguy," suits well the painter's disturbing, heteroclitic assemblages of forms. "The wires are cut that connect us with slumber.... // You've set new traps for ancient dreams / Oh tame them and train them before they get caught! / ... There are too many monuments of broken hearts." The final poem is in rhymed couplets. "The tree with the umbilical eyes / Voids the dress of sunrise" ("Pastoral for Pavlik").

Subsequent collections—*Flag of Ecstasy* (1972), *Out of the Labyrinth* (1991)— generally follow the same aesthetic principles as *Poems for Painters*. Oneiric imagery supports a new, open rationality. Devices such as echoes, rhetorical questions, and regular stanza structure provide a frame for the surreal. As Germain argued, Ford wrote poems "with his unconscious mind." (Germain does not confront the difficulty of distinguishing between the truly unconscious and what is deliberately constructed to appear so.) Williams wrote that Ford's "world, to which the usual mind is unfamiliar, [is] in active denial of all the unformed intermediate worlds in which we live" (quoted in introduction to *Flag of Ecstasy* 8–9). Commenting on Ford, Wallace Stevens asserted that "there is no end of intermediates, but to be master of disorder requires so very much more than to be the master of order" (quoted in introduction to *Flag of Ecstasy* 9). Behind such perceptions and the poetry connected to them are not only psychological questions but those of ontology, the very character and order of being. Probing what human beings are, how they see and think, what they can understand, Ford's verse offers many lenses, many insights.

One further vein of his poetry must not be overlooked, that of his social conscience and sense of southern history. The fine poem "Plaint," included in both collections mentioned above, bears the subtitle "Before a Mob of 10,000 at Owensboro, Ky." The voice is that of Rainey Betha (or Bethea), minutes before he was hanged, in 1936, for the crime of rape (he had confessed to murdering the victim also, but was not charged with that crime). A drunken state employee who could not carry out his task added a horrible *frisson* to the public spectacle, which drew considerable attention. In two short stanzas plus a final couplet, italicized, the man speaks from "the top branch of race-hatred." In "the orchard that excluded me / now I climb death's tree." "*Oh, who is the forester that must tend such a tree, Lord!*"

JOHN P. FREEMAN

John P. Freeman calls himself a modernist, not a postmodernist. His effective use of local, everyday objects and scenes to investigate subtle concerns of mind and existence is a significant contribution to contemporary philosophical poetry.

Freeman (born 1942), a native of Jackson, is partly of Native American blood, through a paternal great-grandmother. For three years as a boy he lived in the country, including two crucial years on his grandparents' farm in the isolated community of Lake. His parents were then in Bethesda, Maryland, so that his father could receive treatment at Walter Reed Hospital. The boy ran free over farmsteads and woods and developed his love for nature. He considers himself to represent rural Mississippi; but he knows also the towns and cities of the state: he has lived in eleven. Reared as a Baptist, he was at one time pastor of an independent nondenominational church in Jackson. He still views himself as a Christian, though not a fundamentalist.

Freeman graduated from Madison-Ridgeland High School, north of Jackson, then took a BA in English (1964) at Millsaps College, where he studied with James Whitehead, "the greatest teacher I've ever encountered." Freeman subsequently earned an MA at Mississippi College. He did additional graduate work at the University of Iowa and the University of Arkansas, studying again with Whitehead. Over time Freeman taught English and creative writing at Arkansas, Tarleton State College (Texas), Mississippi State University, and Hinds Community College. He was also a professional musician and songwriter. In 1976 he began teaching English at Oakley Training School, the state school for male juvenile delinquents. After eighteen years, he was obliged to retire, suffering from chronic fatigue syndrome. He later settled in Harvey, Louisiana (greater New Orleans.) For years he was poetry editor of the *Magnolia Quarterly*. He has been married five times (one of the dedications in *Illusion on the Louisiana Side* mentions "three damn good wives"). He has a son and stepchildren and grandchildren. For Freeman, the body plays an important role in poetry, which is partly visceral. "Good poetry should elicit some form of somatic response.... It is the way the sound effects work on the images that most elicits [this] response" (Interview).

In addition to profiting from Whitehead's guidance in poetics, Freeman learned from reading the work of Yeats, Eliot, Dylan Thomas, and Hart Crane. He also read Theodore Roethke, John Crowe Ransom, Donald Justice, and Richard Wilbur. The greatest influence on his work is that of Carl Jung. After studying Jung for nearly forty years, he concluded that no other system of ideas could make so meaningful "the workings of my psyche and the intuition of the purpose of my existence" (*In the Place of Singing* 46). His work is recognizably southern but not limited to regional material. Ben Gilstrap wrote that "his sparse yet elegant language and thematic poignancy rank highly among contemporary poets" (*Mississippi Encyclopedia*). Freeman has published three collections; in addition, with three friends he brought out *Quartet* (2012). He generally uses free verse, in identical or variable stanza forms, with an occasional loose sonnet. His book titles all suggest localization. "My poetry is tied to place" (Interview).

Whitehead described *Illusion on the Louisiana Side* (1994), Freeman's first book, as "lyrical, theological, sexual, and often wise. The wisdom is of the fire of experience" (endorsement). The "illusion" of the title poem is produced by driving from the bluffs of Vicksburg to the flat fields across the river, framed by the windshield like a museum display. Louisiana is "alluvial, / musty as a vault, flat as a shelf / except for levees humped like burial mounds." The levees lead to thoughts of aboriginal men; a thousand-year-old mummified hand and forearm look human only by "the rack of fingers / writhing toward the palm like a living cramp. / My own fingers clenched, testing their grip." To dispel the illusion, the driver must pull over and stop, "relieved at the cry of a mockingbird / and a tugboat's horn from the river."

Existential, even theological, notes are prominent. "Exile" announces the themes of love and blood, that is, genes, or physical existence in the world. "On a Pier in Biloxi, After Hurricane Grace" deals with "the bare flanks of the land" on barrier islands lashed by the storm and "the Eye / of this strange God who may or may not be, / but who rules in our psyches with an iron rod." Yet "grace" is present, perhaps; the speaker says, "It is I, Lord / you are letting pass, walking these boards to safety / beneath the calm latitude of your Eye." "Evolution and Theology" proclaims that "the memory of God is in our genes." "Holy Spirit" notes that "it would be as easy / to catch this wind in a butterfly net / as to hold on to the Spirit passing." Yet such wind "might billow out the net's resonant cords."

"Grandmother's Quilts" shows a speaker revisiting his deceased grandparents' house, empty and dilapidated. In "Armadillo," the speaker, eating wild
plums, a bit wormy, muses on a dead, rotting member of the species, deplor-
ing its lonely suffering and death. Liquor plays a role elsewhere. The speaker
describes how, when he breaks the seal on a bottle, "the heat of bourbon slides
onto my tongue." Then, he adds, "I drink to my darkest desires—/ love, God,
integrity—/ addictions I can't live without, dedications / to which I am not
faithful ("The Sanitary Landfill.") Trees and leaves, birds, a rain pool and "dream
waters" seem Jungian correlatives for experience just beyond reach. In "The
Other Shadow" the speaker finds with him, as he mows his grass, another
figure, a previous incarnation, or an ancestor in his genes, "an alien branch."
He cannot put it out of mind, "a door left ajar, too dark to see into." In "The
Ship Island Ferry: A Love Poem to My Anima," the persona watches the boat
"on the edge of the world," then slipping over—"a door shut in my face." "Once
more I send my heart churning over the edge. / I strain to see what is out there.
/ A door closes, a mouth / shuts."

Jung's influence is visible in poems on eroticism, often expressed by images
of nature—tree, grass, storm. It is clear that the poet's understanding of sexuality has not been deconstructed. Desire is well suggested in the sonnet "La
Belle Dame Sans Merci." The man-woman relationship is, on the surface, conventional, unquestioned; the persona in "Old Flame" calls himself "a hardened
veteran of more / than a dozen campaigns." The ideal lover may be he who has
"lucked on Archimedes' fulcrum, jarring the planet / just enough, but not too
much, / leaving her vastly shaken, but not hurt" ("Getting It Right"). Woman
likewise can appear in a Jungian perspective. "She rocks in the primordial
rhythm / locked in the memory of her genes" ("Anna Over Me").

A lovely villanelle, concerning the flow of thought, opens *Standing on My
Father's Grave* (2001). The poem reintroduces motifs of liquor, illicit lovemaking, and despair. In contrast stand poems, some featuring "Anna" in the
title, showing domesticity and love's contentment. Family and places and their
association with the dead appear. Grandfathers in old photos, a great-aunt and
a visit to a cemetery "used before the War," the persona's parents—these figures
and their fate, in which he sees his, convey angst. In "The Dispossessed," the
irritants of the body (ragweed, mosquitoes, aching bones) remind the persona
of Eden ("Genesis reports that I / was designed to govern this world") and the
Fall, by which earth is cursed. Yet there are times of grace, "as light slants down
a hillside streaked with pine shadows"). "I can almost know the earth / by her
lost holy name." The spectacle of a dead German shepherd is gruesome, but
the speaker imagines his "translation . . . / out of the language of the physical
/ into the unknown tongue of angels," and, sensing how he himself is spared,

plays "songs of the living" on catgut strings taut as the animal's ribs. Looking at the stars brings, or correlates with, anguish, as in "Nightfall at the Reservoir": "Wind grazes my skin with a shill / skimmed from the lake. Waves of ancient / starlight travel on black water / to shore over primordial stones...." But Light is not absent, even for those who look through clouded glass or are drawn to destruction ("Gypsy Moth"). "Posthumous Instructions for My Wife" offers wise insights into grief and survival. "Dig up my bones. Lay them among rocks / in the throat of a dry river as amulets / (perhaps the water's voices will come back)." The persona asks, however, that his ribs and a shinbone be saved, to be fashioned into a marimba, a flute, "through which you'll breathe in me an ancient music."

Freeman was quoted earlier as saying, "Mississippi is the very subject of my poetry." The first part of *In the Place of Singing* (2005) is "These Roots." Sights (a horizon shimmering with heat in "Delta Summer" or dark, leafy woods in "Heat Wave"), sounds ("Truck Voices at Night"), tastes ("Wild Scuppernongs"), sensations (shivering on cold mornings, in "Waking to Country Music") provide evidence of somatic memory and the deep sources of being. These localized images fit Freeman's underlying psychological and metaphysical concerns, expressed in Virginia Woolf's words (quoted as an epigraph): "What is the meaning of life?" No great revelation comes, Woolf concluded; at the most, one is granted small revelations, little daily miracles. Similarly, Freeman offers modest illuminations—but with wide ripples. Another epigraph, from Hermann Hesse's *Siddhartha*, proposes a different vantage point: "Meaning and reality [are] not hidden somewhere behind things, they [are] in them, in all of them."

Part two of *In the Place of Singing* comprises "Thesis" and "Antithesis," both involving the Rational Empiricist, who (as one title of "Thesis" puts it) "takes the end of belief to its logical conclusion." In March "it is pointless for seeds to thrust / their stalks through stony dirt, for chicks / to prod their beaks through shells." In December, "truth is laid bare in the oaks." When, sensing "the faintest stirring of a hope," the Empiricist parts the grass, he finds a dead mockingbird, "the wing feathers ruffled by the wind." History brings no meaning; in Vicksburg National Military Park, green woods, in the "relentless passion" of earth's genes, cover ridges "like picked bones." (One of Freeman's ancestors fought at Shiloh, one at Antietam, on opposite sides.) The death of the Empiricist's wife extinguishes hope once imagined among the stars. A Milky Way poem shows that dreams are "as cold and pale / as old light from a dead sun." Yet "Antithesis" suggests that souls are like electrons, which touch all their potential space at once. Lights gather in patterns; perhaps the voice saying "I am here" is not an echo but an answer to the Empiricist's appeal. Trees, scattering patches of shine and shadow, are "twisting runes" until he recognizes himself ("On Palestine

Road, Hinds County"). The moon on a pond's surface, a reflection in rainwater, a road all speak at once to man's insignificance and his value, struck by the fire of Pentecost ("The Road").

Part three, "Chahtah," concerns Freeman's Indian ancestry, of which he learned in his forties. Faced with the paucity of evidence about the Choctaws and their lore prior to their conversion to Christianity and assimilation, the poet calls on his imagination to explore his nearly lost heritage. A prologue explains how he attempted to do so at the psychic level, in the Jungian sense, by grafting the "semi-Oriental branch" onto the trunk of his "solidly Western psyche." Three *Apokni* (ancestress) poems illustrate this attempt; one, lovely, gives its title to the book. It is set on a hill in Attala County (Attala = *place of singing*). There, the speaker stands, at dusk, in autumn, looking at the fading sun, one of the many faces of Hushtali, or God (for Choctaws, any occurrence of fire is a theophany). An alepa, or drum, beats in his pulse; he invites his ancestors to sing with him, in praise. Another figure emerging, Freeman says, from the recesses of his mind, is the Alikchi, a modern man, doubtless an authorial projection. He is accompanied by familiars, animal, plant, or mineral. The series ends with Alikchi meditating on the waters of the Bok Hucha—the Pearl River—where his end will come, as he topples like a chopped tree, his image rising in the air "to meet him / passing through the dumb flesh / to lift him into the wind, an osprey fledgling / stretching his wings as he spirals up the sky." These Choctaw poems are outstanding. As Gilstrap observed, following William Faulkner's line in *Requiem for a Nun*, "The past is not past."

ELLEN GILCHRIST

Ellen (Louise) Gilchrist is a well-known prose writer who, like Richard Wright and William Faulkner, began with poetry rather than prose, but is far better known for her fiction.

Born in 1935 in Vicksburg, Mississippi, Gilchrist is the only daughter of Aurora (Alford) and William Garth Gilchrist Jr. ("Ellen Gilchrist," Biography. com). Her father was an engineer and professional baseball player. Much of her childhood was spent in Illinois, Indiana, and Kentucky with parts of summers in the Mississippi Delta, at Hopedale Plantation, with her mother's family. Gilchrist taught herself to read by piecing together words from nursery rhymes and poems, which she loved. "Long before I went to school I knew passages of Wordsworth by heart and the lyrics of many songs and would make up my own and write them down" (*Falling through Space* 70). At fifteen she contributed columns called "Chit and Chat about This and That" to the *Franklin Favorite* in Franklin, Kentucky. In 1953 she graduated from Southern Seminary in Buena Vista, Virginia. For the next two years she attended Vanderbilt University, the University of Alabama at Auburn, and Emory University, without receiving a degree. In 1967 she graduated from Millsaps College with a BA in philosophy. One of her courses was creative writing, taught by Eudora Welty.

Although reared as an Episcopalian, Gilchrist refuses to discuss religion but often expresses a Zen-like spirituality. In *Things like the Truth* she mentions two near-death experiences during which she and others around her were bathed in a "wonderful bright light, brighter than the sun," and although she felt as if she was going to die, she knew she was safe (204–5).

Gilchrist has been married four times (twice—1955 and 1959—to Marshall Peteet Walker, her first and third husband, who fathered her three sons). In 1958 she divorced Walker and for six months was the wife of Judge James Nelson

Bloodworth, whom she married "for his books and newspapers and because he was a judge" (*Things like the Truth* 25). In 1968 she married Frederick Sidney Kullman, a wealthy Jewish attorney, and moved to New Orleans. She marks 1975 as the beginning of her professional career. "Ever since the afternoon in 1975 when I pulled my old portable typewriter out of a closet and went off to the Caicos Islands to write poetry, I've been writing or wishing I was writing every single day from dawn to noon" (*Falling through Space* 41). Noting the date, Mary McCay believes nevertheless that "all the years she spent in New Orleans were certainly grist for her fiction and for much of her poetry" (8).

When Gilchrist was in her thirties, she sought treatment from psychoanalyst Gunther Perdigao. As she went through psychoanalysis, she recalled later, she was "writing poetry, writing it fiercely, praising the beautiful world in which I was confused and suffering, praising all creation while trying desperately to figure out how to become a person I could bear to be" (*Things like the Truth* 35). She attributes to her psychoanalysis much of the depth of her work (*Falling through Space* 90). J. A. Bryant underlines "her masterful explorations of the female psyche and its effects on human relations when allowed to run free"—qualities best displayed in her fiction (205). As her poetry, journals, and fiction developed, Gilchrist drew more and more for her writing on "a deeply personal past that gives her stories and many of her characters an autobiographical cast" (McCay 4).

In 1976 Gilchrist enrolled in the University of Arkansas to study writing, at the invitation of James Whitehead. Although she divided her time between Fayetteville and New Orleans, in essence she ended her marriage also. Later she explained why she "left a very nice, very wealthy man. Although I loved and honored him, I could not fulfill my work as a writer until I was alone, with no one looking over my shoulder or being afraid of what I was writing" (*Things like the Truth* 40). She worked with both Whitehead, whom she came to consider as among her best friends (his poem "For Ellen after the Publication of Her Stories" attests to the friendship), and William Harrison, who encouraged her to write fiction (McCay 15). Gilchrist had not written any prose before she arrived. Her most significant literary relationship, however, was with the poet Frank Stanford, who committed suicide in 1978. Gilchrist offered financial backing to his press, Lost Roads, which published her first book of poetry, *The Land Surveyor's Daughter* (1979), when she was forty-four; Stanford had helped her shape it. She left the University of Arkansas without earning a degree but has been a "clinical professor" there, teaching creative writing for eighteen years (University of Arkansas website).

In the Land of Dreamy Dreams, her 1989 collection of short stories published by the University of Arkansas Press, launched her national reputation. (She lacked the confidence required to send it to a commercial press.) Its favorable reception "freed Gilchrist from her psychological dependency on New Orleans; in effect, she had exorcised the ghost of the rich southern belle. She had gone to Arkansas to become a writer, and she had succeeded" (McCay 17). Presently, having published over thirty books (two of poetry) and having won the National Book Award for her *Victory over Japan* in 1984, Gilchrist is recognized abroad as well as in America.

The Land Surveyor's Daughter presents twenty-eight poems about dreams, relationships, New Orleans, and artistry. The eponymous poem of sixteen unrhymed lines begins with a father's advice to his daughter: "Keep your feet / firmly on the ground, hold your head up." However, the persona acknowledges bluntly how she betrayed him, and then shows how he betrayed *her* by being a hypocrite. Her father has spent his time "spying on a hippie" and criticizing the persona's gaunt cheeks. Noting that his hands slide into his pockets and jangle his coins "against / his penknife," she intimates that his money has controlled her in the past. She ends the poem with the observation that "his hips were dried up / like a cow pond in a summer drought," emphasizing his lack of virility and, thus, power in her life. This poem reflects Gilchrist's conflicted relationship with her father, acknowledged often in her memoirs and essays. A second poem about her father is "The Terrible Heart of My Father," in twelve unrhymed lines. The persona, called Judith, asserts vainly that her father "placed [his heart] under my tongue," noting that it "will melt in time." He had poured her first wine. "Now I drink with anyone, with any boy / whose eyes are hungry as possums." The father's lack of compassion and connection with her seems to have sent the speaker into a promiscuous life of drinking and "wild schemes." A hardcore, deep resentment comes out in these poems. "The Calling" depicts a woman becoming a poet and leaving her husband. The speaker says that she "will not be here / when you arrive" because she will be "writing / three poems a day." Now, she knows that she holds "the future / in my arms like a warm baby, / already it sucks my breast."

The thirteen poems of *Riding Out the Tropical Depression: Selected Poems 1975–1985* (1986), Gilchrist's second collection, display a different tone. They bluntly recognize the persona's flaws as a mother as she simultaneously shows her deep love for her children and regret over her lost youth. The dedication, as well as various poems, shows that her relationship with her father remained problematic: "For my father, William Garth Gilchrist, Junior, of Jackson, Mississippi, the finest man I have ever known. If there are any words he doesn't like he can mark them out as usual." The title poem appears to treat Gilchrist's relationship with a man whom she mentions often in her nonfiction prose, eighteen years younger than she. Her parents and children did not approve of the liaison. In seventy-six lines, the persona, addressing her wine glass, says there is no help for the two of them. She acknowledges how the "poor little rich boy, / [says] we can erase the mothers, / fathers, children, trust funds." But the persona realizes that such connections cannot be erased "like pansy colored butterflies." Thus, she wishes to "sew" the two of them together, but he counters with the suggestion that they "will wear wrist radios" instead. Three scenes depict them together, rediscovering touch, planting corn in the front yard, and buying trees. In the final stanza the persona asks the "Birdfeeder, Treeplanter, Mad Corngrower" if they "can't just call it a day." At the end she is still torn between loving the man and breaking with him: "Oh, let me go away. / P.S., I love you anyway." This second book shows poignancy and evidence of emotional growth.

Lacking rhythm and artistic structure in many instances, Gilchrist's expression is often closer to prose than poetry. Prose was, indeed, a better choice for her.

MELISSA GINSBURG

Melissa Ginsburg (born 1976), originally from Houston, is an assistant professor at the University of Mississippi. She is a former editor of *Yalobusha Review*, a journal promoting new writing, founded there in 1995. After graduating from high school, Ginsburg left Houston, but then returned and took a BA in English at the University of Houston (2002). There she studied with the poet Marie Howe, a visiting professor. In 2005 she received an MFA from the Iowa Writers' Workshop, where she held a fellowship. In 2012 the Mississippi Arts Commission awarded her a grant. Poems of hers have appeared in the *Denver Quarterly*, the *Iowa Review*, *Field*, and other magazines. She also writes fiction; her crime novel *Sunset City* appeared in 2016. Her teaching responsibilities are in creative writing and American literature; special interests of hers include feminist noir writing and experimental poetry. She has published two chapbooks, *Arbor* (2007) and *Double Blind* (2015), as well as a full-length collection, *Dear Weather Ghost* (2013).

Ginsburg combines a minimalist stance with a deconstructive approach to her material. She is often wry. All her poems are in free verse. Lines are short, language generally spare, signifiers unstable, the signified even more so. In *The Rumpus*, Amy Pence wrote that Ginsburg's universe was slightly "off-kilter"; her word choice "disorients, then reorients readers." The direction of the new orientation is not always clear. Contradictions, dismantling, and other negation mark many lines. *Arbor* operates largely by anti-logic. Nouns functioning as verbs may point to the absence of genuine action, or its contrary, names becoming active. Connections among words and phrases and between the occasional stanzas are frequently loose, open, or nonexistent, to all appearances. The poetry displays some kinship with that of the surrealists. In "One Day," for instance, sun "went out into the street," and mouse hides "waved / on stalks." These notations may be read as elliptic or synthetic; shafts of light may move; pods and leaves can be furry. But they seem isolated; they do not adhere well to others. Petals are mentioned merely to say they "cover" nothing at all. Broadly speaking, the poetry, through its uncertainties, suggests inconclusiveness, even stasis.

Sentence fragments, quoted here in full, marked off by periods as though definitive, are numerous: "And I seven times"; "His was a frozen"; "Despair a willow of icicles machine"; "Our trees were." The last line of the title poem reads "The world is full of this." Such fragments and other liberties may be interpreted as mockeries of language, insofar as it fails to stick to reality, or reality resists being grasped. They may be construed by reference to Jacques Derrida's *différance*—the deferring of meaning. They would be invitations to those who, denying that discourse is adequate for reality, wish to collaborate creatively, as it were, with the author in subverting its conventions. In "Arbor," bones ground together to make "a paste" could conceivably point to a strange recycling of linguistic or imaginative materials.

Dear Weather Ghost, which reprints some work from *Arbor*, contains poems as short as two or three lines; others are a half-page or so. The cover features a pheasant staring at a cat in a gilded birdcage. Ginsburg's voice, wrote Mary Ruefle in an endorsement for the book, is both "gentle and terrified," her prose "deceptively simple," her poetic music "mesmerizing." In a second endorsement, Mark Levine observed that the book was "a subtly beautiful address to the air." Titles such as "How to Pet a Porcupine," "Dear Decay," and "The Moss Thief" suggest negativity in approach; again, notations dangle without attaching themselves to much. Again, individual lines often defy understanding, nor is the whole clearly the sum of its parts. "Their falls dark paper . . ." ("Drift," the opening piece) depends first on a homonym; "Inside it seasons" (from "Pink Book") plays, perhaps, on the two meanings of *season*, one disconcertingly used as a verb, and, in a reversal like that of pheasant and cat, puts weather inside (the mind?). Everyday materials—a courtyard, medicine, a hospital, a birthday (three poems)—are metamorphosed almost entirely. Rabbits furnish a recurrent motif, connected now to the sea, now to a milliner. (No tie with Lewis Carroll nor the magician's art is visible, but the headgear reference cannot be overlooked.) Section three, "The Weather Ghost Letters," consists of eight poems, one with staggered lines, addressing "Dear Weather Ghost." Various meteorological phenomena of skies and seasons appear in passing; but emphasis is on the "I," the subject who, apparently noting these phenomena, challenges them, turns them inside out, even denies them. "On the beach I watched / the bluff erode"; "I poured escape / on your downturned /glass" (nos. 2 and 3). Elsewhere, bits of natural beauty, expressed in part by natural details, add appeal to the book; such is the poem "Heron," with trees, minnows, a marsh, and conifer needles.

Insofar as images are negative, empty, voided of their referents, the approach is not metaphysical; the world is not a full treasure-house pointing to meaning beyond. *Nihilistic* would be a better description. The notations are not entirely unlike those of phenomenological poets such as Francis Ponge, who take cognizance of the being around them, without further pronouncements. In its way, however, the stance of questioning or denying significance is itself significant, not neutral, not mere acknowledgment.

Readers may observe similarities between Ginsburg's writing and that of Adam Clay. While some, though not all, of his publications precede her collection, it need not be a matter of influence, constituting instead simply a sharing of thought and poetics. By their age (two years apart) and their nearly contemporaneous training in creative writing programs, which exposed them doubtless to some of the same poets on the circuit or at least the same fashions in poetry, literary theory, and linguistics, including postmodernism, they can easily have developed common views. Clay's lines such as "An astray wasn't there anymore" and "Colors have run elsewhere" illustrate the close kinship. Metamorphosis, namelessness, and disappearance of objects, metaphors without referents, and fragmentation characterize the work of each. Such features illustrate the primitivism, or infantilism, of much postmodernist writing.

The ghosts of the previous book recur in a later poem (2016), "Séance." Ginsburg told an interviewer that she liked to imagine poetry as a "successful séance" ("Conversation with Melissa Ginsburg")—the calling up of the nonexistent or at least invisible. Icicles (again), doomed to nonexistence, are just "ghosts communicating." A buzzard in the same poem reintroduces the motif of decay. "Your message has no content," the voice announces. Yet the specters do communicate; decay feeds life, and the law of the conservation of energy may have a poetic application here.

Ginsburg's poems are a prima facie challenge to readers. Yet, as a rock tumbler rounds rough stones by the lengthy process of turning them in water, might her work—appearances to the contrary—offer a way to smooth verbal and epistemological asperities (conventions, clichés, which veil the real) and discover new contours and coloration? In "Dear Weather Ghost" no. 1, after mentioning a "smoother," the poet writes, "You beat a rock and show / its insides. . . ." Are there new ways of seeing the world? Can one find agates or crystals by rejecting common perceptions and conventions, or create new ones? This is the crux of the postmodern project. As Jean Cocteau wrote, however, art consists in knowing "how far one can go too far." Readers, present and future, will decide.

ROBERT W. HAMBLIN

The versatile author Robert W. Hamblin was born in Jericho, Mississippi, in 1938 and grew up at Brice's Cross Roads, where his parents owned the general store across from the famous Civil War battle site. After graduating from high school, he attended a community college and then Delta State University (BA in English education, 1960). He taught and coached baseball in Maryland before returning to his home state to take an MA in 1965 at the University of Mississippi. He joined the faculty at Southeast Missouri State University, where he spent the remainder of his career. He has written numerous scholarly works on William Faulkner and edited various works of his, and in 1988 he founded the Center for Faulkner Studies. For nearly twenty-five years, he served as an editor of *Cape Rock*. Among his publications are some six collections of poetry, books on William Carlos Williams, basketball coach Ron Shumate, and the novelist Evans Harrington, and a prize-winning account of restoring an old house, written with his wife, Kaye.

From the Ground Up: Poems of One Southerner's Passage to Adulthood, Hamblin's initial collection (1992), introduced readers to his style and outlook. The epigraph is from Robert Frost: "Earth's the right place for love." Frost's style clearly exerted more influence on Hamblin's creative work than did Faulkner's. The poems, nearly all in free verse, are crafted simply. Lines, many declarative, are divided arbitrarily or shaped according to syntactical elements—substantive or verbal phrases, modifiers, or a parenthetical comment. "Farm Mother" offers a good example: "On Sunday mornings, dressed / in his best shirt and pants and only tie, / he sat stiffly between his mother /and father on a wooden pew...." "The Mantel Clock" mentions family stories "repeated / for children on front verandas on hot / summer evenings...." Metaphoric values are not rich; Hamblin is a plain speaker. Not all juxtapositions are effective. In "The Lovers," an empty, rusting garbage can on the curb, "like a thorn," does not serve well as a correction to young lovers' casual talk on the campus.

History is the focus of "The Cannons," which describes the battlefield Hamblin knew as a child, seen again by an older man. Elsewhere the poet evokes, in the third person, aspects of a personal past: the necessary but bloody ritual of killing chickens, the disappearance long ago of a flaming redhead in the family, and the discovery of an uncle making love to a café waitress. Numerous additional figures appear—a father and son, perhaps, a boy dreaming of London (which reappears in "World's Stage"). In many poems, including the little lyric "Mississippi Autumn," direct and appealing glimpses of the rural past contribute to readers' appreciation of the state.

Meditative verse, much in short lines, touches on such topics as children, road travel, a white rose that escaped destruction in a terrific storm, a picnic beneath a rock shelter where prehistoric men may have camped. "We find nothing of ourselves / in conjecture of those ignorant even / of the bow and arrow / and the taming of the horse" ("Family Outing: At Giant City State Park"). Dated January 1991 (the launch of Operation Desert Storm), "For Steve, a United States Marine" connects the poet's personal world to events overseas. The surprising survival of a premature child elicits thoughtful reflections in the midst of "our misdirected and fragmented lives." At its baptism the speaker recalls how "your body marvelously blossomed, / first gram by gram, then ounce by ounce, / until it matched the invisible flower / of your incredible heart's desire." "Underground Poem," set in the London tube, is addressed to Dylan Thomas, whose poetry has been displayed there. "In That Winter" is a rhymed love lyric structured around birds.

Crossroads: Poems of a Mississippi Childhood (2010) combines new poems with selected work from previous books. A map of Brice's Cross Roads (also a poem title) and the three part titles—"Places," "People," "Memory"—reinforce the subtitle. Topics in both new and old poems are often appealing or important: the damage done by racial segregation in baseball ("Robert Freeman"); strict codes of behavior in the past ("Southern Boys"); overflowing rivers and tornadoes ("Flood: A Southern Parable" and "Storm House"). Portraits are warm: a high-school Shakespeare teacher, a "southern lady," blacks at "Bethel C.M.E. Church." Diction and structure remain, however, more characteristic of prose than of verse, with plain statements, little figurative language, and few notable verbal effects. The opening of "Playmate" furnishes an illustration: "Today he would be suspected / a pervert, this large, gentle man / who preferred the company of children / and seemed to have no adult companions. . . ." Hamblin's strengths are his understanding of his home area and its people and the authentic impressions his writing gives.

DERRICK HARRIELL

Derrick Harriell, who lives in Oxford with his wife and son, settled there in 2012 when he was appointed assistant professor of English and African American studies at the University of Mississippi and director of the MFA program. In 2018 he was promoted to associate professor. Born in 1980 in Milwaukee and reared there, he has two degrees from the University of Wisconsin–Milwaukee (BA in English and creative writing, 2003; PhD in English and creative writing, 2012) as well as an MFA in creative writing (poetry) from Chicago State University (2006). His antecedents are southern; both of his parents (whom he thanks in *Ropes*, along with his sister) were from Alabama. Poems of his have appeared in numerous anthologies and journals, including *Callaloo* and *Red Clay Review*. He is the author of three books: *Cotton* (2010), *Ropes* (2013), which was named poetry book of the year by the Mississippi Institute of Arts and Letters, and *Stripper in Wonderland* (2017).

The title word of *Ropes* alludes initially to boxing rings, where "Jim Crow / don't go in the ring" ("Letters to Jack Johnson from Joe Louis" 3). Behind that allusion is the negative phrase "Being on the ropes." The poem "Uncle Sam Shows Joe Louis the Ropes" illustrates a third metaphoric application. The cover reproduces fragments of newspaper articles of 1940, one of which announces, "Joe Louis Scandal Continues." (The scandal rose from his involvement with other women while he was married to Marva Trotter.) Behind those three references is a fourth, to rope used in lynching. It is pertinent that the mother and stepfather of Joe Louis (Barrow) moved from Alabama to Detroit through fear of Klan activity. (See the first of "Letters to Jack Johnson from Joe Louis.")

Each of the four parts—or "Four Rounds"—of *Ropes* concerns a famous fighter, in connection with others, whether opponents or models. Mike Tyson comes first; following him are Joe Frazier, Joe Louis, and Jack Johnson. Many poems, which follow facts closely, bear dates, some of famous fights. Among additional figures, glimpsed or prominent, are Muhammad Ali, Tupac Shakur, Sugar Ray Robinson, and Sam McVey. Endnotes provide information. Women include Etta Duryea, Veronica Porché, and Monica Turner. The boxing terms *round* and *ring* fit well: figures appear and return, giving a sense of recurrence; in turn, such recurrence fits a quotation from Jack Handy, used as an epigraph, who said that boxing was like a ballet.

All poems are in free verse, which occasionally is close to prose; but features such as rhyme, assonance ("A Prison Lullaby"), and stanzaic construction (couplets, for instance, in "Undressing the Belt") furnish poetic interest. Wordplay is frequent, as in "Tupac Shakur Reads Letter from Mike Tyson," featuring *rapper* and *rapist*; and boxing terms serve as metaphors, as in "uppercuts of desire" ("Letters on Love"). A tendency toward aphorism is not out of place, since the epistolary poems furnish advice and encouragement: "When life becomes a drag / it is best to race it" ("Michael Gerard Tyson's Rap Sheet").

What are ostensibly the boxers' voices are heard, whether directly or in letters to family members and other fighters. In "Not Joe Frazier: Tyson Writes Apology Letter," dated the day before Tyson fought Frazier's son Marvis, the diction is perhaps too elegant ("along the hallways of my ambition"; "when angels come to visit"); yet a verb is omitted, as in vernacular speech, displayed often here. Similarly, in "Letters to Joe Frazier from Mike Tyson," a phrase such as "Boxing is a symphony / of wills, an orchestra of skills" sounds out of place. Yet Harriell's re-creation of famous prizefighting figures is valuable, particularly since it involves also, necessarily, the burden of racial prejudice and struggle against it—that is, as a title puts it, "Constructing the New Negro." A recurring aspect of this theme is the risks run at the time by black men who dated or married white women.

In endorsing *Stripper in Wonderland*, Patricia Smith called it a "pimp-walked odyssey of a book." Allusions to rapping and blues connect the poetics to African American music. As Harriell "wrestles with love, fatherhood, the American Southland, and the bruises of black masculinity," he lets his vision "shine through like a strobe light, bringing us flashes of light before reminding us how to live through the dark." The range of this broad vision has its parallel in wide-open form and diction. Few capital letters appear, except in titles. Punctuation is minimal except for slashes within and ending lines, a use Harriell may have borrowed from Sterling D. Plumpp or Etheridge Knight. (Such slashes appear here without spaces, to distinguish them from line breaks in quoted lines.) Loose form is both emphasized and controlled by gaps (a half-inch or so) within lines, arranged in such a way that vertical blank columns may result. Variable left-hand margins, indented blocks, and other variations in form draw attention. Similarly, language is stretched, partly through wordplay and sound echoes. "holy growl how it crooned the watchful night swoon / in its day/how it invisibled right before / hunter and tourist and lens and moon and ghost / . . . christened its chops rare" ("Bigfoot at the Edge of the Projects"). James Matthew Wilson calls such phrasings "non-sequiturs in lines," or "ill-configured disjunctive sentences" (45, 47).

The field of motifs, characters, settings, and themes, many recurrent, is similarly broad and varied. The entire book valorizes popular American culture, mostly in a narrow range, at the expense of all other. The three parts ("Stripper in Wonderland," "Astronauts in Mississippi," and "Pimping Through Eternity") deal loosely with tangential or overlapping materials; but the main connecting element is a speaker's voice. Strippers, patrons, rappers, drinkers come and go; scenes change from Las Vegas hotels and airplanes to rural Mississippi and Atlanta. That Mississippi stands apart is made clear; Martians alight there because they want "a piece / of what we've come in peace for / an anthropological undertaking / . . . a tasting zoo of graveyard and yardbird" ("Astronauts in Mississippi"). Although "all strippers reincarnate to Mississippi" (a poem title), the state does not come off well: "front confederate flag tells all I need to know / about the soul of this South/get it young country / bumpkin/ make grandpa proud/push that pedal / like propaganda/like a hate you can't understand" ("Links Rd to HWY 6 to Jackson Ave"). Similarly, in "Unnamed Things," "antebellum architectured language barked / on this balcony." What is, presumably, deliberate strangeness, worthy of "anthropological" study, is reinforced by scattered allusions to time machines, robots, and a mothership. This very modern streak—something like the machines Italian and French painters introduced into their canvases in the early twentieth century—bespeaks both familiarity and alienation, which, for Harriell, may always be that of a black man in Mississippi.

Harriell's poem "Langston Hughes and all that Jazz," displayed in Square Books in Oxford (April 2018), is more accessible. Addressing "Langston," the speaker expresses understanding of "what it was about the music / that caused them to examine your aesthetic / through a magnifying glass." Blues as well as jazz serve as metaphors and correlatives for effort and weariness. The free-verse line structure conforms to the sentence phrasing, with no startling enjambment. Like Plumpp's and others, the poem connects a music genre created by African Americans to their poetry and thereby underlines the weight of oppression and racial prejudice on both arts even though they are liberating. That is the aim of Harriell's work in general.

BROOKS HAXTON

Brooks Haxton, born in 1950 in Greenville, is the son of the composer and writer Kenneth Haxton and the novelist Josephine Haxton, who wrote as Ellen Douglas. Their marriage appears to have been unhappy; the poet mentions divorce in that connection. He had two brothers; he and his wife, who married in 1983, have a son and twin daughters. His dedication to his paternal grandmother of translations from Else Lasker-Schüler's *My Blue Piano* indicates that his father was Jewish; Brooks and his wife were wed in a Jewish ceremony. In 2001, however, he wrote of God, "He does not exist" ("I Swore My Love on the Appointed Day," from *Nakedness, Death, and the Number Zero*).

Haxton graduated from Greenville High School (1968). Bob Dylan's protest songs and poetry by e. e. cummings and T. S. Eliot attracted him. He took a BA at Beloit College (1972) and in 1981 he earned a master's degree in creative writing at Syracuse University, where he has taught poetry composition in the MFA program since 1993. He is also on the faculty of the Warren Wilson MFA Program for Writers. Previously he taught at the Georgia Institute of Technology, Sarah Lawrence College, and George Mason University. His numerous honors include awards from the Academy of American Poets, the Richard Wright Award, Mississippi Institute of Arts and Letters awards, and NEA and Guggenheim fellowships. He is a member of the Fellowship of Southern Writers and received its Hanes Award (2013), although he pursued his career outside the South.

Haxton's verse has appeared in *Mississippi Observed*, the *Atlantic Monthly*, *New Yorker*, *Sewanee Review*, *Southern Review*, *Poetry*, and elsewhere. Among his topics are civil rights struggles and associated matters. He has published eight volumes of poetry, as well as translations from classical Greek, German, and French and the nonfiction book *Fading Hearts on the River: A Life in High*

Stakes Poker (2014), based on his son's experiences. He was the screenwriter for the PBS documentary film *Tennessee Williams: Orpheus of the American Stage* (1994). In 1990 he resigned, with eight others, from an NEA literary panel in protest against restrictions on artistic expression by Congress when it demanded that projects it supported meet "general standards of decency."

Haxton launched his career with a narrative poem, *The Lay of Eleanor and Irene* (1985). Given the century-old dominance of personal poetry, generally short lyrics or complaints, one could easily overlook the continued vigor of the long poem, usually narrative or dramatic. In France, St.-John Perse set an unexcelled standard with his *Anabase* (1924). Eliot, Hart Crane, Ezra Pound, Robinson Jeffers, John Ashbery, and Stephen Vincent Benét are among twentieth-century English-language practitioners of the genre. In *Obdurate Brilliance*, Peter Baker argued that, unlike its Romantic predecessors such as Wordsworth's *Prelude*, fixed on the self, the modern long poem is characterized by exteriority, that is, others' experience. In recent decades in America, it has been utilized for historical topics. Robert Penn Warren's *Brother to Dragons* constitutes a small-scale national epic featuring Jefferson and family members. John Gery's *Davenport's Version* (2003), David Mason's *Ludlow* (2007), and Jennifer Reeser's *The Lalaurie Horror* (2013) offer recent examples.

The Lay of Eleanor and Irene is set on the Upper West Side of New York City. Portions of the work appeared in the *Kenyon Review*. The medieval term *lai* or *lay*, perhaps of Breton origin, designated a short poem in octosyllabic verse, or a lyric; love is a principal topic. Haxton similarly uses short lines (though not with regular beat or syllabic count), and love is at stake; in other respects, the work does not imitate the model. A male narrator, using past tenses, relates the story—that of an unusual sexual triangle, of whom only two partners are seen directly. A lengthy seduction process, in which the agents alternately lead and hold back, constitutes most of the text. A digression on Rome is interesting. Haxton develops his scenes skillfully, with little clichéd language; and the dialogue may have psychological interest. But the commonness of adultery plots and the particular emphasis here on body parts lend sordidness to the work; whether the verse presentation redeems the work for future readers is uncertain.

Dead Reckoning (1989), likewise a narrative, which Haxton called both *poem* and *novel* (Acknowledgments), is divided into sections named for units of time. It is in linear free verse—close sometimes to blank verse—and he capitalizes words at the left margin. Critics' appraisals quoted on the cover—"definitely entertaining fiction ... fast paced, gritty, and appealingly downbeat," wrote one; "as compelling as ... hypnotic pulp prose," wrote another—indicate, if nothing else, what the literary press wanted to see there. Close observation of details does create effective, sometimes lyrical descriptions, often of scenes familiar to Mississippi readers: fog over cotton fields, the levee, the borrow pit, willow woods and water on one side, the flat Delta on the other (39, 83). The motif of birds, used in the text and especially chapter titles, provides emblematic continuity. Other aspects of the text work against the poetic effect.

That feature is in keeping with the characters, several of whom are common and coarse. Contrasted with them is one of good character and conduct, a decorated Vietnam veteran with considerable intelligence and learning as well as good will. He has made for himself a modest existence, with which he is satisfied; it does not, however, satisfy his father and shrewish stepmother. His unwilled involvement (stemming from an idiosyncratic decision) with crooks, petty and not-so-small, and other local dregs furnishes the heart of the plot, carrying readers along. Certain scenes are comical, and secondary plots contribute human interest. Furthermore, a generous poetic justice puts much to right. Whether this conclusion came from the author's wish to please readers or his conviction that justice may, after all, prevail cannot be said. Although the hero's Vietnam experience and its effects are secondary, they may be the most persuasive and most valuable strains in the book (Haxton founded the war episodes on first-hand accounts such as Tim O'Brien's *The Things They Carried*).

Dominion, Haxton's first collection of shorter poems (personal lyrics, narratives, and social-conscience poems), appeared in 1986. In free verse, the poems are generally stanzaic. Two qualities are clear: his poetic control and the undergirding learning. A sense of mystery, somewhat dreamlike, metaphysical at times, emanates from many pages. Figures and objects from mythology and lore such as Perseus, the Hero, Death, the Quest, and "Sacred Mountain" introduce ancient, persistent myths ("Easter Mass for Little John" secs. 8, 12). Memory is a principal inspiration, although "the memory deceives us / Because what is most essential / Memory most fears, knows best, / And fails most often to remember" ("Easter Mass" sec. 8). The book title comes from Psalm 8, citing Genesis and "dominion over the works of thy hands." Such sovereignty is illustrated in the long opening poem, "Breakfast ex Animo," a narrative with centered lines, which demonstrates Haxton's bona fides as a Mississippian familiar with country life, its sounds, smells, peculiar lighting, and animals. "Justice," which follows, concerns an altercation in a school locker room between a white and his victim, a small black boy, during which a stronger black intervenes, successfully; the sorrow of it comes when the latter is convicted of manslaughter after having killed a Chinese grocer. The Ku Klux Klan and all it implies appear in the third poem, featuring in its long title Strom Thurmond. Occasionally, Haxton treats small domestic scenes, such conjugal squabbling, and rural topics—hunting, a pond, a watery baptism. A drowned child is central to one poem.

Haxton's outlook is, clearly, grim, and nostalgia is infrequent. "Walking Home in the Dark" repeats like a knell the word *doomed*. "Glee" ends with the death of an incompetent hunting dog. In "Witness," concerning an accidental death when an auger catches someone's trousers, the poet accuses the Divinity of responsibility. Nor is Hell a matter of "belief"; witness the urban scene of an addict burnt by ignited hairspray. In disabused tones, the series "Serenade Airborne" depicts modern life, citing in particular a New York City blackout. "Still Life with Fruit, 1969, Missing in Action" imagines a soldier's unrecorded death. "Beans" treats the topic of coffee bean cultivation in South America, where ill-treated workers suffer so that Americans can drink the brew. "Peaceable Kingdom" contrasts Edward Hicks's multiple canvases by that title with the removal of Native Americans from their lands. Late in the collection, "Economics" summarizes the brutality of beasts and human beings.

The Sun at Night (1995), Haxton's fifth book of verse, contains stanzaic and centered poems and some with staggered margins. "Aubade of the Blown Rose" is in rhymed quatrains. The thematic reach is broad, as are the temporal and geographic reaches. Historical and mythological subjects (for instance, Osiris) are put to use; planets and animals appear, such as the puma. Poetic botanicals include pussy willows, trout lilies, wild geraniums in a lovely lyric and, in "From the Outside" and "One Fall," brown leaves. Through these materials Haxton ranges with authority. The title poem makes a historical sweep, from Joshua to Antietam Creek and Khe Sanh. There is unease. The speaking voice departs from the personal to become nearly cosmic in "Garden," a biblical drama, where the persona puts a seed in the ground and corn grows; but Satan appears "by twilight in the body of a coon, and said, / Ah!, hissing from his throat, upreared on hind legs, / black lips curled back from the pointed teeth," and the flowers are "orange as minute live coals." Even a tulip tree in late March, among fine poplars and magnolias, is disturbing: "and the wind came trembling / into the dusk among the leaves" ("Liriodendron Tulipifera").

The title poem of *Nakedness, Death, and the Number Zero* (2001) concerns Archimedes, his "Eureka!" moment, and his death, leaving the legacy of nothing, if not the cipher itself. The lines, unrhymed, are long, the narrative lucid; philosophy and history proceed side by side. Elsewhere in the collection the poet mixes his long lines with short ones, prose, and centered lines. "Song of the Rose" is a villanelle. Maintaining the grimness of previous collections, death weaves in and out; "Catalpa" concerns suicide. The short lyric "First Thing," on a flower, and the series of brief impressions called "Now and Again" deal with mortality, as do, indirectly, "Memorizing 'Lycidas' Under the Warhol at the Walker" (in Greenwich Village) and "Molybdenum," concerned with the Chernobyl accident. The book includes three lengthy poems. "Teenage Ikon" is rich in boyhood nostalgia and awful drama (drugs, sexual rivalry). "I Swore My Love on the Appointed Day," presumably autobiographical, deals with marriage and children. "Tweeg" relates, in quatrains, a dismal love story, told from the man's viewpoint, that borders on incest—at least as the woman sees it. The poem is episodic, with a totem animal and a subplot that challenges plausibility. The poem illustrates by contrast the superiority of fiction in setting out psychological processes.

The *New York Times* review of this collection by Emily Nussbaum, "High Lyrical, Low Cynical," serves as an example of misreading, probably willful. While noting, justly, the weakness of the long poems, especially "Tweeg," she panned the book chiefly on different grounds. Her ad hominem reasoning is instructive. She confuses what she calls the speaker, or "narrator," with the poet; thus, she can accuse the man himself of "obsession with the mossy underside of middle-aged sexual obsession" and can dismiss most of the book accordingly. (In his reply, Haxton pointed out the flaw in her approach and defended his character.)

They Lift Their Wings to Cry (2008) shows that Haxton's lyric abilities remained keen. Nature provides many images; it is the foundation of the poems. Even various social-protest poems are connected to that foundation (see "Prospectus: In Lieu of the Mall Expansion"). The book deals with both body and soul, to the degree the soul can be found; "Breathless," on the common cold, Descartes, and various glands, is pertinent. The book title refers to "The Cry of the Snowy Tree Cricket" and the males' mating calls, made by scraping their wings. Strangely, the female is unable to hear them; she is attracted, instead, by a scent, which the male secretes upon lifting his wings. What these complications mean is not said. But, "her ministrations / hushing him, they mate." Not unlike art, perhaps: "This poem also / cries, and hushes as your mind draws near." "Storm," in four quatrains, creates a dark landscape from such details as cattle egrets, a bull, and forked lightning. In "Screech-Owl Pie," the bird's remains lie on the roadside, mangled by a car and half-devoured. Trying to seize a mouse (perhaps of the sort trained to sing), it had been spooked by headlights. Its corpse "contains / no more an owl than shut books do." Yet, "year-round after nightfall / the white-footed mice are singing."

Such evidence in the collection of transcending limitations offsets, perhaps, the loss of friends, gone like the grass, like the flowers ("Bert, In Memory, and Herb Robert"). Something lingers out of reach, sending occasional signals. In "When I Came Awake," a short lyric, the speaker is, implausibly, in a well, which joins rock to water. "The stone floor made sleep difficult / But when I put my ear to it / I heard waves far off breaking / into the face of a cliff." While "we do all fade as a leaf" (an epigraph, from Isaiah 64:6, to "Gift"), that very poem, describing the speaker's maternal grandfather's Bible, makes faith shine. "If I May" expresses thanks to the Divinity, "if He exists, which I believe / He does. He may not. Probably not. / But I would like to thank Him."

ELMO HOWELL

Elmo Howell (1918–2013) combined his pursuit of poetry with grassroots study of literary and cultural history in his state. He was born in Itawamba County. He graduated from Tremont High School, then took a BA at the University of Mississippi in 1940. He received his MA and PhD (1947, 1955) from the University of Florida. From 1955 to 1957 he taught at Jacksonville State College in Alabama, then moved to Memphis State, where he remained until his retirement in 1983. His chief interests were the English novel and southern literature. Among his scholarly publications are studies on William Faulkner, Flannery O'Connor, William Gilmore Simms, and Mark Twain. He contributed to literary history by publishing three volumes, *Mississippi Home-Places*, *Mississippi Scenes*, and *Mississippi Back-Roads*, all with the subtitle *Notes on Literature and History*. His poetry collections include *Winter Verses* (1989), *The Apricot Tree and Other Poems* (1993), and *Tuesday's Letter and Other Poems* (2000).

Like that of certain other figures in this study, Howell's work is for those who remember or wish to document the rural Mississippi past and who, having rejected modernism, surrealism, the confessional school, and postmodernism, look for directness in poetry. Writing in plain style, during his retirement years, he was the equivalent of a "Sunday painter." He is quoted in the preface to this study regarding "Mississippi lay poets" who, at the end of the twentieth century, still wrote "with Victorian clarity and fervor" (*Mississippi Scenes* 53). His own work has both clarity and, often, fervor. Most of his volumes are self-published. His verse is not without merit, however, by its accessibility, authenticity, and documentary value.

The Apricot Tree illustrates Howell's style and purposes at their best. The poems, mostly in free verse, are well structured. Moments from history furnish scenes and topics for reflection. "On Finding a Confederate Note" follows the thoughts of someone who discovers the banknote in a fruit jar in a closet, with a few Mexican coins. He fingers the paper, reads the inscriptions, and imagines riders arriving with news "that morning in '65, when the word came down from Richmond." "The dead, the dead have died again! / ... / The lares are taken!" Memories may be personal, revolving around boyhood, or deal with other figures. In "Hearing Once the Whippoorwill," the speaker, awakened by the bird "in a great city," recalls the countryside on a May morning, "when there was pasture and tillage and men calling to mules." "How is it," he asks, "that the past cannot be summoned / But comes when it will, unsought ... ?" Tennessee Williams comes to life in a sketch of the dramatist as an adolescent, with his grandfather, after church.

The present furnishes similar moments, emblematic, nearly ideal. In "The Guest" (after Primo Levi) someone accepts graciously an austere hospitality. "I like a bare floor and lamp oil / And a hearth that dies out in the night. ... / But most of all to be in an honest man's house." In the checkout line at a Kroger's store, the speaker wonders, "How could any moment be endured without a symbol? / That full, perfect and sufficient sacrifice. ..." ("When I Saw the Gentle Nun"). Particularly well-noted details mark "Sunday Afternoon in the Quarter," where the present and the past of New Orleans meet. Trees are a frequent motif. In "The White Oak," a tree and a man are share kinship. "They become like one another. / A tree and a good man are happy and do not wish to be anywhere else. / They know the horizons and where the weather comes from. ..." According to "The Cherry Trees of Audubon Park," the trees, in the right season, the right light, "rise up to greet you / And turn on the whole country! / Visibly breathing, pulsing in a sweet levitation— / About to break free!"

Tuesday's Letter is concerned pointedly with Mississippi—its counties and towns, its houses, figures of the past and present (Grant, Polk, Forrest, Faulkner, Eudora Welty), and dramas, real and imagined. An epigraph from V. S. Naipaul on history residing "in the heart" is apt. The poems are accompanied by various paratexts: literary maps, numerous photographs, copies of old poems, useful endnotes, quotations from Faulkner, Shelby Foote, and others. Some borrowed texts are integral to the poems—for instance, a quotation from Stark Young's *Heaven Trees* in a poem of that title. This compositional principle is not without rationale, but its effect is to cast on the collection the shadow of a guidebook. The poems have a casual air and are, often prose-like, with long lines tending toward paragraphs. Plain, direct descriptions characterize many pages. Fortunately, the tones, whether of the narrator's voice or quoted speakers, are often just right. "Towards the Definition of Culture," for instance, recounts briefly how the boy at Mr. Felix's store "fixed" a car and accepted no payment, though the plate was "strange" (out-of-state). The little poem rings true. Yet, although the back cover proclaims that Howell "goes beyond the facts to a closer involvement with the past," as a whole, *Tuesday's Letter* sacrifices poetic imagination to information.

T. R. HUMMER

T. R. (Terry Randolph) Hummer occupies an important presence on the poetry scene today. He is, in one critic's view, "a master storyteller and essayist" (Marshall). He was born in Macon in 1950 and reared on a farm in Prairie Point, Noxubee County. His father was a postman as well as a farmer; the poet pays homage to him in the sonnet sequence "Carrier" (*The Angelic Orders*). His father's ancestors settled in the state in the late nineteenth century; his mother, née Slocum, had Louisiana antecedents, and, as a boy, he visited his grandmother in Tangipahoa Parish. A poem published in 2019, "Louisiana," shows that he has not forgotten this connection. He was aware of the social divides around him, centered on class (the privilege of land ownership) and race. He does not identify himself as a "southern poet"; he happens to be from the South but has renounced most of its southernness, especially "rural Mississippi in the bad old days" (Hoppenthaler). He has tried to exorcise "the demons of his Mississippi upbringing" (Marshall).

Nevertheless, Hummer acknowledges his attachment to Prairie Point. In his boyhood he was keen on jazz and blues music and managed to buy an electric guitar; later, he became a good saxophonist. His interest in music has remained lively; in *The Infinity Sessions* numerous poems bear titles borrowed from albums of popular music genres. "Nobody's Sweetheart" (a part title) is dedicated to the bass saxophinist Adrian Rollini, and the series "Lives of the Angels" is subtitled "Duets for Saxophone and Sky." His book *Available Surfaces: Essays on Poesis* deals with the creative process in both music and verse. Yet he was suspicious of attempts to assimilate poetry to music; he identified what he wrote as poems, not song lyrics (Donovan).

Hummer studied at the Center for Writers at the University of Southern Mississippi and earned both bachelor's and master's degrees (1972, 1974). His teachers there included D. C. Berry and Gordon Weaver. He has a PhD from the University of Utah (1980), where he studied with Dave Smith, who has championed his career. Hummer was married and divorced; from that marriage he has a daughter, Theo Hummer. Well into middle age, he had a second daughter. For years he moved, as teacher or writer in residence, from one appointment to another, with stops at Oklahoma State University, Middlebury College (twice), the University of California–Irvine, Kenyon College, the University of Oregon, Virginia Commonwealth University, the University of Georgia, plus Exeter College (UK). The landscapes connected to these places are prominent in his poetry. In 2006 he joined the creative writing program at Arizona State University. He has since retired and lives in Cold Spring, New York. During his career he edited the *Cimarron Review*, *Kenyon Review*, *New England Review*, and *Georgia Review*. He was a Bread Loaf Fellow in 1983. His work has received recognition in the form of an NEA Fellowship (1987), a Guggenheim Fellowship (1993), and the 1999 Hanes Prize from the Fellowship of Southern Writers. In 2012 he won the Mississippi Arts and Letters Award for Poetry. He has published a dozen collections of verse, chapbooks, and two volumes of criticism, one of which deals with James Dickey, whose influence on him is evident, as is Robert Penn Warren's. Other influential figures he cites are Wordsworth, Hopkins, Yeats, and Wallace Stevens.

Hummer's writing, which valorizes viewpoints without overlooking aesthetic considerations, is concerned with social issues and what he refers to as the body politic, which he treats in the context of American decline. A rough model might be Warren's *Audubon: A Vision*, which likewise evinces disappointment, since the romantic promise of the nineteenth century, far from being fulfilled, has given way to an unjust society. Such titles of Hummer's as *Bluegrass Wasteland* and *Useless Virtues* suggest disillusion. No doubt his standing in critics' eyes is due partly to his jaundiced view of his nation, with its waste, ugliness, and exploitation. Certain poems are nearly what Eudora Welty called "harangues" (154).

The 18,000-Ton Olympic Dream (1990) is a meditation on contemporary America in the world. Hummer uses free verse, stanzaic or in long blocks, often with very long lines; certain poems approach prose. He does not practice concision; words flow abundantly, and his voice is strong. The expansive form invites ranging thoughts and images. The lengthy title poem, which constitutes one part, arose from reflections on the 1987 sinking of the oil tanker of that name, of which Hummer learned while staying in St. Ives in Cornwall. The speaker is ill at ease abroad, "vaguely ashamed / Of my country, of the language / I can't help speaking" (12). The shabbiness of his hotel contributes no doubt to his malaise, which becomes distress as the shipping disaster unfolds through the "snow-grain / Of bad reception" of the ancient television set (12). His vague sense of culpability seems to extend to the catastrophe itself, "widow-making unchilding unfathering" (13). The previous evening he had admired the sea, embracing it mentally: "Cloud-scattered sky, full moon, / The deep-moiled windstroked / Opalescent midnight January Atlantic. . . ." Now he imagines it aflame, smoky, stained by oil "veined / from [the] ruptured hold" (13). The disaster is organically connected to the contemporary world, its microwave towers, relay stations, and (it is implied) American travelers. The poet speaks of "illusion / Of dramatic guilt, this pitiful / And suspicious effort / To be political, liberal . . ." (16). Friends, visiting him, driving—thus using petrol—get what he calls "Wordsworth's Revenge": "emetic motion regurgitated intranquilly."

That indisposition gives its name to the second part of the book, which contains further echoes of the title poem, as in "the oil-scummed image of the surface of the river" ("Slow Train Through Georgia"). The poems border on free association, even surreality. In "Spring Comes to Mid-Ohio in a Holy Shower of Stars," the poet writes of "the unpragmatic crystal ball of my larynx" and "the rusted iron wheels of snow plows" that "gave their spiritual groans in the heat-dead midnight streets." Hummer relies often on loose verbal associations (as when the word *white* weaves through "The Mist Trees Vanish Into"); elsewhere, the associations seem arbitrary, held together by repeated motifs and the voice, in an onrush of words, as in "Salt Flats Crossing: Homage to Vachel Lindsay."

Yet the expansive lines, however word- and image-oriented, convey messages; the poem just cited uses critically such phrases as "sonic-booming" and "sea to shining sea." "We are stunned by the salt of the lost American // Sea that might have drowned Manifest Destiny if the continental plates / Had given the slow bump and grind of their tactical shifting / a rhythm politically correct." Man has ruined the environment: "The sky dumps an essence the color of pleurisy // On the working man's car, congesting / What vision anyone might have of the country / Beyond . . ." ("The Mist Trees Vanish Into"). "Mississippi 1955 Confessional," a reminiscence, depicts a boy with an unnamed illness, on a farm in summertime. Within that setting arise questions of race—distinctions between black and white, social separation. Titles such as "Poem in the Shape of a Saxophone" (it is not) and "Politics" are reminders of Hummer's interests.

The twenty poems, untitled, called "Bluegrass Wasteland"—the final part of *The 18,000-Ton Olympic Dream*—bear Roman numerals. They are in tercets; line length varies. They are built, roughly, on a lovemaking scene, a "passionate illusion," in an office building in Mount Vernon, Ohio, next door to Gambier (Kenyon College). Certain poems and other passages, italicized, seem to constitute an interior monologue, in first- or third-person discourse, centered on a male figure. Those poems in roman are generally performative. Yet the interior monologue overflows into these scenic accounts. Episodes elsewhere—past moments in a boy's visit to his grandmother in Louisiana, and a bluegrass band playing in a barroom—serve as counterpoint, or "countervoice," as the poet writes apropos of puberty, the hating and misunderstanding of life becoming loving of life. The body is valorized. Yet a more pointed concern seems to be not eroticism but American culture. One page reproduces the legends on four sides of the base of a "phallic" statue in Mount Vernon—"Manifest Destiny's Urban Sprawl" (xiv)—which honors those who triumphed in "The War of the Great Rebellion." In the bar, the narrative voice asks, "How can the voice justify the world to the world . . . ?" (xviii).

To deplore "the machine in the garden," in Leo Marx's phrase, and the results of what Kirkpatrick Sale called "triumphalism," is, ironically, to give way to Romantic idealism. Hummer is, or wishes to be, a meliorist, providing by his poetry the insights needed to reimagine America; he has said that he wants to write "poems of conscience" (Hoppenthaler).

Walt Whitman in Hell (1996), an ambitious collection, features several lengthy poems and a wide range of voices, settings, topics, and lore. The chief rhetorical resource is juxtaposition of incongruous, often strong images. Hummer uses various stanza forms, sometimes numbered, with the syntax of one stanza carrying over to the next. He also calls on a favorite distich form, where the even lines are indented, without initial capitals. The book opens with "Zeitgeist Lightning," concerning the unauthorized autopsy of Whitman, the removal of his brain, and its ruin when an assistant dropped it onto a tile floor. The title poem, printed last, in tercets, occupies twelve pages. Hummer's note alludes to "four years of composition" and mentions numerous sources on which he drew for erudite and odd references; among them are Hobbes, Federico García Lorca, Michel Foucault, and a tract handed out at a New York subway entrance. The latter fact may have inspired the setting of the poem: the inferno is that very subway complex.

Between these two key poems one finds little but evil and despair—wars, Nazi tortures, tattooed camp victims, petroleum trucks and other damaging industry, schizophrenia, anonymous murder victims, and historical figures associated with human loss, such as Hart Crane and Emma Goldman. "It is written in the Gnostic *Gospel of Truth* that life is nightmare" ("The Antichrist in Arkansas"). Love fails; religion fails; everything fails. "The bluesman's 'Love in Vain' was lost / In the noise of boots on concrete, sirens, horses and drums, O brother, // Son of dust, cog in the wheel . . ." ("First Assembly of God"). This is the postmodern age, as a curious poem title, very lengthy, suggests when it speaks of throwing into a river Frederic Jameson's *Postmodernism, or the Logic of Late Capitalism.*

One is not surprised to find in *Useless Virtues* (2001) many of the same tones and postures as in *Walt Whitman in Hell*. The message of "The End of History" is clear enough. Two series mark the book. Five poems, scattered, appear under the title "Half-Life Study"; twenty constitute "Axis," concerned with Martin Heidegger. Lest readers misunderstand his intentions and take the series as an homage, Hummer specifies in a note that Heidegger's active connections with the Nazi party are well documented. Nonetheless, the poems, in modified sonnet form, printed 8 / 6, without rhyme and fixed beats, introduce something essential to the poet's worldview. "Axis" is, of course, that of three belligerents in World War II; but it is likewise that of the earth, spinning in the cosmos. In poem 2.1, a boy (called the speaker's "father") is "born in ignorance, stunned by Being, thrown / Out of nowhere into the center of a horrible story / Being written around him in blood, by no one. / The Philosopher [Heidegger] smiles." In poem 4.2, the Philosopher "scorns" such phenomena as the disappearance of a modest colleague, "a Kabbalist?" who had come to him, desperately seeking a favor. "Rumor had it they'd taken a train / Somewhere into the heartland." What occupies the Philosopher's mind is not such contingencies but, rather, the question: "What sits at the Center of Being / Governing Being's revolution?" The poet continues: "Whatever it is, / he will name it. It is there, just beyond his perceiving. / The Axis is time. The Axis is not time."

It is obvious that the evil men do lives after them on many of Hummer's pages. Might *The Infinity Sessions* (2005), concerned, in some sense, with music, offer a different tone and perspective? Not entirely. The poems, all short, are arranged in six parts, preceded by an introductory poem. In addition to song titles, the text features names of various musicians, including Jimmie Lunceford and "Big Maybelle" Smith. Surely the poet intended to pay tribute to these figures, their art, their skill. The poems are not, however, lyrics (either as poems or songs), nor are they biographical sketches. A powerful, malignant fate is everywhere, arising from, or presiding over, the universe; dark forces wait in the wings, then pounce. In "Arkansas Blues," children sing "songs that would make a fiddler's hair stand on end. / They're dancing on graves. They're knocking angels down. / Somewhere the wrath of God is looking for its big black belt. . . ." Nor do the human figures—to the degree that they seem alive at all—evince much consciousness of themselves as such. Hummer's characteristic concerns and diction resurface: "That being impenetrable" [noun], for instance, appears in "The Prisoners." "Zero" sketches a hellish scene, with "clouds of dark matter" and a Kafkaesque figure waiting for "the dead to file their forms." The scene in "The Other Night" is "emptied out now, as after the Rapture, / or postapocalyptic. You can call and call, / You can scream a chord: no angel will answer." Music may remain, but the choirs are "without blue notes" and syncopation has "vanished / . . . a deadbeat purity."

Ephemeron (2011), *Skandalon* (2014), and *Eon* (2018) constitute a coherent group, though not, formally, a trilogy. The first title means, simply, a piece of ephemera; the book is a meditation on the passing of all things. The second title, which meant, in the Greek, a snare, signifies, in Christian theology, a disgrace, stumbling block, or offense, as in Matthew 18:7 (called "le scandale" in French). *Eon* is, of course, an eternity.

The prosody of *Ephemeron*, which the cover terms "pyrotechnic," varies among prose poems, centered lyrics, distich poems with the even lines indented, and those composed of two-line prose verses, many without clear transition to the next. The poems appear to constitute a postmodern atheist's manifesto. The tone is dark, the images often unpleasant, the human condition, or at least today's moral and physical environment, awful, as the poem title "Toxins" reminds readers. Jarring metaphors and irrational, blunt, and sweeping statements place Hummer's writing in today's fashionable literary mainstream, with its emphasis upon deconstructing certain cultural givens. Visions of past loss and doomsday to come swirl around. The writing suggests likewise the darkest existentialism of nineteenth- and twentieth-century predecessors; one section is "Either/Or," a title of Kierkegaard's. While David Kirby's endorsement asserts that "Hummer's world is bright with the beauty of decay, charged with the force of his unrelenting intellect," some readers may conclude that it resembles assemblages of unattractive materials removed from context and recontextualized arbitrarily, meaninglessly.

In the title poem, printed initially, the speaker appears to be a man nearly fifty whose wife expects a child. (The voice varies; one line says "*I am pregnant*"). Terms such as *DNA* and *amniotic sac* emphasize that this turn of events is contemporary, even as it is ancient, written in immemorial biological law. In the reaches of time, what is one child? Nothing. The outlook is not good. According to "Abandon," which seems to cry over God's absence: "Soon, but not yet, the incremental creaking of hinges, the end of molecular / bonding, release of form. . . ." "Ad Hominem" evokes a room, with human paraphernalia but apparently abandoned. "Now that people have vanished, who will deal / with the swarm of tiny annoyances that defined / Human existence?" Despite the title, the poem "Argument from Design" does not concern creationism but rather the proliferation of means and places for committing suicide. The final poem is "Abandoned Draft."

Skandalon earned even higher praise from endorsers than *Ephemeron*. One was Andrew McFadyen-Ketchum, himself an apocalyptic poet. Hummer, he writes, is among the visionaries; his name "will be cherished and passed down by the generations we can only hope are to come." The book is an *"in memoriam* to civilization." As an epigraph, Hummer quotes Richard John Neuhaus: "Our divisions are a *Skandalon* ... an evidence of our disobedience." War is among the evils ("The Fallacy of Composition"). It is modern warfare: soldiers are "vaporized." Everything is "particles." Racial persecution, against blacks and Jews, is a further source of conflict (see "Pandrol Jackson"), as is religious fanaticism (in "The Inquisition," concerning the Cathars). The eighteen poems that constitute "Victims of the Wedding," scattered throughout the collection, are like a knell.

Eon introduces contrasting notes. Whereas, in the two previous books, hope and love were nearly ruled out, they reappear here in an elegiac or simply peaceable mode. Following an opening poem, dedicated to Seamus Heaney, three parts, "Murder," "Urn, and "Eon," trace a moral arc, completed by a poem under the rubric "Coda," dedicated to Philip Levine. All poems occupy only one page, most less than that, and all display the two-line arrangement introduced in preceding collections, the even lines indented and beginning with lower case. The arrangement is pleasing, not monotonous; it suggests continuity, the step-by-step emergence from a black hole. Titles on pages are printed either in all capitals or using lower case for all but the beginning word, a gesture toward ordinariness. Figures from Hummer's family, and the poet himself, appear along with Robert Oppenheimer (thus the shadow of atomic explosions), Heidegger, Rilke, Cabeza de Vaca, and Hermes Trismegistus.

"Cheap Glass Vase at the Jazz Singer's Grave," the coda poem, celebrates music, as sung by the black singer and the speaker, who, picturing his own plot, soars emotionally with a raptor overhead and sings. In the previous poem, "The most ordinary life," which expresses similarly a sense of reconciliation and acceptance, the persona, not solitary, goes out onto a porch "watched over / By a patient beagle." Stepping over the jamb into sunlight, he sees someone addressed as *you*, "there as always, looking up and smiling." The prophet of doomsday is moved. There are such things as poetry, music, love, perhaps even spirit, "that other world / ... where when we go / we go nowhere that is not already human?' ("Charles Vernon Hummer, 1921–1994"). Poetry is "numinous" ("Erato, Dates Unimaginable").

ANGELA JACKSON

Born in Greenville, Mississippi, in 1951, Angela Jackson is the fifth of nine children, the last born there before the family moved to Chicago. In addition to her birth connection to the state, she is associated through her poetics with two fellow Mississippians who went north, Sterling D. Plumpp and Etheridge Knight. Brought up as a Roman Catholic on the South Side, she received a BA in 1977 from Northwestern University. She had entered as a premedical student but was drawn toward literature by the influence of Margaret Walker and William Fuller, visiting professors there. In 1995 she received a master's degree in Latin American and Caribbean studies from the University of Chicago. She is single and has lived in Chicago with her mother most of her life—eventually becoming her mother's caregiver.

Jackson's creative works are primarily an exploration of the African American world of the United States. She writes plays and novels as well as poetry, but she has said that poetry is her primary medium, although she hides it in her other writings (Solomon). A part of Chicago's Black Arts movement, she has participated in the city's Poets in the Schools program, and her works have been included in the Dial-a-Poem and Poetry-on-the-Buses campaigns there. In 1977 she was selected as a United States representative to the second World Festival of Black and African Arts and Culture in Lagos, Nigeria. The Organization of Black American Culture (OBAC), which had its first home in the South Side Community Center, has been an important part of her life, influencing her style and thought.

Jackson has won many awards and grants. In 1974 she won the Academy of American Poets Prize. She was also awarded the 1986 Illinois Arts Council Literary Award for Poetry, the 2002 Shelley Memorial Award (Poetry Society of America), as well as grants from the National Endowment for the Arts. She received the Daniel Curley Award for Recent Illinois Short Fiction in 1979, 1980, 1986, 1988, and 1997. In 1985 she won the American Book Award for her poetry collection *Solo in the Boxcar Third Floor E*; in 2009 she again received that award for her novel *Where I Must Go*. Her poems have been published in the *Chicago Review, Callaloo, Black Collegian, Black Creation, Black World*, and *Nommo*. She served as writer in residence at Stephens College in Columbia, Missouri, and she taught at Columbia College of Chicago and Howard University.

Jackson's poems, in free verse, "weave myth and life experience, conversation, and invocation" (poetryfoundation.org). In addition to *Solo in the Boxcar Third Floor E*, her published poetic works include the brief *Voo Doo / Love Magic* (1974); *The Greenville Club*, a chapbook published in *Four Black Poets* (1977); *The Man with the White Liver* (1987); *Dark Legs and Silk Kisses: The Beatitudes of the Spinners* (1993); *And All These Roads Be Luminous: Poems Selected and New* (1998); and *It Seems Like a Mighty Long Time* (2015).

In *Voo Doo / Love Magic* Jackson uses African American vernacular. Initially, she inserted slash lines within words and lines, as well as at the ends of lines, intending perhaps to create a pronounced rhythm. (Such slashes appear here without spaces, to distinguish them from line breaks in quoted lines.) Both Plumpp and Knight, likely models, used them to suggest caesuras, silences, or a rhythmic blues quality. The title poem begins by announcing: "I'm gon put a hex on you/work some voo-doo magic/on/yo mind." Double slashes appear later: "Gonna do to you/what/you done to me//and mo //." Further examples are "Watch/out" and "Doing Black//Woman/Love." Gradually, Jackson abandoned the practice. Her poetry thus became more polished and thoughtful, suitable for examining seriously African American achievements and challenges and other topics. According to Donna Seaman, "She portrays family members with tender radiance and uses poetic form and narrative drive with particularly cunning intent as she addresses racial violence past and present."

By 1993, with *Dark Legs and Silk Kisses*, the winner of the 1993 Chicago *Sun-Times* Book of the Year Award and the 1994 Carl Sandburg Award, Jackson's writing was stronger. The collection, a tour de force, features cleverly crafted poems that use the spider as a connective theme, capturing events that span hundreds of years. Many poems are related to African American Woman Guilds. "The Institutional Spider" is "craftless, save for a malice-mischief" and "wild / with ambition. Yet cannot create; / she mimics compassion and begs / it for herself." The poem shows clearly the lack of creativity, the malice, and the jealousy of this familiar institutional type. "She likes to get even with you / because she cannot make what you / make."

And All These Roads Be Luminous includes poems from previous volumes as well as new ones. They are centered on various topics: food, civil rights, religion, weather, family, love, and fire. Although most are in free verse, as in previous volumes, one is in couplets and another is a quasi-sonnet, Shakespearean. Jackson's artistic discipline comes to fruition here. Her joy of words and her cleverness in playing with them—for instance, splitting compound nouns (as Plumpp does) so that readers rethink words—create entertaining, engaging poems. "Memories/The Red Bootee," published first in *Voo Doo / Love Magic*, notes the importance of family. Thoughtfully dedicated "for Mama," it centers on the image of a "little biddy/red bootee" found in the drawer of "important papers": "birth certificates / life insurance / and / all our old report cards"— salient elements of family life. The image captures the reader's heart. When Mama tells the children that it is Emma Lee's shoe, "a baby sister / older than us / who we'd never // seen," they make the discovery of a heretofore unknown sister and have a sense of her importance.

Jackson's latest collection, *It Seems Like a Mighty Long Time*, contains her finest poetry, centering often on civil rights issues. The poems, in free verse or prose, concern such African Americans as Bessie Smith, Rosa Parks, Ida B. Wells, Emmett Till, Bobby Seale, Phillis Wheatley, and Trayvon Martin. "A Woman Was Being Raped," in prose, emphatically captures prejudices, the tendency toward violence, and the predatory nature of human beings, which Jackson often calls to her readers' attention. The central incident is a rape occurring on an El platform in early morning. "Look at that bitch— // and she hollerin it's so good," exclaim passengers as the train passes. The victim's race is understood. "Others tittered at the sight of public sex, / her skirt askew, coat thrown open, spread, blouse torn down to the bra // underneath the ragged scream she screamed, wild turbulence." Ominously and callously, life goes on. "The train kept on its way, / blue fire licking out little tongues on the sides." Later, hearing news reports on the radio, listeners who cannot discern the race of the victim show sympathy for her. "The first commuters / on their way to work heard it on their radio, between the time / they punched the time clock in and out. The memory of her kept them / awake throughout the day." It's a juxtaposition of dramatically different reactions to the violence of rape—at first *witnessed* by people from the El windows and then *heard* on the radio. Jackson ends her poem, powerfully, with two lines in italics, pulling the poet-persona herself into the tragic event: "*Do you remember her face? Would you know her if you saw her? / Did she look like me?*"

It is unfortunate that Jackson's verse is not more widely known. Carefully and artfully, she captures her love for her family and race and conveys the wrongs done to blacks and, indeed, people of all races.

LARRY JOHNSON

For Larry (Lawrence Edward) Johnson, poetry is, foremost, an art; and, in his hands, that art is directed preeminently to representing history. Through historical re-creations, his poems invite, or rather oblige, readers to discover things they would not attend to otherwise, things that are lastingly human. By his style as well as his subject matter, his poems bear resemblances to some dating from the periods he writes about. He makes no apology for his historical bent, nor for the artistic side of his writing. "Though poetry is the oldest form of literature and the one most apprehensible by our intellectual and physical processes," he writes, "it is, like all human creations, *artificial*, 'made with art.' Its language is necessarily elevated, it uses literary devices, and its characters no more speak 'ordinary speech' than do auctioneers" ("Comments for *Hellas*" 1; his italics). His work is thus distinguished from most prevalent currents of contemporary writing. His solid knowledge of Latin and certain other foreign languages has allowed him historical reach, and he has—perhaps as a result of studying the classics but also, surely, of wide reading among contemporaries— excellent poetic taste. Readers can appreciate the poet's broad knowledge of ancient history, classical literature, and music—composers and performers, such as the New Orleans figure Louis-Moreau Gottschalk. It is not a question of showmanship or artifice; for him, erudition is a gateway to poetry, not its core.

Johnson was born in Natchez, in 1945. Four years later, his family moved to Jackson, living sometimes in the city, sometimes outside. He attended schools in Clinton, paying tuition when necessary. His native state has remained important to him. "I'm almost always happy to be in Mississippi. Those of us who still live in the South can see it steadily and see it whole ... and we take beauty and irritation as they come, knowing that time changes everything," Johnson remarked (Abbott, *Reflections* 400–401). Memories of his boyhood feed his poetry, as in

"Near Eastabuchie, Mississippi" and "Once," from *Veins*, where he describes a dead ivory-billed woodpecker, ridden with shotgun pellets.

Johnson has published poems in the *Iowa Review, New Orleans Review, Transatlantic Review, Town Creek Poetry*, and elsewhere, and two collections of his have appeared, *Veins* (2009) and *Alloy* (2014). He took a BA, with honors, at Mississippi College in 1967, then enrolled in the graduate writing program at the University of Arkansas, where he studied with James Whitehead, to whom he dedicated a poem ("the very best of teachers," as his note in *Veins* puts it), and participated in workshops with James Dickey, Robert Pack, George Garrett, and Paul Engle. He was awarded an MA and an MFA (1970), the second such degree given there. From 1969 through 1972 he taught at Alma College in Michigan. From 1973 to 1981 he was in Knoxville, completing doctoral work, except for the dissertation, at the University of Tennessee; his concentration there was in modern poetry. For most of the next two decades he lived in Hattiesburg and New Orleans, where he was instructor in English at UNO for two years. He served a term as poetry editor of *Mississippi Arts and Letters* magazine. In 1999 he moved to North Carolina, where he taught at various institutions. In 2006 he read from his work at the Library of Congress. After his retirement in 2017, he settled in Pomona, California, where he works with his wife in contract editing.

Veins consists of two parts, "Adrenalin Night" and "Adrenalin Light." The book bears laudatory comments from Donald Justice, Garrett, and Fred Chappell. Justice called him "an American Cavafy." Chappell praised, appropriately, Johnson's "vivid and startling vision of the past." Garrett saw the "intelligence" and "compassionate resonance," the imagination, strength, and suppleness of the poems. Extensive notes on the poems furnish information for those unfamiliar with the topic or the language (German, French). The poems of the first part are grouped according to reverse chronology, going back to 966 BC. Johnson's writing does not convey an ossified past, however; his craftsmanship, including choice of details, brings it alive. Furthermore, he writes also on distinctly modern topics such as a blues singer and the speaker's infatuation with her ("Blues Poem").

Johnson's technical range is similarly broad, and his accomplishments are striking. He expressed well his own aims: "The best poetry contains a language of polychromatic density and a fixed but variable meter in order to produce an artful semblance of corporeality" ("Comments for *Hellas*" 1). In his free verse, instead of being arbitrary the line breaks contribute to the meaning. His rhymed verse is without awkwardness. The traditional sonnet form suits him well, printed as a block. The sonnets are tight but not hidebound. In "Moorish Idol" he uses rhymed couplets. The villanelle form stands out in "Earth" and elsewhere. "Withdrawal" is a short prose poem. The little lyric "Honey"—eleven short lines—appeals to the senses of vision, hearing, and taste. A few poems are multipage. "Frozen Danube," a blank-verse narrative in the voice of the Roman poet Claudian, extends for nearly ten pages.

Johnson's metaphors are expressively bold: "... words are souls themselves, / they tune the eons of our hiving blood" ("For All Hostages"). The poem "Beginning" calls up "thought-dolmens ranged behind a silver beach / where the omnilingual sea transpires with ease: / I visit there by heart each day / when other men's dark grains become my own." The poet's stance within poems varies; he may stand apart, like an anonymous painter of historical subjects, or may use the first person to inject himself (a certain self) into the poem, even addressing the other characters, present-day or historical. Favoring scenic presentation over summary, he re-creates settings and characters.

The title word, *vein*, is set off in the last line of "To Her Husband," where it is associated with both anger and desire. The burden of anger against oneself in the form of shame and despair reappears in "Withdrawal," which begins "Dead night. Night of inked stars." The possible role of poetry in such emotions comes to the fore in the question, "Do poems do this?" Johnson's treatment of the love theme is not facile; the convolutions of body and mind that characterize erotic relationships come out brilliantly ("In Lieu of the Truth"). In connection with the theme of death, especially suicide, Villon, Wilde, Keats, Ezra Pound, and Weldon Kees draw Johnson's attention. "Morte d'Oscar" illustrates his skill. He places Wilde, who muses in the first person, in his room at the L'Hôtel (its full name) in Paris, as he, his century, and Queen Victoria are in their death-throes. Wilde's weariness resembles that of the century, materialized in the decor and furniture of the room. His question conveys his aesthete's stance, not toward art but toward life: "What does the (wine) glass matter, provided that one get intoxicated?" (The line is translated from Alfred de Musset's "La Coupe et les lèvres.")

In *Alloy*, in three parts, Johnson maintains his muscular poetics, pursuing lines explored in *Veins*. "Few poets have made so deft use of history," writes John Wood in his endorsement; Frederick Turner observes, "These poems show us how the past is, after all, the hottest and edgiest new thing." Johnson's historical imagination takes him easily into a subject such as Ealhswith and Alfred, in the year 877—a long narrative poem spoken in the woman's voice, filled with direct language about the female body, sex, and birth. Following immediately this reenactment, which uses both historical facts and psychology, comes "Aztec," a dense rhymed sonnet dealing with blood and sacrifice. Roman emperors and other ancients appear again, along with such figures as Pachelbel, Keats, and John Berryman. "Alexandria Eschate" ("the Furthest"), evokes the king's most northerly outpost in Asia, left to its devices, marking the edge of the Greek world. The value of historical awareness appears in the sonnet "April 4, 1984. Last night to the flicks. All war films," which recalls obliquely George Orwell's warnings about Fascism. That Johnson reads the present and its obsession with conflict in terms of "ancient mores" does not mean that the collection offers little novelty. The range of topics is wide, as is the variety of tones and forms (among the latter, a haiku, a sonnet divided 6 / 8, and the "Abecedarian Poem," the final piece, the five lines and twenty-six words of which, beginning with letters of the alphabet in order, suggest airily an *ars poetica*.

While Johnson's output is small, it is serious and of high quality. It demonstrates how high literary art, directed toward a discerning and well-read audience and thus routinely challenged as elitist, may serve truth better than popular writing that is accessible, but shallow.

ETHERIDGE KNIGHT

Etheridge Knight, an important African American figure whom Sanford Pinsker called "the kind of poet who gives poetry a good name" (711) was born in Corinth, Mississippi, in 1931. He was one of seven children of Etheridge ("Bushie") and Belzora Cozart Knight. Relatives of the mother, a poet and songwriter, had founded Wenasoga, a community near Corinth. An unsuccessful farmer, his father moved the family to Paducah, Kentucky, in an attempt to support them by working on the Kentucky Dam. When the boy ran away from home, repeatedly, his parents, as a countermeasure, sent him and his siblings back to Mississippi to live with family members. At age sixteen, he quit school, though he had been eighth-grade class valedictorian, and took to the streets. However, "his education in the uses and joys of language continued as he explored the world of juke joints, pool halls, and underground poker games. He began to master the art of the toast, a form of long, improvised, humorous poetry of the nineteenth century that has its roots in African storytelling" (poets.org).

His drug and alcohol abuse had its roots in that difficult period. Realizing that he did not wish, really, to live thus, he forged his parents' signatures (1947) in order to join the army. He scored so high on intelligence tests that those in charge reexamined him. After war broke out in Korea, he was shipped there as a medical technician. Wounded by shrapnel, he was given morphine, to which he became addicted. When he died on March 10, 1991, he had fought drug addiction most of his life. Following his discharge from the army in 1951, he settled in Indianapolis, where his parents lived.

Unfortunately, his drug addiction continued; he committed theft to get drug money and also became a dealer. In 1960 he was arrested for armed robbery; he received a ten- to twenty-five-year sentence, which he began serving at Indiana State Reformatory. Soon he was transferred to the Indiana State Prison, where he arrived angry and belligerent. Owing to his emotional state, he retained later no memory of his first few months there. But then, "realizing prison could destroy him, he pulled himself together, read voraciously, and committed himself to poetry" (Anaporte-Easton 942). Beginning in 1965, poems and prose of his appeared in *Negro Digest*. In 1968 he wrote there that the black poet must create new values and legends, not using those of the European literary tradition, and that he should be accountable only to other blacks. (However, he later not only married a white woman, but also gave poetry readings to white audiences and included a white inmate in his anthology *Black Voices from Prison*, 1970.) While Yusef Komunyakaa asserted that "with the Black Arts Movement, Etheridge was really on the sidelines," he added that Knight's poems were "a lot more grounded than the voices coming out of [that movement]. Etheridge is not reactionary in his poems. He is confrontational . . . seeking a level of truth that pretty much defines the essence of him—an individual, an artist" (*Blue Notes* 131). In this he was among the avant-garde; even Gwendolyn Brooks did not move away from conventional writing styles until the late 1960s.

Stephanie Burt notes that "prisons are part of a state, and a system, and a set of communities," as she shows how Knight even "imagines a community far beyond the prison" (237). While in prison, Knight was a journalist for prison publications, wrote letters for illiterate inmates, recited toasts, corresponded with poets Dudley Randall, Sonia Sanchez, and Brooks, and received visits from them and other writers. It was "poeting," as he called it, that allowed him to turn his life around. He declared: "I will write well. My voice will be heard and I will help my people" (Gates and Smith 613). Before he was released, Randall's Broadside Press, in Detroit, published his first collection, *Poems from Prison* (1968). In it he notes, "I died in Korea from a shrapnel wound and narcotics resurrected me. I died in 1960 from a prison sentence and poetry brought me back to life." In the following years he often introduced himself to audiences with that statement (Hayes 22). He was paroled in 1968 (1969, according to some sources) for good behavior; Sanchez helped secure his early release. She married him soon thereafter.

In publishing other inmates' work with his own in *Black Voices from Prison*, Knight fulfilled his obligation to fellow prisoners who were also writers, "whose love and words cracked these walls" (*Black Voices from Prison* 10). The 189-page volume includes eighteen contributions by Knight (both poetry and prose, including the preface), filling 104 pages, and eleven contributions by nine others. The introduction is by Roberto Giammanco, an Italian sociologist and historian who had contacted Knight to produce such a book. First published as *Voci Negre Dal Caracere* in 1969 in Bari, Italy, it appeared in English the next year at Pathfinder Press in New York.

Certain fellow poets, such as Haki Madhubuti (Don L. Lee), who belonged to the Black Arts movement, did not approve of Knight's use of dictionary words and references to Greek classics. But many black poets praised his poetry. Michael Harper, who used jazz inflections in his own writing, praised Knight for his unusual wisdom and lyrical treatment of a marginal society (Gates and Smith 613). Brooks, prefacing *Poems from Prison,* called Knight's poetry "vital," "a major announcement," and "certainly male." Komunyakaa said that Knight had "such an unusual voice because there was a kind of earthy, Mississippi-informed diction there. . . . Etheridge wanted to appear as if he had not been really educated; that was part of his persona. But he read a little bit of everything" (*Conversations* 137). Elsewhere, Komunyakaa remarked that Knight "came out of the Southern tradition and consequently, he remained in the Southern tradition, even when he was . . . elsewhere" (*Blue Notes* 127). Influential, mainstream white poets such as Donald Hall and Robert Bly also praised his work. "If one accepts Bly's claim that Knight at his best is as strong a poet as Wallace Stevens . . . then Knight's writing demonstrates that there is no need to choose between aesthetic achievement and political engagement" (Collins 38).

Knight's marriage to Sanchez ended after only two years, apparently because he remained addicted to drugs, although he sought treatment at veterans' hospitals. In 1972 he married Mary McAnally, a white South African activist who had adopted two children. Their marriage ended in 1977, and the next year, he married Charlene Blackburn, with whom he had his only biological child, Isaac BuShie Blackburn-Knight. "No matter how often he himself failed it, love remained Knight's weapon of choice" (Collins 50).

From 1969 to 1972 Knight was poet in residence at the University of Pittsburgh, the University of Hartford, and Lincoln University. He toured the country, giving dramatic poetry readings with audience involvement and leading Free People's Poetry Workshops. In 1972 he received a National Endowment for the Arts Grant (and another in 1980). He went on to attain recognition as a major poet, receiving both Pulitzer Prize and National Book Award nominations for *Belly Song and Other Poems* (1973). Six poems in that collection are signed "E. K. Soa" (Soa is Sword/Servant of Allah), indicating his allegiance to the Nation of Islam and its leader, Elijah Muhammed. This volume was inspiring to those who viewed poetry as a collective and oral undertaking, led by a strong central figure. Knight also composed poems about Malcolm X, his hero. In 1974 he was awarded a Guggenheim Fellowship to study the oral traditions, speech patterns, and music with which he had grown up—African American performance experiences that he considered fundamental to black poetry. In 1985 he received the Shelley Award from the Poetry Society of America and in 1986 the Before Columbus Foundation American Book Award in poetry for

The Essential Etheridge Knight. Awarded an honorary bachelor of arts degree in November 1990 in American poetry and criminal justice from Martin University in Indianapolis, Knight was also chosen as that university's poet laureate.

Most of Knight's poetry is in free verse, but he also wrote many haiku. Claude Wilkinson suggests that his grasp of that form and improvisational skill surpass Richard Wright's (Zheng, *African American Haiku* 100). Knight's free verse often has a Whitmanesque boldness and lyricism. From *Belly Song* onward, he used slashes within lines to introduce a pause or serve as punctuation. The slashes, which appear very frequently in his last two volumes, act as a "break," akin to a musical break (Collins 17). He may well have borrowed this device for creating a jazz- or blues-like rhythm from Sterling D. Plumpp, who used slashes abundantly and very effectively in much of his poetry. (Plumpp's poems began appearing in the 1960s; his first collection, *Portable Soul*, dates from 1969.)

One theme in Knight's early volumes is prisoners' vulnerabilities. Two poems, each included in both *Poems from Prison* and *Black Voices from Prison*, illustrate them well. "For Freckle-Faced Gerald" portrays a young, defenseless man, preyed upon by the "wiser and bigger buzzards / than those / who now hover above his track / and at night light upon his back." A mere child, he is "pigmeat" for the hardened criminals to whom he is exposed: "Sixteen years hadn't even done / a good job on his voice. He didn't even know / how to talk tough, or how to hide the glow / of life before he was thrown in as 'pigmeat.'" Commenting on the poem, Komunyakaa observed that "prisoners have to create their own cycle of victims out of situational greed" (*Blue Notes* 17).

A contrasting poem, "Hard Rock Returns to Prison from the Hospital for the Criminal Insane," has parallels with Ken Kesey's *One Flew Over the Cuckoo's Nest* (1962). Instead of a sweet voice and freckles, Hard Rock has split purple lips, lumped ears, yellow eyes, and scars. Because of his toughness and the fact that he is "known not to take no shit," the doctors perform a lobotomy on him. The other prisoners, who have admired Rock for his toughness, wait for him to be tough once again, to take up for himself and others, but, more importantly, to be their hero or role model again. The "testing came": "A hillbilly called him a black son of a bitch / And didn't lose his teeth, a screw who knew Hard Rock / From before shook him down and barked in his face. / And Hard Rock did *nothing.* Just grinned and looked silly." Other evidence accumulates, and the men mistakenly think that Hard Rock has "wised up" and is playing a game with the "screws." But finally, reality hits home: "He had been our Destroyer, the doer of things / We dreamed of doing but could not bring ourselves to do, / The fears of years, like a biting whip, / Had cut deep bloody grooves across our backs." While gentle Gerald is molested by fellow inmates, the prison system eradicates the bravery of the prisoners' hero, stealing his very inner being as well as theirs. Knight uses black vernacular as spoken in prison, a badge of authenticity.

Born of a Woman: New and Selected Poems (1980) begins with acknowledgments to those who helped him after prison. It includes poems about all three of his wives. "A Love Poem" (1972) captures his love for McAnally, as she comes to rejoin him after stormy times. The first line, punctuated with Knight's slash-line breaks (printed here without spaces, to distinguish them from line breaks), reads "And Mary/is/on the High/Way." The "High" here is the high one gets with the anticipation of seeing one's love, not merely the "highway" traveled. "High" does not, presumably, allude to an altered state of mind for either him or Mary; the line was composed while Knight was not taking drugs. The strong beats created by slashes may be read as imitating a traveling sound. The next line is "coming to me/thru the rain." "Joyously," the poem ends by the phrase "We are Singing." Even though the two people are separate, the gap is closing and they sing together as one.

While the short prose poem "Rehabilitation and Treatment" was attributed to Joe Martinez in *Black Voices from Prison*, it is the final piece in *The Essential Etheridge Knight*, his last book (1986). Either it was appropriated from Martinez or the name was Knight's pseudonym. The book, divided into five sections, describes how a convict chooses among the prison doors programmed to doom him: Correction, Treatment, Adult, Democrat, and finally Black. Those "choices" cause him to fall "nine stories to the street." Knight chose to end his *Essential* collection with that final indictment of the prison system, once again fulfilling his pledge to his people.

"Various Protestations from Various People" reveals the persona's honest assessment of his own flaws and his realization of how others perceive him. The phrase "too much" rings like a hammer at the end of every line. Like many others, this poem uses black vernacular even for the persona, incorporating misspelled words, subject-verb agreement errors, and other irregularities. In an easy beat, with rhyme, it begins, "Esther say I drink too much. / Mama say pray dont think too much. / My shrink he say I feel too much, / And the cops say I steal too much." These characterizations are followed by further accusations, showing how beleaguered the persona feels. Perhaps he is honest; perhaps, rather, he does not accept the portrait. "Social Workers say I miss my Daddy too much, / That I dream of driving a Caddy too much. / White folks say I'm lazy and late too much / Not objective—depend on fate too much."

He thus sums up others' criticism and, presumably, what he called elsewhere his "fucked-up" life ("Feeling Fucked Up"). The poem concludes ironically with the lines: "Reagan say I talk about me too much, / Singing songs 'bout being free too much. / I say—sing about me being *free* too much. / Say sing about me being *free* too much?" Thus, after summing up well the unfavorable descriptions he has heard of himself, he ends the poem with the poignant acknowledgment of the burdens under which he has lived: his color, his poverty, the prison system, and drugs. The speaker may intend those words as an accusation of others and the social milieu around him. Certainly, he has *not* been "*free* too much." Is there whine here, or just a hard-core acknowledgment of how life has been?

PHILIP C. KOLIN

A glance at Philip C. Kolin's poetry reveals that his Christian convictions are central. "God's blueprint calls for / nature to cooperate with Grace" ("She Taught Her Classes Proverbs," from *Benedict's Daughter*). His faith is not simply a hidden wellspring of creative energy or a subtle thread; it is proclaimed repeatedly, without shading or circumvention. References to scripture and ecclesiastical tradition and practice are everywhere. Faith, which is an agent, illuminates quotidian experiences as well as perennial human predicaments and mysteries. He uses "plain style" (as Yvor Winters called it), that is, direct expression, in easy-moving unrhymed free verse. The modes and tones of the poems vary among meditative, laudatory, prayerful, and didactic.

Kolin, born 1945, comes from the Czech immigrant community of Chicago. His chapbook *Pilsen Snow* (2015) presents scenes from the neighborhood, now turned Hispanic, where both immigrant groups have lived "two lives at once" (Interview). His BA is from Chicago State University, his MA from the University of Chicago, and his PhD from Northwestern University. He is now professor emeritus at the University of Southern Mississippi, where he taught English for some forty years. A productive scholar, he has published widely on Shakespeare, Tennessee Williams, Edward Albee, and African American playwrights. The latter interest is connected to his concern for social justice. His handbook of technical and business composition, *Successful Writing at Work*, has gone through numerous editions. His poetic production comprises books, chapbooks, and hundreds of poems in periodicals such as *Michigan Quarterly Review*, *Louisiana Literature*, *Christianity and Literature*, and *Anglican Theological Review*.

Deep Wonder (2000), which Kolin considers one of his two premier collections, won an award from the Catholic Press Association and was endorsed by church figures as well as Susan Ludvigson, Jerry W. Ward Jr., and Ann W. Astell, who asserted that "Kolin's poems are prayers that can be prayed." Some poems end with the word "Amen." Kolin explains in the preface that he had composed very few religious poems until he lost a woman he loved and fell into a desert of the heart. Advisors counseled him to obey and "listen to God." His poems turned into love poems for God. "They are His words, not mine."

Kolin's style, which contrasts with older devotional poems and liturgical language, reflects changes in Catholic thinking and writing following Vatican II. His principal resources are similes and metaphors. Many poems have everyday settings and allusions and use familiar diction, especially in addressing the Deity. In "Christ, the King of Doors," Christ is to be given control "of all / The handles / And knobs" that people try to turn for their own purposes. (The poem seems unconnected to the image of the door in St. John's Gospel.) "The Father's Love" identifies its topic as "the song / You hear on / The radio . . ."; it is "the green / Light to go on / With your life. . . ." In "Gethsemane," he elaborates on Jesus's suffering in the "garden of thorns" and today, wherever Christ feels "Our thorns— / Divorce, abortion, / Child abuse / Blasphemous cruelty . . ." and even indebtedness. These human sufferings are not without value: tears become prayer, a sign of faith; pain becomes "stigmata / Inside your heart." In short, "Every time you cry / He bleeds."

Kolin does not shrink from the hortatory mode. "Women at the Well" admonishes women to "harvest," not abort. "What He soweth / They need to labor / Reaping lives / For eternity." Lazarus's modern equivalents must return from "defeat, doom, despair." Their "tombs" are sometimes an office "where calumny / Is bought and sold / In a marketplace of deceit," or a church "where back- / Biting and harping / Sing slander willfully / In the choir of shadows." Or the tomb may be a marriage "dead to love. . . ." ("The Anointing of Lazarus"). Contemporary diction and images may startle readers, in such phrases as "a dictatorship / of clocked consumption" and this plea to Christ: "Set your alarm / Of hope to wake / Us up to life / In You. . . ." Enjambments are sometimes infelicitous: "God be my prayer / Book for life. . . ." (the first line is the poem title). Phrases from well-known hymns are juxtaposed: "O Sacred wounds / . . . / Let me hide / Myself in thee" ("Christ's Wounds"). Kolin underlines the Christian use of paradoxes in the Bible and such canonic poets as Donne. "I feasted on / Your paradoxes: / The less I struggled / The more I was free" ("The Desert"). Bold metaphors may be pleasing: "Can't your Son / Rise earlier this / Morning in my soul?" ("Goodnight, Abba"). "Unhook Me, Father" addressing God as "Fisherman," is suggestive of Donne and Hopkins.

Kolin published three chapbooks in the period from 2007 until 2013. *Wailing Walls* (2006), illustrated in color and by woodcuts, intentionally naïf, no doubt, contains innumerable contemporary allusions—to a child's experiences in Chicago, the events of September 2001, and Hurricane Katrina, for instance. Chiefly, its concerns are social. It enumerates present ills, begs for divine assistance, and suggests remedial measures (for example, the word *reparations* in the first poem where one might expect *repentance*). In "Ransom Us," in couplets, the speaker begs for rescue "From the fiery furnaces / Of domestic violence and rage // From the bullet-lined walls / Of ghettos in Watts and Cabrini-Green" and, later, "From false prayers / That put wealth in pastors' back pockets // From coyotes taking immigrants across / The border between dreams and death." The agents of such evils include child molesters, angry bosses, terrorists, and lying politicians. Victims of human evil and circumstances, not overlooked, are cocaine addicts, jobless youth with large student loans, those with cancer, and spouses "whose marriages were voided / By partners in transition." Abortion, adultery, hungry children, low-class nursing homes, and the 2001 attacks are treated with the same moral conscience and similar directness.

The cover of *A Parable of Women* (2009), the second chapbook, reproduces Rubens's painting "The Holy Women at the Sepulchre." Certain title figures are biblical, others contemporary, illustrating social ills and individual unhappiness. "Edith," a first-person portrait, uses an old trope by imagining illness as a lover, wheezing a swoon. Of note is "The Secretary," in which rancorous businessmen—"pinstriped despots"—"martyr" the woman. Some poems combine past and present; in "Herodias Throws a Party," the speaker, displaying her good clothes and good connections and boasting of having "spent a tetrarch's ransom on Salome," watches her turn heads and set men on fire. A ghoulish note follows: "The first platter is coming in. / It's a delicacy to kill for." The transhistorical imagination exemplified here is startling. A mention in "Wondra's Dolor Bills" of "Wal-Mart Plantation" (providing a better job than a waitress's) and "Last Esperanza St. // In the Lower Ninth" ("Odeila's House") presuppose blacks' situation as little better than slavery.

The religious spirit is again visible in a third chapbook *In the Custody of Words* (2013), where the first poem title, "God's Word," again emphasizes communication between men and the Divinity. The poem piles up details, many biblical. Some phrasing, such as "fatted / incense," requires readers' indulgence.

Reading God's Handwriting (2012) enlarges Kolin's field of inspiration by asserting that God's communications come from not only from scripture but also the book of nature (preface). The cover shows Moses with the tablets of the Ten Commandments (a reproduction of Philippe de Champaigne's canvas); Kolin also quotes Psalm 10, "The heavens declare the Glory of God," and Hopkins's line "Glory be to God for dappled things." The diction is less breezily familiar than in *Deep Wonder*. Longer lines provide formal variety.

"Genesis," in prose, rapidly surveys events from the first book of the Penta-
teuch. To the tale of man's first disobedience are added ravens, rams, "covenants
honored," "tomorrow's seeds, and stars, always stars." Feathers, a river, flowers,
leaves draw readers' attention to the natural world and its meanings. Section
titles—"Oremus," "What Prophets and Saints Foretold," "An Advent Wreath
of Prayers," and "Epiphanies of Madonna and Child"—announce the Christian context. In "Praying the Icons," an old shawl-draped woman furnishes an
image of the piety that resisted and survived "monk murders," "unharvested
children's moans," and further atrocities under Stalin. A man visits a comatose
woman ("Visiting Hours"); a drifter ("Requiem for a Homeless Man") dies "of
an overdose / of neglect," with emblematic mustard seeds and a brown lily
in his pocket. In "St. Anne's Oratory," the lily is explicitly connected to Mary,
mother of Jesus. "The Grandfather from Pilsen" sketches what may be the
poet's own ancestor.

Sue Brannan Walker, writing from the Baptist tradition, found *Reading God's
Handwriting* impressive, its poetic language displaying "majesty and mastery"
(204). She applauded what she viewed as the central poem, "Lectio Divina,"
emphasizing, as Kolin put it, the "sacred ritual of meditating on God's word,"
including its manifestation in nature. Praising the poems on Habakkuk and
Ezekiel, she concludes that Kolin, like them, is a prophet. "He takes the ordinary
and makes it redemptive" (202–3). Reading the book is "transformative" (206).

Departures (2014), which Jack Bedell, David Kirby, and William H. Greenway
endorsed, is varied. Lines begin with lower case except when standard usage
calls for capitals. "Pecata mundi" and "The Performance of Waste," featuring
enumeration, are quick impressions or snapshots. Again, Kolin uses surprising
images. In "The 19th Century," "caged poetry" drapes the Crystal Palace; "obse-
quies with opaque lattices" resemble "a peacock's morbid desire." Snow is like the
"white meat" of a hazelnut; "silver bells tinring / through time." In "Sylvia Plath's
Epitaph," poems (hers, or perhaps those of Ted Hughes) taste like turpentine.
Of a mixed-race woman who is beaten, the poet writes: "Now she's blue as well
as black"—an audacious and infelicitous play on a term describing skin color
("Odessa" 7). Statement is often blunt: "The 19th century was a fabrication of /
arrogance and abnegation." "Passover in the Camps" recalls Hebrew traditions
and texts and draws parallels between the prisoners' condemnation and that of
Christ. The final line, "Pilate washes his hands at Wannsee," confirms the equiva-
lence by its reference to the conference in the Berlin suburb that agreed on the
Final Solution. "A Eulogy for the Buffalo" is another accusation of the nineteenth
century, Victorian England and the Empire, and perhaps the American South.
Love, illness, death recur in varied guises. Mississippi and other southern places
appear in "A Delta Christmas" and "Memorial Day on Panama City Beach."

"Odessa" features a creole of color in New Orleans circa 1939, too dark to be accepted by whites, too light for those darker than she, but proud of all the races whose blood runs in her veins. Kolin works out well the social and psychological conflicts she endures in her "twilight world" and asks, the authorial voice sliding into hers, "Who defines race? Who measures / blackness?"

Kolin's important collection *Emmett Till in Different States* (2015) demonstrates his concern for African Americans' welfare. Third World Publishers brought out this book, one of few in their catalogue by white writers. Among the endorsers were Ward, Sterling D. Plumpp, Natasha Trethewey, and Devery S. Anderson, a historian. The poems illustrate Trethewey's observation (quoted above in connection with Ann Fisher-Wirth) that the story of Till's murder "belongs to all of us and should be sung by many different voices" (Hearne 208).

Kolin and his subject have in common their birth and upbringing on the South Side of Chicago, and the poet is well acquainted with the small Delta town where Till's family originated and where he died, the victim of brutalization and murder. Kolin compared his work with those of others who have written about Till, especially Marilyn Nelson in *A Wreath for Emmett Till*. Whereas she concentrated on Till's murder and victimhood, he chose also to "extend the time line from the 1950s to the present to honor Till's legacy as a Civil Rights martyr. . . ." The figure thus becomes "a heroic commentator on subsequent acts of racial violence"—murders of prominent black figures, the particular difficulties of black soldiers in Vietnam, the disadvantages from which children suffer in today's African American neighborhoods (Zheng, *Arkansas Review* 189–90).

The collection title puns on *states*, referring to Illinois and Mississippi (by extension, the rest of the Jim Crow South, ultimately the nation), but also to the conditions of life and death at the time of Till's martyrdom. More than one figure speaks: Till, introducing himself in the initial poem, for instance; his mother, Mamie, in the triolet form once; his Uncle Moses; an anonymous third-person narrator; Mahalia Jackson; victims of lynching; the Chicago River itself. Sometimes, the narrator addresses Till. This multiplying of speakers is an effective device for the purposes of exposition, lamentation, and eliciting emotion.

The spirit behind the poems is fidelity to the facts and their place in civil rights history. The book opens with a chronology of Till's life and pertinent events thereafter, including the murder of Medgar Evers, Martin Luther King's delivery of his "I Have a Dream" speech, and the reopening of the Till case in 2004. Scripture and other Christian markers establish the context. A compendium of verbatim press statements from the 1955 trial of Till's murderers furnishes facts, which, enriched by the poet's imagination, create a new Till, a "commentator." He appears, for example, as a night watchman guarding the

Vietnam Veterans Memorial, and he speaks to Trayvon Martin. The analogy between the Madonna in a Pietà at the Art Institute and Till's mother in Mississippi after her son's death is apt ("Emmett and Mamie").

Incongruities include (in "Facts About Me") mention of James Dean, who died a month after Till: "I wonder if he was a breech baby, too." "Scars and stripes" may be viewed as effective or inappropriate ("What Emmett Would Have Sung"); "roof / and sheets to put over their heads" works well; *pro malo* (defense lawyers worked without fee) less well ("Slop Jars"). The allusion to Jean-Paul Sartre—"skin precedes essence"—is ironic; to the hostile Mississippi whites, black skin *was* essence. "Aunt Aretha Remembers" contains an apt, imaginative metaphor: "A Negro's face is a scroll unfurled, / a history of consecrated soils / that birth souls. . . ."

The second collection Kolin identified as his most important is *Benedict's Daughter* (2017). The free verse is often arranged into regular or irregular stanzas. Along with rather plain statements, Kolin introduces image clusters, particularly that of wings and feathers, whether of birds or angels (see "The Gulls' Oratory"). The motifs of fishing and garden convey evangelical overtones. The poet combines contemporary syntax and expression with traditional Christian metaphors: "We are all flesh of flesh until / the bridegroom comes clothed in clouds. // Continue to search for God on these grounds / and let him find you at the crossroads. . . ." ("In this Place of Stability"). Poems on the canonical hours in "Prologue: The Liturgy of the Hours" set the tone of piety, underline prayer and service, and emphasize the interpenetration, as Kolin sees it, of the holy with the quotidian.

The second part, "The Journey," depicts a woman of faith, based on a real model, Margie, here called Midge. Obliged to end her Benedictine novitiate—because she is deemed too frail—she must live *in* the world but, as an oblate, not *of* it. The book is, as Mark S. Burrows asserted in his endorsement, "both biography and encomium." Interspersed among poems treating episodes in her life and her family's are others on explicitly Benedictine topics; the saint himself gives a homily on the temptations of the flesh. Midge marries a former Marine, "Mr. Al," rears their children, and, beyond her role as wife and mother, serves God in prayer and work, as teacher, caregiver, spiritual counselor, and general Samaritan. Their son appears in the poem "A Nurse Called Joseph." Suffering from Alzheimer's disease, Mr. Al goes to a nursing home; Midge wears his wedding ring over hers ("The Month of Blue Moons"). The journey ends in their death, in their eighties. Their resting place in St. Bernard Cemetery (Cullman, Alabama) is evoked in the final poem. The poet's voice is heard in "A Manual for Oblates," regarding a book he inherited from the figure portrayed.

Kolin's work commands respect. He makes plain his conviction that poetry must lead to change in oneself or society. The limitations of such edifying literature are as obvious as its earnestness. Critics who would evaluate it on literary grounds face a difficulty. To set aside, for purposes of assessing the rest, the elements of scripture and church tradition, with their unique authority, on which Kolin's work draws liberally, is to dismantle many individual poems and ignore his clear intentions. The message is the medium. What would remain, could such a reductive separation be performed, would be a mutilation.

C. LIEGH MCINNIS

C. Liegh McInnis was born in Clarksdale, in 1969, to Claude and Claudette McInnis, who met in a class at Jackson State University after Claude had returned from Vietnam. (He had volunteered for service, after his family learned, from the sheriff, that he would do well to leave town; the family viewed Mississippi as more dangerous than Vietnam.) The poet owns a copy of Margaret Walker's *Jubilee* that belonged to his mother at the time. Although his parents divorced when he was an infant and his mother had custody, both were, he states, "great parents," and his father spent as much time as practical with the boy, an only child. His father was a juvenile youth court counselor for forty-two years and was active in politics; Claudette, who was certified as a special needs teacher, taught in Coahoma County (Interview). Acknowledgments in the poet's books express firm belief in God and appreciation to his family and friends, who include his wife, Monica Taylor-McInnis, his parents, and Jerry W. Ward Jr.; in that spirit, the tone of many poems is upbeat, hopeful, pointing even to the transcendental.

McInnis earned a BA and MA in English (1992, 1994) at Jackson State, where he is presently an instructor. He pursued studies in creative writing at the University of Southern Mississippi. He lives in Clinton. His principal concerns are African American writing and the black experience in Mississippi and elsewhere. The history of American blacks, from slavery to the present, offers landmarks for the poet's rhetoric. The NAACP chose him as one of nine to appear in Washington, DC, for its "Inaugural Poetry Reading," celebrating the election of Barak Obama as president of the United States. McInnis was a runner-up for the Amiri Baraka/Sonia Sanchez Poetry Award, sponsored by North Carolina A&T State University. He is the former editor of *Black Magnolias Literary Journal*, and he wrote Ward's biographical sketch for the

Mississippi Encyclopedia. McInnis has given numerous readings in Mississippi and elsewhere and has poems and video readings on the Internet. His writing has appeared in the *Southern Quarterly, New Delta Review, New Laurel Review, Oxford American*, and anthologies.

McInnis has published four collections of poetry, the most recent in 2007, as well as creative and critical prose, including a book on Prince Rogers Nelson. All his books bear the imprint of his own press, Psychedelic Literature, and thus have not, apparently, gone through even a modest sieve of editorial reading or peer reviews. The absence of such validation might suggest artistic unworthiness, though, of course, it does not demonstrate it. The fact matters little: McInnis views poetry not as an art, essentially different from rhetoric and expository prose, but, rather, as activism, integrally connected to social and political causes. Literature should be "socially moving" and "impacting" (McNeil). His position echoes that of W. E. B. Du Bois, in "The Criteria of Negro Art," that all art is propaganda. An article by McInnis is titled "Continuing the Analysis of Art as Socio-Political Engagement." There he cites Henry Louis Gates Jr. on Etheridge Knight's belief that "poetry should be a functional and communal art with a strong oral artist in the middle of the circle." In that light, whether the verse has present and lasting merit according to criteria of poetic accomplishment is immaterial, if it affects readers and listeners as McInnis wishes; it must be approached accordingly. For at least two hundred years, however, poetry has been the least suitable genre for changing minds. Even though Victor Hugo's popularity as a poet was enormous, when he wanted to arouse readers' sympathy for the lower classes, he wrote not lyric or epic poems but *Les Misérables.*

Matters of Reality: Body, Mind, Soul (1996), McInnis's first collection, endorsed by Nikki Giovanni, illustrates his style, which partakes of the homily and polemic. His voice, which comes through quite transparently, is direct and appealing. He uses free verse, with occasional scattered rhymes. The language is hortatory. Although metaphoric, the poems are statement-like, without artistic shaping. Expansive and edifying, they feature second-person pronouns and use American, sometimes black, vernacular, as in "My Blooze for You."

McInnis does not spare his blame. "A Bullet for the Drug Dealer" expresses his loathing for those who undermine families and neighborhoods and, literally, kill young people. "You," he tells the dealer, "are just a second-hand, remote controlled Trojan / Horse attacking Black villages worse than HIV. // . . . We are a caged community attached / by the shackles of dope." Indiscriminate sex, especially among young people, is another target. "Children are parenting children who are pirated by adults" ("A Matter of the Dissolution of the Ghetto"). Meanwhile, the grandparents work a late shift to pay the rent; no one is at home. Proper family instruction is missing; schools are inadequate. One poem is titled "Vote!" Casting aside such topics sometimes, McInnis can write a tender love poem ("Black Angel") and frame an existential complaint ("[i] Want to Know Why: It Ain't Existential, Is It?").

Searchin' 4 Psychedelica appeared in 1999, only three years after *Matters of Reality*. The title word, *psychedelica*, combining McInnis's website and publishing imprint name with *a*, would suggest hallucinatory drugs. That interpretation is mistaken. A prose poem, "Psyche/Psychological/Psychedelica (Definition)," explains the term as "D mind functioning as d center of thought, feeling, & behavior, consciously or unconsciously. . . ." The title poem elaborates on aspects of experience, many in a contemporary context. The poems play with language, which, in a postmodern spirit, is somewhat deconstructed, although McInnis generally follows standard syntax. A typographic idiosyncrasy, printing the first-person pronoun as [i], may be intended to reduce the presence and force of an ego; using *language* as a verb is understandable. The typography features images of hearts, stars, and eyes (for "I") to replace the respective words. Abbreviations (perhaps inspired by text-messaging, although in 1999 the technique was still young), such as *r*, *u* and *2*, are ubiquitous.

The level of speech ranges from standard English to heavy black vernacular, including many vulgar terms. Subversion of standard language in poetry dates back a hundred years or more; Giovanni, Sanchez, Knight, and A. B. Spellman are among recent predecessors of McInnis, and it remains current among poets publishing at presses large and small. He is, however, not so *outré* as many others, and he does not make his poems impossible to understand.

Might McInnis have adopted these uses, especially the vulgarity, to appeal to students and other young rebels who, at the end of the twentieth century, had rejected good manners, good speech, and various standards of behavior, intent upon denying everything bourgeois and much of what was white? A cover endorsement mentions a student who said, in praise, "C. Liegh is Da Bomb." The typographic features are not audible, of course. But the slang and indicated mispronunciations, along with rhetorical features such as repetition, re-create for listeners many effects of the written words. One may view McInnis as a performance poet, like Bob Kaufman, using the Internet and reading circuit as a contemporary "street." The altered typography and spellings and the vernacular re-create the poet's voice on paper.

"Mississippi Like . . ." calls on colloquialisms and repetition and uses history to good effect. The lengthy poem is a "defense and illustration," an apology for the state, directed toward its residents, who need to feel pride; it is also, one assumes, intended to enlighten those elsewhere. It acknowledges shameful incidents of the 1960s and figures such as Ross Barnett, but gives greater prominence to those who worked for improved racial relations and better living conditions for all. What contradictions! Mississippi is "black folk hating Ole Miss and respectin' Archie Manning. / Dat honky sho could play coudn't he. / It's white folks hating JSU & admirin' Walter Payton. / Dat Nigger sho could run" (25). McInnis seems particularly incensed by accusations that Mississippians are "dumb & stupid." To refute the charge, he cites a long litany of figures, black and white, famous and modest, in political activism (Medgar Evers), music (B. B. King), literature (Eudora Welty), broadcasting (Robin Roberts). Local manners and customs, trees, music, ways of speaking—all belong to the poem. Optimism prevails; courtesy and generosity make a difference, social mobility is real; and "an education / is d sledge hammer 2 knock holes n / d walls of njustice & oppression" (27).

McInnis is both an idealist and a pragmatist. His art springs from the conjunction of the two. He takes it seriously, assuring his readers that he "will not pimp poetry" (the phrase is a poem title). His scale of values is his own; within his Mississippi context, it emphasizes love, loyalty, even tradition, devotion to God and others—and, of course, poetry, which beats a Lexus any day. "It's d substance dat keeps / d world balanced & ordered 4 me." His earnest efforts to express the truths he holds and persuade his audience of their worth command respect.

WILLIAM MILLS

William Mills, who lives in Addis, Louisiana, is an important figure in southern letters. A poet early in his career, he then turned to fiction, publishing novels, including *Those Who Blink*, and a short story collection called *I Know a Place*. Subsequently he wrote and illustrated with his photographs *Bears and Men: A Gathering* and *The Arkansas: An American River*. He was also a literary critic, with books on Howard Nemerov and John William Corrington.

Mills was born in Hattiesburg in 1935. He was reared in Baton Rouge and began his college studies at Centenary College before spending two years in the army. In Korea, his hearing was damaged by the pounding of artillery. Poems in *Watch for the Fox* (1974) reflect his foreign experiences in Japan and Germany (where he studied). Following that service, he earned his bachelor's degree at Louisiana State University, then a master's, then a PhD (1959, 1961, 1972). His first wife was Sylvia Broussard, who accompanied him on a venture in Central America. The couple returned to Louisiana, and they were subsequently divorced. Mills later wed Beverly Jarrett, then on the staff of LSU Press. When she became director of the University of Missouri Press, they moved to Columbia. In the course of his career Mills taught at the University of Arkansas and Oklahoma State University, where he directed the Graduate Poetry Workshop.

Watch for the Fox, the poet's first collection, displays fine control of his medium, which is the short lyric in very free verse. James H. Justus wrote that the book "achieves a resonance of both the natural and human worlds by the sparest of language" (Rubin et al. 541). Mills does not strain to create poetic effects. Words are usually capitalized at the left margin but not always. Lineation is uneven and unpolished; lines may end with *and*. Punctuation is sparse. Few poems occupy a full page or more. Voices vary from that of an anonymous narrator to those of figures sketched. Occasional mentions of Mississippi and Louisiana locations simply reinforce what readers sense: that this is a southern poet, with the gift of narrative, and to whom a certain perceived decadence is not foreign. A reminder of James Dickey, in "When I Read the Man from Atlanta, What He Wrote," comes with an allusion to Sherman.

The diction is contemporary, the syntax familiar, and images generally uncomplicated, without suggestions of surrealism. Yet the poems have touches of the strange, a strangeness which is that of the everyday and something else also, a shiver. The fox skulking around in the title poem represents a primitive fear, inherited from men's ancestors, connected to the need for fire. ("Smoke" reintroduces the motif of fire and its taming.) In "Go, You," a hunting poem, the fox is the necessary victim in a natural order that subsists on killing. (See also "Pity," on skinning fish.) In his cover comment for the book, Miller Williams wrote that Mills was more taken with the physical than the metaphysical world. But Mills, like other poets, often sees them as tangential, intersecting, even interpenetrating. One poem is titled "Theology 101." Generally, however, Mills suggests such interfacing without metaphysical referents.

Whether expressed through images or characters, themes appear and recur easily. Below most of them runs the deep theme of happiness. "The Aerialist," concerning Brahms, illustrates Mill's delicate treatment. Politics appear (in a poem of that title) obliquely, tied to exploitation of nature and greed. Religious allusions, such as the burning bush ("Summer Garden"), are not uncommon. (In the title poem of *Stained Glass*, Mills alludes to his "Protestant period," although in "Sir," from the same volume, he suggests his atheism.) Calvin appears in "Careful." The names of St. Thomas Aquinas and Hume are linked in a title. In "No Riders," a man carrying a knife, two fish, and a heavy cross thanks the speaker for a ride, calling him "Jefe." Dying is the topic of "Sprung Rhythm": "John Tullos is / Rotting in the ground." (The Hopkinsian title must be a euphemism for death.) Love, particularly in the past, colors several poems, among them "Kyoto: Twenty Years Ago" and the melancholy "Between Touch and Think." "Sad breasts / Of the middle years," writes the poet in "Hymn to Someone Else's Wife." The recurring theme of aging is announced poignantly in another theological poem, "On Turning the Same Age as Our Lord When He Got His," where the "great historical Fish" moves, dramatically, from depths to "Ascension."

Certain poems are nearly fables. Such is "A Thin Line, or Love Is a Gun," concerning an unhappy dog whose sufferings move its master but others discount. "You'd think it was human," says someone, derisively. "From life to life / Is not far," the narrative voice says. Moreover, love "most often hits its mark / . . . / Where reflex / And quick draw / Count." "Listen Love," first evoking yellow leaves of late summer, declares then that "the green came back. / This is a metaphor."

Stained Glass (1979) pursues the philosophical strains of Mills's earlier book and displays versatile wit. Justus found it less staccato, more leisurely than *Watch for the Fox*, broader, warmer (Rubin et al. 541–42). The title poem uses its image for existential meaning; broken, monochromatic pieces of the past are saved and refashioned, with color added, to create a different life (perhaps a new marriage). It is "no window at Chartres" but furnishes pleasure on some days. The moral, however, is not encouraging: "A fact of stained glass and light: / Stained glass dies at night." The short lyric "Seven Red Apples," which mentions Cézanne, is at once an effective poem of desire and a comment on the presence, "noumenal yet luminous," of things, the *Dasein*. As the five lines of "Bare Black Limbs" show, things have "a certain way of being and of letting you know."

In this collection, Mills introduces a slightly modified poetics, with longer lines and irregular rhymes, ending couplets (rhymed sometimes), and lengthier poems, which contrast with the short lyrics. The lines of certain poems— "Among This All" is one—have a strong beat. Highly lyrical tones characterize certain pages. In "For You Whom I Have Just Met," the poet, having evoked intimate conversations at evening by the Gulf, adds: "All this above the sea sound of the world's breath." "Wedington Woods," a four-page poem, explicitly relates erotic love, illicit in this case, to poetry: "For those whose passion must stop short / Let art, pantheon of our humanity, / Keep permanent what the flesh could not." (This is one of few poems by Mills that address directly the art they illustrate.)

The settings in *Stained Glass* are at once familiar and particular. "Since the Blond Lady Decided to Leave Me to Look for Her Individuality" offers an effective sketch of a miserable man in New Orleans in February, suffering from the cold rain and abandon; but then, "wanting to pay / Love and Beauty's cartage," the poem depicts Jackson Square, its nearby saints and its pigeons, after the rain. Elsewhere the poems move outward to foreign scenes. While a friend in Louisiana is dying, the speaker recalls Teotihuacan and meditates on the passage of time and those who built the Mayan pyramids. In "Sutra," he contemplates his own life, running out. On a night train from Moscow to Vilnius, he has a revealing experience when two hostesses, who have led him to the dining car, get him food and drink. Grateful, nearly overcome, he displays a book of his poems. Having no English, they are still taken with the book and carry it off to examine it. Is it Russian admiration for poets or wish to check him out ideologically? "He begins to know / The importance and danger of what he does."

While Mills is interested, as a poet, in the human condition, that interest rarely takes the form of concern for social conditions. History, however, is not absent. He honors the past of his native state in the four-page concluding poem, "Our Fathers at Corinth." Like his Louisiana friend Corrington and numerous other twentieth-century southern poets, he pays homage to an ancestor who volunteered and fought in the battles of 1861–65. Addressing his great-grandfather, the speaker summarizes his war career: eagerness to fight, his first experiences as an infantryman, the miserable times near Corinth, the fall-back to Tupelo, and his death, imagined. "You rest in your sons / Who must keep you to themselves."

BENJAMIN MORRIS

Benjamin Morris is the author of the poetry collections *Coronary* and *Ecotone*. He has also published essays concerning literature and cultural heritage and is the author of *Hattiesburg, Mississippi: A History of the Hub City*. His poems have appeared in the *Southern Review*, the *Edinburgh Review*, and elsewhere. He has been active in literary circles in New Orleans and elsewhere and has won numerous prizes and awards, including two fellowships from the Mississippi Arts Commission, an artist's residency grant from A Studio in the Woods, and the Chancellor's Medal for Poetry from the University of Cambridge.

Morris was born in Hattiesburg in 1982 and went to school there. He enrolled in Duke University, where he graduated magna cum laude in 2004, with a BA in English and minors in Latin and philosophy. In 2005 he earned a master's degree in creative writing at the University of Edinburgh. He spent the following five years at Clare Hall, Cambridge (MPhil in archaeology, 2006, PhD in Archaeological and Cultural Studies, 2010). He returned to America (New Orleans) but went back to Edinburgh in 2012 to be a postdoctoral fellow. Until 2016 he was an affiliate member of the OpenSpace Centre for Geographic and Environmental Research in Milton Keynes, UK. He now divides his time between the Crescent City and Mississippi.

Morris is one of few Mississippi poets writing today who have cultivated formal verse extensively. *Coronary* (published privately, 2011) consists of twenty-one sonnets concerning a patient, addressed as "Dad," hospitalized for heart fibrillations, and a first-person speaker, a son, who can be identified with the poet. The son visits his father and pays close attention to his condition. While the theme of illness is current in poetry today, sustained sequences focused on it are less so. Morris's noteworthy series can be likened to Julie Kane's fourteen linked sonnets, "A Hobo's Crown for Robert Borsodi," in *Jazz Funeral* (2007).

Morris's poems bear one-word titles, some from ordinary medical terminology. Printed as blocks, they are rhymed, often loosely. The first relates succinctly the man's symptoms at home, the arrival of EMTS, the rapid procedures at the hospital, and the summons to the son: "Driving / past the limit is the least that I could do." Following sonnets dwell on such matters as the patient's inability to speak distinctly (for instance, inability to pronounce *infarction*), the tubes and cables that keep the heart pumping, the insertion of a pacemaker. The hospital takes on the features of home: relatives spend hours there; they eat and, in effect, sleep there. In his frustration, the helpless speaker broods on the past in terms only slightly less incoherent than the patient's dreams. Metaphors are neat: "In the light your mind's dark tooth grows long" ("Rat"). The ordeal ends not with death but with a return home, the "nightmare" fading. Yet the penultimate line of the last poem—"Home again, home again, home from the sea"—bears, although apparently triumphant, a caution, since it recalls Robert Louis Stevenson's "Requiem" and thus presages death.

These well-crafted sonnets constitute, as one reviewer wrote, "a strange body of flesh, time and memory" (Bailey). In fact, the poems are not strange, not disconcerting; the tone is conversational but not colloquial. Morris's strength here lies in expressing the familiar (and the tedious, unpleasant, and awful) in terms both precise and concise, by which one recognizes reality and understands it better.

Ecotone (2017), a chapbook, is a collaborative work by Morris and a painter, Myrtle von Damitz, who lived in New Orleans for some fifteen years, according to the biographical note. The work was "inspired by the landscape of coastal Louisiana," described as "a mysterious wilderness, racked by disaster" (back cover). "Entry," the opening poem, mentions hills; but the poems reflect the setting where, according to the acknowledgments, they were composed: an artists' colony on the lower coast of Algiers, in "endangered bottomland hardwood forest." The poems involve "a journey into the unknown" by a group of travelers, "seeking the truth," facing conflict and "a fateful choice." Morris follows here the still-powerful Romantic tradition, illustrated by numerous nineteenth-century Louisiana poets, of the wild landscape, the trek into darkness, the uncertain outcome.

The poems, all in couplets with regular rhyme or sound echoes, bear titles. The paintings are titled separately. Von Damitz's art is carnivalesque, to the point of surrealism and beyond; the cover illustration is identified as "Not Mardi Gras." The poems, chiefly descriptive but with an uncertain narrative line, similarly evoke alike the familiar and the alien, beginning with an imaginary cityscape, disquieting, where wanderers set up their tents. Such terms as *batture* are familiar to those who know New Orleans; disturbing images, however, constantly challenge the known. The unsettling images in "Market" include a tonic that will cure or induce blindness—the merchant is unsure; "a twitching leg . . . / freshly harvested from the last // round of operations at the clinic." Amputated limbs reappear in the poem "Circus." A voice announces that "this is the only place in the land // where those like us feel at ease." Use of the French term *quartier* instead of *neighborhood* or *district* adds to the sense of alienation. Lake and river and wrecked vessels mentioned can pertain to a Katrina-like landscape, although the strange devastation goes beyond any plausible hurricane damage. A "Directorate," installed in the bizarre settings, recalls the French Revolution and, vaguely, Nazi authorities. "Protection" furnishes many parallels with post-Katrina New Orleans and the Gulf Coast, such as the reopening of a neighborhood when the Directorate, having sealed it off as unsafe, deems it nontoxic and sound. "Scavengers" and "Invaders" give similar impressions; the latter poem suggests also racist oppression and profiteering.

Morris's ecological concerns are evident, and his poems are among the most unusual reflections of the devastation wreaked by hurricanes—Katrina surely is the model—and other consequences of harmful human activity. Whether myth, in the form of journey and discovery, or the depictions of real storm destruction presented by other poets is more effective in conveying the accumulated human and environmental damages is the reader's decision.

WILLIAM ALEXANDER PERCY

William Alexander Percy (1885–1942), long known in southern letters for his autobiography, *Lanterns on the Levee* (1941), was foremost a poet. Although his work, praised by John Crowe Ransom and Allen Tate, had a significant reputation in his time, it has not endured well. It was included in the first edition (1952) of *The Literature of the South* (edited by Beatty, Watkins, and Young) but omitted in the 1968 edition. Since the mid-twentieth century, the long poem, a form Percy favored, has not competed successfully with short narrative poems or lyrics, and his diction and rhetoric, not without charm but rather old-fashioned, even for its time, have come to seem antiquated.

Like others, however, he should be taken on his own terms. His standing in Mississippi letters of his time justifies his inclusion here. He was a traditionalist in his poetic practice, social ethics, and, generally, views on race, now out-moded; yet he was antitraditionalist in his freethinking views on sex. Today's context requires that he be recognized as a homoerotic writer, although he did not identify himself as such publicly. He has been praised, by Benjamin E. Wise and others, for striving to reconcile conservative, even elitist social, economic, and philosophical ethics with sexual freedom, and for achieving in his writing both self-concealment and self-revelation. To Wise, he presents an important example of survival. Others, particularly John Barry, have damned him for his obsession with sex joined to self-hatred, an inferiority complex, lack of self-control, and spinelessness.

Percy came from a well-established line of planters in Greenville. His grand-father, Colonel Percy, had helped drive out carpetbaggers from the Delta and disenfranchise, practically speaking, the newly freed blacks, thus overturning much of Reconstruction. His father, LeRoy, a partner in Percy and Yerger, was an attorney for railroads and other interests and also managed the family cotton plantations. He was his father's opposite, in physique and character, and both sensed the awkward difference. His mother, of New Orleans French-speaking Creole stock, was a Roman Catholic. Will was reared in that creed rather than in LeRoy's nominal Episcopalianism.

The boy had private tutors, then was sent to a military preparatory school in Sewanee, Tennessee. Appalled by the uniforms and drills, he took, and passed, the entrance examinations for the University of the South. In an existential crisis, he came to question his faith. He began searching for a substitute philosophy that would reconcile ideals with reality, including the reality of desire. Studies of Greek texts at Sewanee led him to realize that the Greeks "practiced bisexuality honestly and simply without thought or condemnation" (*Lanterns* 111). He began to develop what Wise (92) calls "a historical and philosophical explanation of same-sex desire that made sense to him." Known for a sense of duty, he must have understood that duty to himself required—in a rather Protestant fashion—seeking *his* truth and somehow fitting it into the world. Bertram Wyatt-Brown speaks of his "Stoic" philosophy. Percy's desires and closeting are key to his poetry.

He did not abandon all traditional belief, however; his verse shows that he honored and often felt close to the Gospels and the figure of Christ. Nature, though closely associated with paganism in Greek literature, is a manifestation of the Christian Deity also. Hearing a bird "at break of day / Sing, from the autumn trees / A song so mystical and calm," he concludes that "No man, I think, could listen long / Except upon his knees" ("Overtones," *Collected Poems*). (Percy noted that "critics and anthologists, almost without dissent, have liked" that poem [*Lanterns* 136], and William Faulkner appreciated it [Faulkner, *Early Prose and Poetry* 72].)

The death of Percy's younger brother in a shooting accident meant that eventually Will would have to take up the family responsibilities. After graduation from Sewanee in 1904, he spent a year abroad, in Paris—doubtless a revealing stay—Italy, and Egypt. He then studied law at Harvard before returning to Greenville and joining his father's law firm (1908). In December 1916, as the Great War raged, he became a member of Herbert Hoover's Commission for Relief in Belgium and briefly served abroad. After the United States entered the war, he was successful in earning a lieutenant's commission and was sent to France, as he wished. He received a *Croix de Guerre* and a promotion, and returned to Greenville as a war hero.

He performed his attorney's duties well and cared about his clients. He was often generous with blacks and defended some in trouble. In 1867 his father set an example by successfully defending an ex-slave, Holt Collier, accused of murdering a federal officer. The younger Percy's sexual bent and complicity with underground life may have made him particularly sympathetic to the disadvantaged. He was publicly friendly with his chauffeurs and his cook's son. He was able to travel widely, finding in cultural differences literary and moral inspiration and freedom from behavioral constraints. He took young men, black and white, to Europe or Tahiti. Glimpses of these travels, notably to Italy, then later to Japan and Samoa, appear in his verse.

During the great Mississippi River Flood (April 1927), his fellows looked to him for leadership. He was in charge of obtaining and distributing relief supplies, and he worked on the levee with the black laborers who had been drafted to reinforce it with sandbags. Taking the initiative, he tried to arrange an evacuation of blacks and whites downriver to Vicksburg. It was a debacle, and he became a party to very harsh treatment of African Americans. In some readers' minds, his image is sullied forever. Percy's parents died in 1929. In 1930, after the death of his cousin LeRoy Pratt Percy, Will invited the widow and her three sons to live with him, then, upon her death, adopted the boys, of whom the novelist Walker was the eldest.

Percy's entry into literature dated from publications in *McClure's* and the *Yale Review*; subsequently, verse of his came out in the *Sewanee Review*. His first collection, *Sappho in Levkas and Other Poems*, appeared at Yale in 1915. The book was praised in Boston, New York, and Edinburgh. Harriet Monroe demurred, writing in *Poetry* that it was "an absolutely artificial product," "full of everything that I most dislike and resent in poetry." Subsequently he was appointed editor for the Yale Series of Younger Poets and served until the great flood.

William Faulkner reviewed Percy's next collection, *In April Once* (1920), finding it flawed, but with many merits. Its title piece is a sort of closet drama in male voices, set in the thirteenth century. Four years later, *Enzio's Kingdom*, which Percy considered his best work, was nearly a critical failure. The forty-page title poem concerns the Holy Roman Emperor Frederick II, who has just died, and his bastard son. LeRoy Percy was a model for Frederick, toward whom Enzio's attitude is ambivalent. Percy denied that the poem was autobiographical; but in stating that the conflict lay, rather, in the emperor's quarrel with the Church for its strictures on sexual behavior, he invited a different sort of personal reading.

In 1930 Percy published his *Selected Poems*, incorporating new verse from the late 1920s. *Collected Poems*, with a foreword by Roark Bradford, who found Percy's poetry "beautiful, charming ... warm and honest and lyrical," came out in 1943; *Of Silence and Stars*, with a preface by Hodding Carter Jr., appeared posthumously in 1953. The title, a quotation from the poet, underlines the editorial choice to display his idealism.

This idealism was not that of political change or utopian visions; "Enzio's Kingdom" reflects his antipathy for democracy and plebeians. He complained to Donald Davidson at Vanderbilt about the expectation that all authors should write about the lower classes (Wyatt-Brown 224). Rather, his idealism was the romantic ideal of the individual, his feelings and aspirations, his soul and its overwrought expressions. Inspired by yearning and nostalgia, he at once celebrated happiness, mourned its loss, expressed covertly the anguish of his spirit and body, and pointed toward the impossible realization of any dream. "What I wrote seemed to me more essentially myself than anything I did or said. It often gushed up almost involuntarily like automatic writing.... I could never write in cold blood. The results were intensely personal, whatever their other defects" (*Lanterns* 131). In addition to being nonpolitical, much of his work is antihistorical.

In essence, Percy wrote like a late Victorian, cultivating the past and its usages. His overblown diction and tendency to statement did not reflect the modernist revolution. He did not cultivate the image, in Ezra Pound's sense, nor what Yvor Winters labeled the postsymbolist poem. He was not unaware that he was out of date. He may be viewed as blind to the need for an altered idiom to suit the speech and tones of his time; or he may be commended for cultivating the English poetic tradition, or certain strands of it, and deftly exploiting it for his purposes.

In his verse, nineteenth-century usages are common, including third-person verbs in -*eth* and -*oth* and words such as *forspent, mayhaps,* and *gathered* in three syllables, but without accent mark, as a rhyme word. Abstractions and adjectives abound, as these examples, from *The Collected Poems,* show. "O joy, the trancèd splendor of the air. . . ." ("A Winter's Night" 73). Rhyme is the dominant choice for short poems, but Percy knew also how to craft good free verse and handled blank verse well. Sonnets are not uncommon, whether Italian or Shakespearian. Apostrophes (to trees, winds, his heart, Sewanee) are frequent. "Strike down into my breast, O sun, and cleanse my soul— / Shadows are here and ailments of the dark!" ("Hymn to the Sun" 227). Iambic pentameter is the principal meter, but meter is not always regular; in "Sappho in Levkas" and other pieces, the lines vary from six to twelve feet. The left margins may be irregular; some result in nearly centered justification, thus reinforcing the artificial effect.

Whereas the idealism and its rhetoric serve in part to *conceal* "the love that dare not say its name," the poems *reveal* much, to those prepared to read them as keys to encrypted homosexual love. Occultation of homoerotic inclinations had been practiced in a different mode by Walt Whitman, then, in the period roughly contemporary with Percy, by Hart Crane and Federico García Lorca, whose posthumous publication, *Sonetos de amor oscuro* (1936), suggests its shadowy theme in its title. Moreover, high-profile British aesthetes of the late nineteenth century such as Walter Pater, Swinburne, John Addington Symonds, and Oscar Wilde had invited readers to associate the aesthetic mode, and particularly its vein of nostalgia, with sexual deviation; the association endured well after 1900, offering language and themes. Two French figures, André Gide and Marcel Proust, used various stratagems, including ambiguity and disguising one sex as the other, to hide, yet express their inclinations and behavior, despite themselves or otherwise. Gide asserted that literature must "manifest," even though that meant violating inhibitions and transgressing boundaries. In addition, he provided rationales for legitimizing individual happiness. Their examples and others' show that "Uranians" or inverts could be modernists, indeed brilliant literary innovators. Percy told Shelby Foote that Proust's *Remembrance of Things Past* was one of three works that had changed his life; the others were James Joyce's *Ulysses* and Thomas Mann's *The Magic Mountain* (Wise 237).

The storehouse of classicism afforded names, motifs, tales, themes, and historical and mythological matter by which Percy, like Gide earlier, could express his moral and aesthetic idealism. He could refer to explicitly homoerotic materials or simply suggest, by using such traditional figures as shepherds, the difference between the modern world and the ancient one—the Greece of poets. Significantly, Percy even saw his chauffeur and factotum in a classical guise, an erotic one: "my only tie with Pan and the Satyrs" (*Lanterns* 296). *Et in Arcadia ego* could have been his watchword, as suggested by "Arcady Lost," from *Sappho in Levkas*. In the title poem of that collection, Sappho falls in love with Phaon, depicted as a "dark-curling head, the shepherd lad," and, perhaps tellingly, "brown." An unidentified voice speaks of "his beauty," "the summer of his mouth" ("Phaon in Hades," *Collected Poems* 78). With considerable breast-beating, she confesses this love—shameful, in view of her station—to her father, Zeus, whose lofty status and prestige are not without parallel to LeRoy Percy's. The simultaneous self-accusation and self-justification in Percy's make-up, couched as an appeal to authority, are visible in the classical setting.

Percy's use of abstractions as well as features from the English poetic tradition made even highly personal poems, charged with dissimulated references, accessible because generalized. Male voices, whether unnamed personae or named characters in the longer poems, dominate; feminine personae are not frequent, though Sappho stands out as an exception (a meaningful one, perhaps, since she also is known for homoeroticism). The speaking *I* may stand for the poet himself, or a persona somewhat removed; the second-person pronoun, frequent, is usually unidentified as either man or woman. Male characters in long narrative and dramatic poems speak ostensibly for themselves; one need not seek a key. Yet no doubt many contemporaries could read more than was said and gave to the pronouns their accurate meaning, in the context of Greek figures and flowery depictions of idealized young men, kisses, embraces, and voiced yearnings.

Percy achieved distancing between subject matter and readers, between himself (and his innermost feelings) and his social milieu, most successfully in his long poems, which retain considerable charm. The choice of blank verse and topics both historically and culturally removed allows readers to view the poems as timeless and not expect modern idiom. In addition, the extended narrative line, speakers' voices (whether using elaborate speech or sounding quite familiar, as with Saint Francis), and variety of tones make these poems more approachable than many of Percy's short lyrics, in which the rush to be poetic takes over the whole poem. Sappho, speaking to her father, Zeus, moves easily from one tone to another, her relatively straightforward statements and evocations offsetting what seems excessive in the rapturous passages. "In April Once" has elegant but natural language. In "Enzio's Kingdom," which Percy considered a "contemporary poem," the lines move rapidly; the diction is reminiscent of Robert Browning's—one of Percy's models, along with Shakespeare, Milton, and Arnold (*Lanterns* 132).

As Percy's art developed, he continued to cultivate both long poems and short lyrics, exemplifying often the appeal of simplicity. Avian imagery is frequent; as Saint Francis says to the birds, "For you, tho' of the world, share not its taint" (47). In "Greenville Trees," a lovely quartet of poems in various forms, each in the voice of a tree, "The Water Oaks" includes the bird motif. Numerous poems, set in France, concern the Great War, its horrible destruction, and the grief it brought. Some can compete well with lyrics by British and French poets, though Faulkner dismissed the entire section (Faulkner 72). "Poppy Fields" (1920) inevitably brings to mind John McCrae's "In Flanders Fields" (1915).

Read in the light of Percy's desires, including that of concealing, his poetry assumes more meaning than may first be supposed and more importance as an undertaking. In another light, it can be judged as an unfortunate diversion from what might otherwise have been his best topic: Greenville and Mississippi in his time. That was not his burden. He needed to write for himself and for kindred spirits, but not as an underground writer—rather, in such a way that his verse could "pass" and appeal also to a general audience. The result is a body of individual verse, some beautiful, that expressed his overt and secret concerns. Many poems stand as testimony to the anguish of difference and the price of dissimulating it. In practicing concealment, he was of his time; in allowing his difference, nevertheless, to inform his writing, he anticipated those who, later, wrote openly of their lives.

STERLING D. PLUMPP

The work of Sterling D. (Dominic) Plumpp deals almost wholly with the black experience in America and, occasionally, South Africa. He said on Mississippi Public Radio that "part of my task in life is to use language to speak about the humanity of African Americans, to affirm that humanity and to be proud of the legacy of the people who developed Negro spirituals, blues, jazz, and gospel" (Zheng, *Conversations* 158–59). Thus he pays homage to the musical genres of African Americans, which express "all my people's dreams. / All my people's hopes. / All my people's joys" (*Horn Man* 20). His writing contains, in John Edgar Wideman's estimation (afterword to *Blues Narratives*), "a philosophic inquiry about the blues as world view, as consolation and rumination, long quarrel and reconciliation with godhead, blues as a path for coming to terms with existence." As the back cover of *Horn Man* puts it, Plumpp is "internationally recognized as Black America's blues poet." Reginald Gibbons called him "one of the most original poets in America, and one of our most valuable" (Introduction to *Home/Bass* xiii). In Jerry W. Ward's opinion, Plumpp is "the most original and gifted blues poet of his generation" and can stand honorably next to Langston Hughes (Zheng, *Conversations* xii, 11). In 2019 the Chicago Literary Hall of Fame bestowed on Plumpp the Fuller Award for Lifetime Achievement.

The Chicago blues are Plumpp's primary model, his chief love, but, as a *Library Journal* reviewer observed, jazz likewise is a source of his rhythms (back cover, *Blues: The Story Always Untold*). Claude Wilkinson and other critics have suggested that whereas blues constitute a mode of acceptance, even complacency, jazz "proposes discontent with the status quo" (Zheng, *African American Haiku* 106). To what degree Plumpp embraces, consciously or unconsciously, this distinction is unclear.

Plumpp, whose blues songs have been recorded (Introduction to *Home/
Bass* xv), was born in Clinton, Mississippi, in 1940. He has retained ties with his
native state, although he has come to view southern society as an "intractable
caste system" (Taylor 138). "Though there will be other places in my life, none
will be home, as close and as painfully or joyfully familiar as Mississippi"
(quoted in Willie Morris 99). Plumpp's papers are housed at the University of
Mississippi. Yet his attitude toward his home state, which he left as a youth, is
necessarily ambiguous. He returned in 2014 as a visiting professor at Mississippi Valley State University. He spent most of his professional life, however,
in the African American studies and English departments at the University of
Illinois at Chicago, where he is now professor emeritus. After his retirement he
taught for some time at Chicago State University. He has also given workshops,
worked for Third World Press, and traveled, notably to Toulouse, France, for
the jazz festival, and to South Africa.

In addition to poetry, Plumpp's output embraces *Black Rituals* and other
prose studies, dramas, and translations from the Afro-Cuban writer Pedro
Pérez Sarduy. Among Plumpp's honors are three Illinois Arts Council Literary
Awards, the 1983 Carl Sandburg Literary Award (for *Mojo Hands Call, I Must
Go*), and the Richard Wright Literary Excellence Award (1999). *Home/Bass*,
which celebrates the Chicago bass player Willie Kent (a fellow Mississippian),
won the 2014 American Book Award in Poetry. In 2015 Plumpp received the
Lifetime Achievement Award from the University of Illinois at Chicago. He
has one daughter, Harriett Nzinga, and two grandchildren. He was divorced
in 1983 from his wife, Falvia, a registered nurse.

Plumpp's parents, unmarried, were Cyrus H. Plumpp and Mary Emmanuel.
He was reared by his maternal grandparents, Mattie and Victor Emmanuel,
on the cotton plantation near Clinton where they worked as sharecroppers.
Sterling had to be told later that Mary was his mother. The father played no
role in the boy's life. (See Ward's chapter and Gibbons's interview, in Zheng,
Conversations.) *Blues Narratives* is dedicated to his grandfather, "the only daddy
I ever knew, man of blues and prayers." It was a very religious household.
The grandparents prayed aloud, lengthily, morning and night, and during
anxious times or threats such as tornadoes. When he first heard blues songs,
he assimilated them to prayers because of their cadences (Interview). Mary
Emmanuel, one of seven children, already had an older son, Wardell Johnson.
In 1948, the boys began attending a grammar school some miles away, during
seasons when they could leave farm work. In 1955 Plumpp's grandfather died,
and the remaining family moved to Jackson. (Mattie died at age 103.) An aunt
used bootlegging money to which she had access to send Plumpp to Holy

Ghost High School, which had a white faculty but was for black pupils. There, he converted to Catholicism and graduated in 1960 as valedictorian.

On a scholarship, he attended St. Benedict's College in Atchison, Kansas. Its curriculum included extensive readings from the ancient Greeks, Dante, and Milton. He also discovered *Sonny's Blues*, by James Baldwin, and started writing poetry. In 1961 he went to Chicago to look for summer work. The next year, quitting school, he moved there, with the intention of studying at Roosevelt University. To support himself he worked at the main post office. He read widely among black writers of the period and earlier. Drafted into the army, he served in 1964–65, then returned to Chicago and was, for a few years, associated with the Black Arts movement. He earned a BA in psychology at Roosevelt in 1968, then an MA in 1971. Having established his writing credentials, he started teaching in the black studies program at what became the University of Illinois at Chicago, where he rose in rank. He was involved in cultural undertakings and publishing enterprises, and he wrote ceaselessly. Asked who had influenced him most, he named Richard Wright, Louis Armstrong, and Amiri Baraka (LeRoi Jones), whose poetic style "renders blues into bebop and uses ellipsis to achieve quick phrasing" (Zheng, *Conversations* xv). To Diane Williams, who queried Plumpp about influential predecessors, he named Hughes, Sterling Brown, and various jazz performers (Zheng, *Conversations* 168).

Uniquely American creations, blues and jazz, both originating in southern black communities (fields, churches) and tied to rhythms inherited from Africa, enormously influenced not only music elsewhere, whether ephemeral or intended to endure, but also other arts. David A. Davis writes of the "blues paradox": "The experiences of poverty and oppression paradoxically yielded riveting cultural products" (in Watkins 113). Plumpp has the saxophonist Von Freeman say, "My music can / give a ride from bruises and pains you try to / hide" (*Horn Man* 44) Echoing Houston A. Baker Jr., Davis observes that "the blues vernacular, the coded language of resisting economic oppression, is central to the study of African American writing" (Watkins 113). Plumpp was not the first to connect blues and poetry. *Blues: A Magazine of New Rhythms*, founded by Charles Henri Ford and friends in 1929, linked them and underlined their kinship by publishing Ezra Pound, Gertrude Stein, and William Carlos Williams. Plumpp, however, built nearly his entire poetics on the assimilation.

Whereas poets may, without further justification, believe in, and seek to realize, a synthesis of arts or genres, critics confront problems when dealing with the theory and practice. Since poetry has become chiefly a written, and silent, genre, whereas music, to be fulfilled, must be transferred into sound (however interesting scores may be to performers), the distinction is considerable. That songs incorporate words, and poetry may be recited rhythmically, in varying tones, does not invalidate the difference. Plumpp's understanding of traditional blues supposes words only *as accompanied by music*. If building a poem concerning music or musicians is easy enough, and if verbal features (vowels, consonants, stresses, and their combinations) may be called, approximately, "musical" (meaning, generally, pleasing to the ear), to transfer into a verbal medium the full sound spectrum of any musical genre is impossible. What Plumpp does is call on musical modes of structuring, including repetition, a call-and-response pattern, the verbal equivalents of syncopated rhythms (not the steady beats of canonic iambic pentameter), perhaps the use of improvisation (letting the poem go, as it were, by itself). Plumpp's *aab* arrangement (two identical phrases, followed by a different one, contrasting or amplifying) is that of basic blues. It is pertinent that Daniel Cross Turner calls songs by bluesman Robert Johnson "poetry" and speaks of "quantum leaps from one image to a markedly different image" in his songs (in Watkins 230–33). (Turner does not mention Plumpp, an oversight.)

Syncopation, repetitions, dispersal, improvisation are modernist techniques with approximate equivalents in graphic art, fiction, and poetry. Davis even speaks of "blues modernism," using "tropes of modernity to depict the challenges of life in a racist, agricultural society within a rapidly developing nation" (in Watkins 113). Although Plumpp does not give up all traditional markers of sense, he jostles and dislocates language often. His slashes, which create visual interruptions (printed here as he has them, without surrounding spaces, to distinguish them from line breaks) are, he has asserted, parallels to the pauses one "hears" in a blues song (Zheng, *Conversations* xii). He uses black vernacular, or nonstandard, speech, he said, as a way of "connecting" to black music (much of which is vocal). "My saxophone is a key. / A collaged territory of / witnesses" (38). That verb *connect* is crucial. Still, as Gibbons pointed out, Plumpp's poems are not "blues lyrics"; rather, they contain "echoes and overtones of blues lyrics" (Introduction to *Home/Bass* xvi). Yet Kent can claim that *his* business also "is language, naming and / renaming, using and / re-using" (*Home/Bass* 23).

The sixteen poems of *Portable Soul* (1969) show, however, Plumpp's determination to go beyond the aesthetics of modernism. This little book, his first, is dedicated to "My Momma" (his grandmother). Technically speaking, the poems are simple and direct, but they display already features to come, such as words divided at the end of a line without hyphens and a parenthesis appearing alone. The message of blackness is strong. "Re-recognized black beauty," he calls it in "Portable Soul Explosion." "Black Resurrection" and "Black Liberation" are among poem titles. "I'll Find Our Way," dedicated to Jones, expresses Plumpp's embrace of his people. What he calls "the festering / brain waves / of white america" are contrasted with the project of "saving blackness . . . / sanctifying awareness" and "blinding out blue / artificial eyeballs" ("Beyond the Nigger"). Brief allusions to slave auctions, law codes, escapes into swamps, sexual victimhood, and heavy work suffice to evoke black misery ("Travelling").

Plumpp's second book, *Clinton* (1976), a poem in sixteen numbered parts, shows how close he remained to his native place. He uses a chastised free verse, in lines of moderate length, with a few oddities of typography such as occasional slashes and words run together. He evokes "talk between the people and the soil," hot, crumbly cornbread, bowls of gumbo and jars of peaches, honeysuckle on fences, morning glories, mud and rain, and "unfurrowed rows of my life" (6, 9). The boy subject and the reminiscing narrator appear very close, thanks to these sensorial details. The key phrase: "Momma says 'She is your momma; / I am your grandmother'" is clear only to the adult (8). Expressions of nostalgia are not unqualified, of course: Jim Crow is present, with reminders of Willie McGhee and Emmett Till (16). The last poems evoke Chicago in the poet's first days there, then the army and afterwards—the sixties, Malcolm X, Martin King, and Stokely Carmichael. Earlier, Nat Turner is mentioned. "History cannot be put off" (21).

The Mojo Hands Call, I Must Go (1982) is an impressive collection in a strong voice. It reveals Plumpp's continued development. The pictures it offers of the black experience rely on correlatives, quick, impressionistic touches, or direct statement. In addition to using black vernacular, he omits standard punctuation and capitalization. Echoes, such as repeated phrases, serve as organizing threads. He takes liberties with images, as in the puzzling "the edge of birth / prying against stagnancy/flowers / jimmying fear to free respect" (11). The book is built around two moral and cultural centers, Mississippi and Chicago. Excepting the opening poem, "Sugar Woman," a homage to womankind, and "Zimbabwe," it consists of complex, multipart poems. In his endorsement, Baraka called the title poem "brilliant," treating "the flashing mojo of black consciousness under the duress of racism." The South African poet Keorapetse Kgositsile provided an introduction to "Steps to Break the Circle," with wide-ranging references to similar poets of black anger. He praised Plumpp for being able to endow a European language "with the weight and depth of the rhythms of our life" (45–46). Plumpp is "this young brother who leaves Mississippi confused, searching for his blackness, his mystical identity, his hocuspocus belief that essentially after he has found his blackness his problems will be solved."

"Steps to Break the Circle" has elements of dialogue and narration, with veins of preaching. The train to Chicago is an organizing principle. Two voices warn against taking that train. The first comes from an old Mississippi woman who visits the city only briefly; her bones have "permanent homes / down deep deep in Mississippi" (52). The second is that of a "reverend." The young man's voice responds, justifying his decision to leave the South. There are many antitheses in theme and images. In Chicago, opportunity does not hide under concrete "like sweet taters" (56); but the South is no paradise either. As Kgositsile says, "There is nothing like the blind, mystical belief in the virtues of the rural South here, or that mystifying pastoral nonsense the Europeans trapped us into" (47). Anywhere, "the Black Man's days are epic chains" (50). This anger contrasts, however, with hope, which Baraka identified in the "historical chronicling that sweeps us along with a sense of growth and recognition." Tender memories are in conflict with "fractured dreams," "crippled winds," and "splintered tongues" (11). Broken syntax and sense correspond to unfulfilled promises of life or perhaps frantic attempts to break out of the circle, or "rock" against it (55). The circle may indicate, in Kgositsile's terms, "deathbound confusion and limpminded posturing" (44), that is, responses to oppression; but it is also oppression itself, the "life cycles my fathers left me" (50).

With *Blues: The Story Always Untold* (1989), Plumpp became fully the admired blues poet. The poems are in free verse of short lines. Sound echoes (not formal rhyme), wordplay, repetitions of words and structures, recurrent motifs provide organizing elements among disparate, sometimes synesthetic images. The punctuation is erratic. "Preface" introduces figures and themes to come. "Martin" and Malcolm X appear, along with musicians, all in "my history's garden." The blues reign "from bases in im / provisation's, arms"; they "wait in distant rooms of / my mind." The second poem, "Identity," has snatches of voices from the poet's past and the collective past, starting with "I/the poor" ... Bowl of / blues at my hours." The voice imagines "long rows of blues / mangled with boll weevils / of greed" and "dirty / blues tangled in my weeks." The poem ends on a colon, suggesting what will follow. "I ritualize:" The word *blues* beats and beats again, as a word might in a sermon. (Plumpp described sermons as a kind of "language" that "spread literacy among embattled souls" [Zheng, *Conversations* ix].) The poem "Mississippi Griot" incorporates similar echoes, as it evokes a "son" of the state, "native of / genocides, emitting / black seeds of prophecy." Local features include a mockingbird, catfish, the levee, and "muddy rhythms." The griot "had the river in / side him and sang it." Among the strongest images is that of the griot taking Till's "decomposing body / from the river" to lift it "with the fork of his cries / to a corner / in my skull."

Certain titles mention singers such as Muddy Waters, B. B. King, Bessie Smith, Howlin Wolf, Billie Holiday, and Big Maybelle: "Her pain in / her voice/ her / people's in / her vein." Their presence mingles with figures from the poet's past: his grandmother, his dying grandfather, anonymous figures in the fields and along the roads. Poems are dedicated to Hughes, Angela Jackson, and William Faulkner. The eleven-page poem "Callings," dedicated to Charlie Braxton, consists of short apostrophes beginning "O"; many are simply the phrase "O blues." Few lines have finite verbs; they are evocations. "O hell bitten land if you are black" (85). Repetition of words and lines creates a hammering effect. Women as well as men are evoked, women of fear, of hard work, of prayer, of courage. Well-known incidents of injustice come alive again with only a few words: "O they told her Constitution Hall could not be used"; "O remember/ conductor said, 'Nigger, you can't ride in no Pullman'" (86–87).

Horn Man (1995), in short lines, incorporates the same poetics. "A tenor ax crosses / over my mind"; "rebellions in voice"; "a ballad of / silence"; "a / be-bopper flung on a low sky" (14–15); "these mirrors I blow" (43) offer illustrations. (*Ax* or *axe* was slang for a saxophone before being applied to other instruments.) Expression is often notational; a poem may rely on very few verbs. Odd expressions call attention to themselves: "reeds" as a verb (13); "I / come horn every ten years" (35). Enjambments may fit normal phrasing, or may break it up, to greater effect. Compound expressions and polysyllabic words are often divided at line ends ("under / stand," 14). A parenthesis may appear singly, and slashes are frequent, as in "Mister/Ragtime" (45). These poetic choices point to a fundamental feature of Plumpp's poetry: an assemblage of threads but not a finished tapestry.

The composition of *Horn Man* is loose. In two of the four parts the poems, many multisection, have titles according to the table of contents but not preceding the poems themselves; elsewhere they are numbered. The tribute to Freeman, whom Plumpp met in 1981, is accompanied by homages to others. Names and nicknames such as "Bird" (Charlie Parker), "Trane" (John Coltrane), "Satchmo" (Louis Armstrong), "The Monk" (Thelonious Monk), and "Bessie" (Smith) carry the poet's tribute and the sense of a powerful, eloquent musical tradition. "Miles" (Davis) is "a cartographer of wind / crisscrossing prairies of self. / A birdwatching renegade / pleating lines from myths" (24). Mentions of key instruments and players contribute to evoking the effect of a jazz or blues ensemble. Plumpp emphasizes Be-Bop (as he spells it) as a subgenre and plays with the term, as in the dedication, "For Von Freeman, Boptized" and an address to Parker and Coltrane: "You bop-tized me / with a tenor ax" (22).

That the blues and jazz were not born ex nihilo, but rather from work and suffering, is clear. "All paths lead to pain / but you gotta dance them" (45). "Yard bird," alluding to Parker, suggests also any prisoner; "stevedore" points to back-breaking labor (11). "The Promised Land" carries the memory of spirituals (13). The phrase "Deep river," repeated, precedes the lines: "I got miles over yonder / past a half century / the Brooklyn Bridge chained / my name" (20). The bridge theme appears earlier: "The bridge / is my minister. Open arms / under tides. Miles down...." Each letter of the word *down* is printed on a separate line (18). Christian terms and symbols are not isolated. "The tenor [sax] is God's voices" (39). Allusions to hymns and prayers precede a brief historical reminder: "One-half block from the slave ship / I practice riffs on and sleep / with pain each night I lie down" (46). Plumpp gives to Freeman words that many artists could endorse: "...into a chordal geography of landscape / I follow. This horn I blow. / This sax I am. This sax. / I am. This sax I am" (47).

Johannesburg and Other Poems (1993) features settings in Mississippi, Chicago, and South Africa. Notes at the end identify unfamiliar references and words. Numerous poems are autobiographical. The long poem "Sanders Bottom," dedicated to Plumpp's grandmother, includes an anecdote from her life (see Zheng, *Conversations* 58). The speaker, unidentified, remembers her "momma" saying that she was marrying and that the man wanted neither the girl nor her brother. "Only wanted his chilluns / by her." The child's reaction is phrased with genius: "Remember how / I looked out and saw a ought/and the ought was me" (33). Elsewhere, the poet evokes his native fields and river. Numerous references to historical figures and events create an impression of monotonous recurrence: Toussaint (L'Ouverture), Turner, Harriet (Tubman), John Brown, Medgar (Evers), Malcolm, human rights (a poem title), and L.A. riot (another title).

Blues Narratives (1999) is extracted from a lengthy family epic, "Mfua's Song," which draws on oral history. (Plumpp has worked on it since the early 1980s.) The book comprises two parts, "Mary (1920–1980): Dialogue with My Mother" and "Victor (1880–1955)." The first person singular is the dominant voice. The typography is significant. Lines, very short, are either centered, aligned at the left margin, or mixed. Poems in part one bear only numbers; those in part two have titles also. While most poems in part two are in roman type, in part one both roman and italic appear, constituting different voices. Roman type, left-aligned, may carry the voice of the presumed author-in-the-text, followed by centered italic text in which the presumed mother responds. Elsewhere, italics carry the woman's words.

Repetitions are frequent. This stanza is printed twice: "My blues so low / down make me / sleep out of doors" (22). The four lines "I ain't a bad girl, / I just / take your broken week / ends / carry them home" are repeated immediately, with one variation ("Said I ain't a bad girl...") (23). For each of these poems, a third stanza, different, finishes the thought. This stanzaic pattern parallels the *aab* pattern *within* stanzas of basic blues. End words in stanzas one and two may have rhyme words in stanza three. The metaphoric vein is strong; speech is colloquial.

Through a pattern of accusations and justifications, the poet makes clear the physical separation and personal alienation of mother and son. One reads of cancer, sees a bedside with a night nurse, a moaning patient, and a watchful son who tells her that leaving a child with grandparents "ain't / no crime" (13). Recurring motifs and themes include dreams, chance, loneliness, absence, and suffering. Mentions of "the white / woman you worked for" and "white folks" suffice to evoke an entire society (23, 27).

The part devoted to Victor begins with what seem to be his words. An adversarial relationship between him and the speaker, as a boy, is clear. "We / do not mend / fences" (52). But it is tender, too: "you / is my Poppa" (the term *grandfather*, says the speaker, is impossible) (53). The persona raises the question of illegitimacy, countering it immediately with the observation that the accusation is a lie. "There is no legitimacy / in this land / for a skin / like mine ..." (55). The burdens of American blacks find expression in such notations as patched overalls and aprons, lynchings, mutilations, "slavery's / chains and freedom's / slippery palms" (57). "Calling You Back," addressed implicitly to Victor, furnishes time markers; his death occurred forty-one years before, and the speaker is eighteen years older than Victor at the time. "I need a voice / to re-invent passion / for toiling in fields / of the spirit," fields without maps, where, as the poet writes later, one must "journey to survive" (66).

Home/Bass (2013) is dedicated to Kent's memory. He and other great performers preside over the collection. Yusef Komunyakaa called the book "a stripped-down utterance ... situated where rural Mississippi meets urban Chicago," in which the poet reaches back into things, "bridging time and pathos," expressing "a longing back to the soil." "These poems convey the true timbre of life's ultimate rehearsal" (back cover). Plumpp introduces Mississippi by evoking the Natchez cemetery and his wish to find "the house / behind the house behind / the big house where my origins / begin in this Republic." He adds later, "Somebody's / hands bleed so I / exist" (prologue). The short dedication poem is accompanied by one to the poet's grandson, which characterizes blues as "truth pulled from experience" and, speaking of its poignancy, asserts that "it heals the impulse / giving the singer / the blues in the first place." The persona and voice in the book are double, both Kent's, as Plumpp imagines them, and his own. This doubling does not interfere with the remarkable unity of the work, arising in part from the strength and will it manifests. "I/never let curses / touch my songs. / I/never let weight of my burdens / determine my pace" ("I Tote," poem fifteen). This is despite—or because of—"blues/some / body's pain." "Pain/I weave. In / to my soul. ... Pain/I give names. .. I/raise. / To/a song" ("Words," poem sixteen).

The prosody of *Home/Bass* is familiar: extremely short lines, numerous multipage poems, repetitions of words, phrases, stanzas, slashes everywhere. All thirty-eight poems are numbered and titled, in three titled sections. Occasionally Plumpp inserts irregularly rhymed line ends, as well as interior rhymes and other echoes; "Magnolia," poem thirty-four, is mostly in rhymed couplets. "Hard Times," poem twenty-three, illustrates the theme of the blues along with its imitated beat: "debt blues, bo / weevil blues, drought blues, / woman/ gone away blues, / mean boss man blues." The poet mixes plain statements with metaphors. The blues are "an/ever / green forest of songs," always offering something fresh. "Blues/lives under / ground/in troubles." The blues take "bad feelings/and moans / or/shouts / some / thing worse"; they "suck out pain" ("Words," poem sixteen).

In *Home/Bass* Plumpp reasserted that he was put on earth "to recover, mold and discover the most private of public languages speaking to me from the Afro-American side of time" (xiii). How this project will be shaped by future social and political trends and his thoughtful reflections is not clear. Perhaps his reputation will rise. That he is not included among the eighty-six poets in Charles Henry Rowell's anthology of contemporary African American poets, *Angles of Ascent*, is unfortunate; any future survey should remedy that oversight.

PAUL RUFFIN

Paul Ruffin (1941–2016), whom Daniel Cross Turner calls a "major poet" (in Watkins 243 n.3), is more properly considered a Texas figure than a Mississippi one. He spent nearly all of his university teaching career at Sam Houston State University and served as the 2009 Texas poet laureate. Nor is he a native of Mississippi. Yet by his boyhood and early career, he belongs there. The fact that with *Circling* he won the 1997 Mississippi Institute of Arts and Letters Poetry Award attests to the connection.

Ruffin, a very productive author, was born in Millport, Alabama. His family moved to Columbus, Mississippi, when he was seven. His creative oeuvre comprises novels, essays, and short stories as well as poetry, his first genre. Additionally, he has edited or coedited critical volumes and important anthologies, focused particularly on southern poetry. His poems and prose appeared in magazines and reviews such as *Michigan Quarterly Review*, *Georgia Review*, and *New England Review*. He has read from his work on numerous campuses.

Proud of his country roots, he wrote that he was "poor and white, but not quite trash" (*Mississippi Writers and Musicians*). After service in the army, he took a BA in English at Mississippi State University, where, two years later, he earned his MA (1968). He married young and had one son; the marriage failed. A second produced two sons, but ended similarly in divorce. He taught high school until 1971, when he enrolled in the Center for Writers at the University of Southern Mississippi; he obtained his PhD there in 1974. His dissertation was a collection of poems, "The Hill." After one year as an instructor at Mississippi State, he moved to Sam Houston State, where he rose to be the Texas State University System Regents' Professor. He founded the *Texas Review* in 1979 and was editor-in-chief for several years. He created as well the Texas Review Press.

Ruffin's *New and Selected Poems* (2010) gives, along with nine new poems, some fifty samples from his three previous collections, *Lighting the Furnace Pilot* (1980), *Circling* (1996), and *The Book of Boys and Girls* (2003). His poems are in a controlled free verse, often with short lines, unrhymed except for occasional couplets or other scattered rhymes. His tone is familiar. A few infelicities, such as awkward enjambments, are to be ignored. He handles well concrete images and figures of speech. The language fits the topics, and individual voices stand out. Ruffin's rooting in the South, especially Mississippi, is obvious; he is unapologetic. He calls California the "Left Coast" and evinces almost no interest in the Northeast. The chief influences on his writing, generically southern, may include James Dickey particularly; the closing line of "He Spins His Tires," a coming-of-age poem, echoes Dickey's "wild to be wreckage forever" ("Cherrylog Road").

Ruffin tells stories well, usually with concision; he draws effects from simplicity. Many poems relate anecdotes, with a controlling metaphor and neat conclusion. Incidents, characters, settings from a southern boyhood appear. One reads of shrimp and oyster catches, an immersion baptism, a sawdust pile smoldering inside; of a boy, supervised by his grandfather, cleaning a well; of gigging frogs and burying a calf, a bottle-fed orphan then rejected by a cow with milk. "The Old Game: Boy in Training" connects boys' early shaping to the biologically and culturally based behavior of the male sex, responsible for hunting and for war. "What moves him is in the blood / engendered by a deeper urgency / than his father's wishes for him." Ruffin does not applaud war; he is a simply a realist, without utopian impulse. Like the inhumanity of Coronado's expedition, with its six hundred Pueblo slaves ("Llano Estacado: The Naming"), the dire visions of the twenty-first century (in a poem of that title) disturb him.

Nature, however cruel, is all that man has, save religion (delicately introduced in "The Mystery for the Magus"); and nature made the human species sexual. *The Book of Boys and Girls* deals discreetly with young sexual yearnings and older love. Addressing a young woman, the poet calls on the Renaissance trope of *carpe diem*: "Your hair lies across your / shoulder, soft and warm / in a yellow rib of sun"; but "children may one day pick up your bones" ("To a Student on the Front Row"). "Nasty Notes at the Academic Conference" pays tribute to married love. (*Nasty* is antiphrastic; the couple, at a hotel, their children at home, can flirt and enjoy a pretend assignation.) "To the Celibate" stresses that "you are bone and flesh, designed to breed / and die, no less than the purest holy man, / no more than the lowly oyster." That sexual love may be empowering—like poetry?—is suggested. In "The Woman Who Made Love on Frost's Grave," a "new-found strength" visits the title character, "who, sandwiched between the living and the dead, / had felt a feverish trembling to all her length." In "Buddy Philosophizes After Cutting the Bull," the sexual drive comes with an indictment, when the cowman points out that in emasculating the animal he has simply "take[n] the rage" from him, adding, "If anything, I sometimes wish somebody'd make / some cuts on me."

The flaws in *New and Selected Poems* come in the new pieces, generally longer and somewhat silly, particularly "When Amelia Went Down" and "A Glimpse of the Stone Age, According to Mack Dryden." Granted that they may bring smiles and applause before student audiences, one still regrets their garrulousness. Elsewhere, Ruffin showed himself to be in command of the southern vernacular and its raconteur tradition, and of much human wisdom.

ROBERT SARGENT

Robert S. Sargent (1912–2006) was successful in each of what C. P. Snow called "the two cultures," science and the humanities. He was born in New Orleans and reared, from age eight, in Mississippi, where he took a degree in electric engineering at Mississippi State (1933). Subsequently he pursued his studies, working on radar, at Bowdoin College and MIT. Interested in the theory of special relativity, he attempted to reproduce the mathematics underlying it; he succeeded in doing so after Einstein, with whom he corresponded, provided a key step. Sargent served as a naval officer with the Department of the Navy in Washington, DC, during World War II, then moved to the Pentagon in the late 1940s and remained there until 1972, working in research and development of radar technology. He received the Distinguished Civilian Service Award from the Navy. He was interested enough in philosophy to study, briefly, with Richard Rorty after he became Kenan Professor at the University of Virginia (1982).

Sargent was married three times. His first marriage, to Lucretia Cork, from whom he was divorced, produced two children. His second wife, Christine Pack, died in 1977. He was married in 1985 to Mary Jane Barnett, the adoptive mother of a Chinese daughter, Lula Jane, of whom Sargent became very fond, as his collection *Lula and I* (2004) attests.

Sargent, an admirer of George H. W. Bush, began writing poetry in middle age when a neighbor, with whom he had shared his interest as a reader, died. His range of topics is broad, including the South, the ancient world, jazz, marriage, and love. He published poems in prestigious journals such as the *Georgia Review, Antioch Review, Prairie Schooner, Poetry,* and *Shenandoah.* In a necrological article, Hastings Wyman, a poet friend, spoke of Sargent's effective public readings and "his enduring southern accent." (Numerous readings took place at the Library of Congress, the Folger Shakespeare Library, and the

Corcoran Gallery.) Sargent was active in area poetry associations, and his verse earned the Columbia Merit Award (1996).

His first collection, *Now Is Always the Miraculous Time* (1997), displays his art well. He excels at short lyrics and meditations as well as narrative poems of two or three pages. Free verse, very well crafted, is the dominant form; some is rhymed, strictly or loosely. He wrote excellent blank verse also. His lasting interest in the South is visible in poems set in Mississippi and one called "A Southern Poet," a sarcastic satire concerning boorish behavior and the Jim Crow mentality. In the title poem, which presents a short lesson on artistic affiliation and development, the poet Thomas Wyatt, credited with introducing the sonnet into England, dreams of Anna or "Anne." (She is perhaps Anne Boleyn, whose name was linked with his). Next, William Faulkner hauls coal at a power plant (and writes *As I Lay Dying*); then Buddy Bolden toots his horn in Storyville or Lincoln Park (Gert Town) and inspires a boy named Louis (Armstrong). The Faulkner motif recurs in the following poem, "New Albany, Mississippi," where the speaker, driving "a crooked concrete road through slanted hills" in "the stepchild state," observes that, even after the Nobel committee honored the novelist, no sign indicated that the "small one-storied town" was his birthplace.

Science inspires two excellent poems. "Forty Thousand Thousand Fathers," in quatrains rhymed abcb, deals, imaginatively, with evolution and genetics. "A Student at Alexandria," in seven parts, is in the voice of a young Athenian banished by his father to that city sometime after the death of Philip of Macedonia. The youthful speaker whines about the career of that "outland Greek" and his awful city. He carries on about missing Athens, two girls there, and good times (the reason for his banishment). But he finds enough intellectual energy to attend the mathematics lectures offered by Euclid, on topics introduced in his proposition twenty-seven and fifth postulation. How, asks the youth, can such be of great interest? He cares more for the girls across the sea. Euclid speaks "as if he believes / someone might care in a couple thousand years."

The gallery of portraits in this first collection includes "Lone Hawk," an old Comanche, speaking around 1700, when Plains Indians had acquired horses. In another poem, two veterans of the European fighting in World War II—one unknown to history, the other "Abe" (General Creighton Abrams)—meet years later at a wedding and reminisce, on equal terms, about what each experienced. "Monody for Bowie" pays tribute to a friend (perhaps the neighbor) who died "in the dying year" quoting lines from Gerard Manley Hopkins. "Medea, at the Kitchen Sink" stages a grave domestic quarrel, beginning with the wife's complaints, her rising tones as she harangues her husband, and her dramatic gesture of throwing her wedding ring into the kitchen sink as she starts the grinding mechanism. A corrective poem is the final one, "Truth in a Parked Car."

In *A Woman from Memphis: Poems 1960–1978* (1979), recurring sources, themes, and tones, some reprised from the previous book, afford coherence. The poems vary between full-bodied and insubstantial. Forms vary, as before; loose iambics are effective in narrative poems. The syntax and other features of expression impart an ancient flavoring when it fits. Short lyrics offer reminiscences by an autobiographic persona of his childhood in New Orleans and Pass Christian. The poet speaks under his name in "The Reunion," which sketches a meeting, in Memphis, of four former school-fellows, now middle-aged. The theme of "this camaraderie of men" and old warriors' fellowship reappears in the narrative poem "Olaf and Sigurd," two Scandinavian heroes who encounter each other in the streets of Constantinople, embracing, just like the speaker and a friend with whom he played football at Durant High (38).

Subjects from both the Old and New Testaments receive cynical treatment (Sargent was, apparently, without religious belief). "Pharaoh," the opening poem, retells antiphrastically, with sarcasm, crucial episodes in Jewish history. Moses, the king's overseer, waves his "magic" rod, brings on pestilence and a decline in public health, and blames the plague of locusts on the king. "Moses swore / That my opposition to him and his Asian god / Caused all these disasters." Pharaoh asks, "Is it / Clear what a problem he was? Is it?" In "Zipporah at Bethpeor," an effective satire, God, called the Employer, throws tantrums "at fancied slights to his most August pride." Vain and dictatorial, he acts arbitrarily; he makes use of Moses, takes the credit for his achievements, then discards him. "The Invalid" corrects the story from Mark 2:3–12: the paralyzed man is not really healed, because he was able-bodied to start with; he was just lazy and liked to be waited on.

Additional themes and motifs include writers and their subjects (Byron, James Joyce, Ernest Hemingway, Constantine P. Cavafy). "A Cavafy Poem" sketches the poet in the library reading room in Alexandria, in 1910, as he takes notes. In three lines, Sargent presents a core challenge for poets: "The problem for him, for us, what is important, / Is what to do with the facts: Their aureate transmutation." Elsewhere, Degas, Whistler, and Matisse appear (with Van Gogh, the latter is surely one of two or three most frequently treated painters in contemporary American poetry). In "Protagoras, in the Agora, Mulling Things Over," the title character critiques sculptures by Phidias, the Athenians' reverence for words, and the teaching of the young Socrates, who proposes the reality of such abstractions as justice and truth. Protagoras, known as an agnostic, depicts the rather brash philosopher thus: "Came in, the intense young man, wary, / Wanting to argue, wanting to win." "Was once one too," he adds. Sargent's Protagoras is a relativist, like the real figure, known for stating that man is the measure of all things. "When the Continents Parted" suggests, in sketching evolutionary differences, that the poet rejected fate or divine intentions for human beings.

In fifteen short sections, the title poem of *Aspects of a Southern Story* (1983) relates the first encounter of a black domestic with the sea, at Biloxi. Her response when she faces the waves, alone (her employers and their children having stayed back, discreetly), is understated (or underfelt): "Ain't near as big as I thought it'd be." Quoting Protagoras again, the poet explains this private appraisal variously. "Was Alberta playing folk-hero, defying the deep / by belittling its size?" Or was it a way of showing her independence? In either case, she was reporting the size of the sea "as she saw it." While spoken first in private, to the waters only, her words were "brought forth" later in the car—presumably drawn from her by questioning; they composed a "story," thus fulfilling a human need, perhaps especially southern. A few other poems are similarly effective, such as the delicate, discrete lyrics "Our Hands Were Occasionally Touching" and "Two Parties," on marriage and love, and "The Lost Poems"—those the speaker did not write, in his youth. "Circe to Ulysses" has a snatch of wit.

Unfortunately, elsewhere the collection is disappointing. In an endorsement, Ernest Kroll, likewise a Navy man, later at the State Department, called Sargent "genuine in an age of phonies." Kroll was not wrong. But simple genuineness in sentiment or character, which can serve well in readings and with friends, may not wear well on the page. Sargent's voice becomes ordinary to the point of triviality, as in "Pennies" and "Wide Bed," where small domestic details do not develop into a poem. The prosody, too, is ordinary, its beat sometimes awkward or sing-song ("The Culprit"); except for occasional rhymes, it is simple without art. That being said, one must admire Sargent's achievements, all in his middle and later years, and honor his contributions to poetry in Washington.

JAMES SEAY

James Edward Seay III, who was born (1939) and reared in Panola County, has carried on his entire career in the South and can be viewed as a representative southern poet of the post-Faulkner, post-Welty generation, close to them in vision and certain experiences, yet molded also by a changed society and landscape. He grew up as a Southern Baptist. He has one-sixteenth Choctaw blood. His father was an operator of heavy equipment and a land-development supervisor, his mother a housewife. He had two sisters. Small-town life in Mississippi marked him. "I guess it's still going on—my childhood in Mississippi, I mean" (Abbott, *Reflections* 411). He portrays his mother delightfully in a poetic essay called "You Dumb Bell"; another essay, "The Weight of a Feather," sketches a satisfactory relationship between son and father, who offers guidance to him as he drives a tractor. Yet "Dial Direct" (from *Let Not Your Hart*) suggests a son's anger and disappointment with respect to his father, neglectful, perhaps, and physically distant. While it is uncertain that the lines should be taken as autobiographical, Seay's writing often involves a speaker who seems to be the poet's self.

His early poems include numerous scenes of rural and small-town life in Mississippi. James H. Justus wrote that no poet of Seay's generation has done better "in not only evoking the village culture of the contemporary South but also transforming its commonplaces into objects and events of talismanic significance" (Rubin et al. 547). Seay writes of fishing and hunting, of Indian dead and bottle trees, of minor incidents in rural life. On occasion (as in "Options" and "The Lame, The Halt, and the Half-Blind," *Let Not Your Hart*) he refers to the loss of his right eye, hit when he was twelve by a stone thrown by a motor—an accident not unlike that which wounded Robert Penn Warren as a young man and led to loss of sight in one eye. The lifelong consequence is certainly part of Seay's poetic as well as physical self. Whether it should be viewed as Edmund Wilson argued in *The Wound and the Bow*—giving a sense of estrangement or inferiority like the wound of Philoctetes and thus motivating the victim to "sing"—is uncertain.

Following two years as a Mercer University undergraduate, Seay returned to Ole Miss to earn his BA in English (1964); classes taught by Evans Harrington were important to him (Interview). After working as a claims adjustor, he entered the English graduate program at the University of Virginia (MA 1966). There he studied with George Garrett and profited from the readings given by visiting figures such as Robert Lowell and James Dickey. In 1967 he married the novelist Lee Smith, a Virginia native. They have two sons. They were divorced in 1981. In 1991 he married Caroline Szymeczek. After teaching at Virginia Military Institute, the University of Alabama, and Vanderbilt, he moved in 1974 to the University of North Carolina, where he remained until his retirement forty years later. He served from 1987 to 1997 as director of the creative writing program. His honors include a teaching award and one from the American Academy and Institute of Arts and Letters (1988). He was writer in residence at La Napoule Art Foundation in France. He has traveled widely in Europe; in 1987 he was part of a delegation of Mississippi writers invited to visit the Soviet Union. Now professor emeritus, he lives with his dog on a four-acre property. He continues to travel in Europe and to fish, often with his son, in the Florida Keys and elsewhere. Politics interest him; he is a sometime activist and occasionally writes op-eds.

Seay's poetry has appeared in four collections of verse and two chapbooks, in limited editions, and has often been anthologized. Poems of his have come out in the *New Yorker, Southern Review, The Nation, Hollins Critic,* and other noted magazines His essays have been published in *Esquire* and *Harper's* as well as the *Oxford American.* The script for the documentary film on big-game hunting, *In the Blood* (1990), was a collaboration between him and George Butler, the director.

Seay presents his poems aloud artfully. Although rhyme appears in early poems, subsequently he wrote generally in free verse, often with strong beat but flexible stanza and line structure, with many breaks and indentations and occasional centering. His love of language, especially as spoken, is obvious, and nothing about his style is cramped. Carefully chosen images complement his rhetoric, never intrusive but important. Many poems are narratives, in the southern storytelling tradition; but he writes understated lyric and meditative verse also, occasionally featuring refrains. He uses the sonnet form (unrhymed) at times. At the outset, he capitalized most letters beginning lines, demonstrating, in Justus's opinion, that he shared with other southern poets of his generation "a residual fondness for conservative forms and techniques" (Rubin et al. 535). In later collections capitalization follows normal rules; further signs of loosening in his prosody include prose paragraphs and one poem printed side-wise (at a 90-degree angle).

The title poem of *Let Not Your Hart* (1970), Seay's first book, is dedicated to George Garrett. It was inspired by a church bus—an old school bus—bearing on its rear door the biblical admonition not to be troubled. "On faith and a curve, both blind," and "hoping against the evidence / of things not seen," the bus passed the speaker's car. The incident is a parable of faith. "My lane, my life on your faith, / My troubled hart." Scripture transmuted appears elsewhere, as in "Valley of Dry Bones" (derelict cars). Various other poems feature African American figures, such as black trusties. "Through My Santa Mask" stresses the "separate but equal" (or unequal) arrangements of a company that manufactures Styrofoam articles; men work side by side but attend separate company barbecues. Seay calls on his own imaginative vision to express "the images that most forcefully outlive / their past"—sketches of the desperate hungry and other marginalized figures, or strange objects, such as "the bleached snake / Bottled in alcohol, / The egg it ate intact" ("The Pomegranate").

Whether depicting incidents, characters, or scenes, Seay's poems often bear glosses, insights, even a moral. Topics range from a coin minted by a Roman emperor and a love affair connected to it, to the freak death of a skilled American airman in the Pacific. A particularly effective poem is "No Man's Good Bull," depicting an animal bloated on wet clover, its methane gas turning to blue flame. Work of many kinds, especially the field and mechanical labor Seay was familiar with as a boy, is valorized. In "No Fluid-Fed Governor," a young man and his father inspect diesel engines on pumps along canals in the Everglades, where portions are to be drained for agricultural purposes. Beautiful phrases mark "The Starlings," with its effective enjambment: "To hold a thing that flies is flight / Itself." The real, as in that example, tends toward the dream, that is, the ideal, "where blood schools at the heart of its deepest dream" ("Circling the Reef").

Water Tables, constructed in seven parts, most quite short, appeared in 1974. The poems vary in length, from brief to multipage. Water is a frequent motif, connected often to the feminine (a recurring thematic element). The book does not constitute a novel departure, although new notes are visible; most evident are the presence of a child, in "Naming the Moon," and repeated suggestions of fractious love. "I don't understand / what passes between women and me / any more than I used to" ("Devices"), the poet writes. Fantasy and the play of the imagination are major constituent elements; certain images may puzzle readers.

Elsewhere, metaphors fit easily. Curves traced in ice skating, for instance, in "The Motion of Bodies" (sec. i), with an epigraph from Newton, are figures for human possibility. "The Ballet of Happiness," a light and pleasing poem, makes explicit one side of the human coin; its obverse, disappointment (with the need to reject the past), marks others. Mention of "a Greek play" ("On the Island," sec. i) suggests ineluctable fate, made visible in character, perversely. "The way it works is this: / we devote ourselves to an image / we can't live with and try to kill / anything that suggests it could be otherwise" ("It All Comes Together Outside the Restroom in Hogansville," one of Seay's most frequently anthologized poems). Yet "Patching Up the Past with Water," the seven-page concluding poem, an oneiric one, suggests, however foolishly (since love seems to have ended), mending and conciliation. Motifs from earlier in the book—the water-table image and hands—recur, as the voice speaks of "that dreamed absence of succession / in which to reassemble the whole being. / And yet our hands are straining . . . ," as though to reach an image, "free and alterable."

Narration is the chief structural principle of *The Light As They Found It* (1990), although thematic composition, centered on travel and the past, appears also. Blocks of free verse are usual, but the last poem, "An Ideal of Itself," is in unrhymed quatrains. Narration is connected explicitly to culture, all under the scepter of "time, open-faced, yet secret before us" (as the title of the fourth poem reads). That poem (which runs to ten pages) and several others are lengthy. Seay's expository skill is well illustrated in "When Once Friends," built on two nearly fatal incidents, unrelated except that in each the speaker and a companion were exposed, in thick mist, to sudden threats (at sea, in the air) that arose quickly, passed, but remained in his mind. The experiences were enhanced by the fact that an eleven-to-one bet on greyhounds had furnished the funds for the sea adventure.

Historical fate appears in "Tiffany & Co.," where Lenin and his Bolsheviks appear at breakfast near Fabergé's shop as they plot to change history. Dealing with both personal destiny and the past, "Time, Open-Faced . . ." winds through story and epoch, moving from a Florida roadhouse to the Blue Mountains of Jamaica and from a father's wartime photographs, lost, taken during the Pacific campaign, to an inscription in a fallen-down house. Scratched two hundred years before, beside an interior bevel, its enigmatic message appeals to the ages: "*In your chimney of love, / count me ten brick.*"

In what appears to be a personal statement, the poet writes of "the obsessive sad riddle of sorting out / the blame for the failure of early happiness" ("Gifts Divided"). "An Ideal of Itself," the concluding poem, featuring the motif of light, acknowledges that "there's a question / of what kind of witness to bear, / what calls on the past to make . . . // in sounding the memory we've made of feeling." Not all can be told, nor recalled. "More and more often all I remember / is this or that landscape we passed through on our way somewhere."

The 1997 volume *Open Field, Understory*, dedicated to Caroline, brings together poems from Seay's previous books and chapbook and adds nineteen new poems, plus a verse epilogue. Endorsements of Seay's writing by Elizabeth Spencer and Reynolds Price suggest his national profile. The subtle composition in the whole and individual poems alike shows how composition *is* meaning. The "open field" is surely that of poetry, or of the poem, as a writer faces the blank page and its vast possibilities. Additionally, the field may be that of general human potentiality. *Understory* has three or four meanings, of which the first is *foundational narrative*. Personal and collective history alike furnish elements of this background. Even the individual poem has its ur-history.

The collection begins beautifully, with "The Fire of Both the Old Year and the New," recounting how the speaker and his wife burn corks saved from the wine bottles of the year now ending. The fire burns with the "pure residuum / of the wine itself" and that of memory, recalling labels that "won us to their cause by their truth in the mouth, the cup of kindness. . . ." The new poems include also sad reexamination of love ending and memories of quarrels among beauty ("On the Steps to Roquebrune").

Twentieth-century history and what may be called the anthropological burden of evil weigh on the poet in the multipart "Nothing He Had Ever Said or Done." The fact of historical destruction and wickedness, from which the poet does not shirk, provides a particular meaning for *understory*. The poem has several panels. A fisherman in Marseilles displays for sale a great blue tuna, dead so that men can eat; that his bristling dog is named Hitler cannot be ignored. A World War II veteran, who had "walked through ashes," comes to visit his buddy, "with whom he had walked out of the ruin," so that they may speak of things ordinarily unmentioned. An inscription on the Nevsky Prospekt in St. Petersburg warning passers-by of German shelling leads to reflection on the use of hair, blond, gathered from residents, for making cross-hairs in bomb sights—then, not incidentally, to introduction of a Russian girl, identified as the speaker's mother-in-law, whose hair was cut for the purpose. Where, the poet asks, are the living things in all this carnage? The theme of warfare recurs in "Flags," with the glimpse of a Japanese freighter in contemporary times and knowledge of a soldier (the poet's father, one assumes) on Okinawa.

The epilogue poem is set in a primitive cave on a limestone cliff in Dordogne, the home of Cro-Magnon (Upper Paleolithic period). Meditating in its confines, above trees and rivers, the speaker, imagining himself in the distant past, rehearses steps in developing civilization: primitive speech, concern for safety, hence careful choice of shelter, with use of fire and stone tools, and ultimately cave-painting. In a far-reaching vision, the persona asks whether another will climb from the *understory* (the material and anthropological sense) to reach and go beyond him—perhaps for practical gain, perhaps "to hear these words / I am working toward song?" Poetry carries, in this vision, the highest cachet.

Seay's sensitive use of language and broad, charitable understanding, added to his craftsmanship, make him a humane poet, considerate of readers, offering much. The evenness and reliability in his writing are a strength, not a fault, and do not exclude surprise; they are doubtless the result of lengthy reflection and effort and concern for the effects of his work as a whole. One remembers his poems.

ALEDA SHIRLEY

Aleda Shirley (1955–2008) was born in Sumter, South Carolina. Her father was in the Air Force; the family followed him to various assignments, including Texas and the Philippines. (One glimpses him in "Reasons for Flight," *Chinese Architecture*.) With their varied settings and multiple addressees, her poems suggest cosmopolitanism and restlessness alike. Kentucky, where she began her literary career, was her home for years. In 1990, however, she settled with her husband, architect Michael McBride, in Mississippi and remained there until her death, from cancer; she is now identified with the state. Appearing always slightly marvelous, even in its ordinary, often rainy or mud-caked reality, Mississippi inspired many of her poems. Among additional backgrounds are Florida, New York, and the American Southwest, with its turquoise, arid panoramas, and Hopi culture.

In 1975 Shirley graduated from the University of Louisville; she then pursued an MFA at Indiana University. In Kentucky she served in the poets-in-the-schools program. In Mississippi she was similarly active in supporting literary activities. She taught at the University of Mississippi and served as writer in residence at Millsaps. She was the recipient of grants from the Kentucky Arts Council, the Mississippi Arts Commission, the Jackson Arts Council, and the NEA. Poems of hers appeared in such periodicals as *Poetry, Shenandoah,* the *Denver Quarterly,* and the *Georgia Review. Chinese Architecture* (1986) received a First Book award from the Poetry Society of America. *Silver Ending* (1991) won a chapbook competition held by the St. Louis Poetry Society. *Long Distance* appeared in 1996 and *Dark Familiar: Poems* in 2006. She was coeditor of *Mississippi Writers* (1995) and edited *The Beach Companion: A Literary Guide* (1999).

In *Chinese Architecture*, Shirley's art is already mature. Gary Davenport characterized her poems as "traditional," not meaning worn-out in form but, instead, using English "in its basic integrity" and respecting twentieth-century "normality," a classic style (Shirley et al., *Rilke's Children*). Eschewing postmodernist maneuvers, cheap appeals to readers, and programmatic verse, she crafts moving lyrics on a wide range of topics. She uses free verse, frequently stanzaic, with natural syntax, which enjambments follow. The epigraph, from Proust, underlines, as an antidote to the real, the importance of desire ("the country which we long for"). Thus the importance of the exotic. The title poem plays with the possibilities of the *pailou* (or *paifang*), the characteristic Chinese archway, an entrance to what is conceived as the ideal space. Poetry provides it, often catalyzed by memory. "Petrarch imagined / an architecture of memory / where images were stored..." ("Finding the Room"). The *you* to whom the discourse is often directed, someone evoked or present, invites readers into the book. Yet the *I* who speaks is not just rhetorical; Shirley's poetry is deeply personal. "However deep and obscure even to the writer," asked Robert Penn Warren, "isn't poetry always autobiography?" (quoted in Simpson 144).

The first poem of *Chinese Architecture* is set in Brazil, at the confluence of the Amazon and Rio Negro. The final poem shows Ralegh off the coast of Guiana on his last voyage. In between are many glimpses of the exotic, which, although foreign, must be domesticated, partly at least, to be grasped, even as it retains its identity as different. Hence the observer's ambivalent position. The exotic is not spatial only; time likewise has its allurement, its mystery. A word such as *tree*, for instance, may transport one back to the past, to a willow and the complex of experiences around it ("One of a Number of Good Intentions"). Or the mind can concoct wonders out of nothing but familiar objects, metamorphosed. "I see the confluence of our sky / with that of another planet, / three or four moons gleaming there" ("White Birds"). Nature, particularly the seasons, offer its marvels, there for the taking.

Psychological dimensions are not lacking. "I am trying to sleep and clear / my mind as one clears a mirror by moving away" ("White Birds"). Confluence, a meeting of waters, is also a mental process. Themes and motifs of love, aging, and loss weave among others. "Sunset Grand Couturier," a beautiful lyric, sets up a scene in early evening, with sounds of boys shooting baskets, Vesper bells, late, dusky colors, fireflies, and a dress of a Rembrandt hue—all of which are transformed in the speaker's mind into a sensual and metaphysical union of setting, self, and the person addressed. "Let Me Tell You How It Happened" rehearses alternate realities in the past.

The chapbook *Silver Ending*, containing forty-five pages of poems, deserves notice for its beautiful manufacture—design, paper, printing. Every poem is in stanzaic free verse. (Some were republished in collections and are cited below.) From the nostalgic perspective of age thirty-five, the title poem evokes the past, the present, and their imagined future prolongation. Descriptions lead easily to personal conclusions. Inventorying features of an island, for instance, the speaker remembers two sea grape trees, their shadows on her face, "and, at nightfall, the shadows on the water / which was always the last thing to darken / as if it were holding the light that slipped from the sky, / as if it had, like me, lost all track of time" ("Cayman Time"). Introspection and retrospection are both profitable. Inspired by some forgotten old letters from a man "on the move," the persona reflects: "I couldn't figure back then // where exactly I'd be in ten years, but I made / an informed guess about the future, and when I looked / toward it, I could find him nowhere there" ("A Gift for Dead Reckoning").

An epigraph to *Long Distance*, borrowed from Henry James, reintroduces the motif of confluence and its obverse, separation, or "fracture" ("A Dwelling in the Evening Air"). Contrasting the familiarity of the past with its strangeness, and one's liking for both, he wrote of "the moment when the scales of the balance hang with the right evenness." Again, Shirley reveals herself as a poet of thresholds and delicate equilibrium. "I lived in two worlds for months. Segue // became not a silence between songs, threshold / not the passage between inside and outside; / they were the slick bridges I skidded across . . ." ("The Sky in the Stone"). The poet muses on the Day of the Dead in Mexico, "the day when life and death intersect / in a way you can see . . . // . . . everything / taking place as if it were not so, a dream, and enchanted world . . ." ("The Day of the Dead Bride and Groom"). In a poem evoking Gulf Coast rain, the speaker broods on a lover. "This is the rain / of the past, with its two stubborn dimensions that flatten // things out and con you into believing there's depth . . ." ("Right as Rain"). The intimation of fluidity and change is strong. "Aware" calls up "that feeling engendered by ephemeral beauty, the way / some things are beautiful because they will change / with the passage of time."

Anxiety prevails in many poems dealing with separations and "this obsession with closure" ("The Spirit of the Staircase"). Death, the irremediable separation, appears, but without such closure, in "All the Voice in Answer I Could Wake." Elsewhere, while details are sketchy—the poems the more effective thereby, doubtless—it is clear that the persona thinks often, and imaginatively, of the past and probably lost loves. In all, "the great invisible machine that is time" ("Monday Morning") is confluent, beginning and ending confused. In "Celestial Ennui"—a noun that must be taken in its strongest sense—the poet writes: "Far off, on the horizon, // I see a boat. It may be glass; it is shining. / This is the vessel that would take us away, / if we could go. And I can't. And I can't." With an inevitable echo of Heraclitus, the strains of "Proud Mary" piped from a calliope on a paddleboat underline ways of understanding the past, the remembering but especially the forgetting as one is carried along ("The Curve of Forgetting"). Yet liminal fields and "moments of transition" ("Aware") may be beautiful. In a park, where a year before two people (lovers) said goodbye, "a boy dunks his ball a final time, tucks / it under his arm; so smoothly does he slide, / on his skateboard, into dusk, dusk might / well be a destination instead of an hour" ("Fourth and Magnolia"). "Fixed in Silver" reveals the truth-value of the past. "I want the past still, // perfected. And only distance is perfect. He's flawless / now, an X-ray, a photograph . . . / shimmering, permanent, largely invisible."

The title *Dark Familiar* recalls previous books and their veins of death and disappointment. Shirley strikes new notes, however. Many poem titles contain color terms, introducing notes of vividness; typographical choices (ampersands throughout, and use of italics for some titles, roman for others) draw attention; and theological concerns run through the collection. According to the first two poems, God apparently is "not looking out for any of us" or is "absent." "Four Darks in Red" describes, on a canvas, "a band of anthracene / that is God or the absence of God / or someone's ingenuous belief in Him." The fundamental identity of the human condition, announced at the conclusion of "Blue Over Orange," is a subcurrent, arising from general ordinariness. The poet reflects that "how you are / is how you are, that the level of joy or meaning / on the most ordinary Wednesday afternoon / is the level of joy or meaning you're stuck with" ("April Fifteenth"). Did Shirley, in the interlude after *Long Distance*, move away from earlier perceptions? In "The Minor of What We Felt," the voice says, "I've lost my taste for the indistinct, / the luminously suggestive. I want heft. . . ."

"Wisdom," concerning the poet's grandfather, a veteran of the Great War, introduces the hard facts of twentieth-century history, perceived from the twenty-first. "In Paris another useless declaration of peace. / We like to imagine the future as something // we soar toward, but it may be more like falling. . . ." The recurring word *distance* obsesses the poet, along with endings. "How is it possible, / from a silence I've never disturbed or escaped, / to locate the precise moment everything ended, / even though it went on & on, forever" ("Three Blacks in Dark Blue"). (One is not surprised that the persona of that poem has undergone regular psychiatric analysis.) Dream may hold both ending and duration. "At night / everyone comes back to me eventually, / this one I loved & that one" ("Song of the Abducted"). In the dream world, "the border between past & present blurs // & we've the chance of a connection, however fugitive, / with people who are far away, the dead, / the gods" ("The Customary Mysteries").

   Shirley's subtle, delicate, searching lines show that her premature death not only deprived her surviving father and husband of her love but also signified for American literature the loss of a gifted poet, devoted to high standards of craftsmanship and human and aesthetic truth.

J. EDGAR SIMMONS JR.

With its "manic governor-less energy with language," as James Dickey wrote, the late work of Joseph Edgar Simmons Jr. (1921–79) stands out in Mississippi poetry of the period (foreword, *Osiris at the Roller Derby* v). Probably less in imitation of modern French poets whose work he knew than through native impulse, fueled by alcohol, Simmons combined a visionary element—resembling that of Rimbaud and the surrealists and rich in cultivated implausibilities—with the frenetic writing of Beat poets, creating a strong, idiosyncratic style. Dickey considered Simmons "authentic," as opposed to the "would-be wild man on the page"—what Dickey elsewhere called the "yowling," and not very good yowling, of Allen Ginsberg (*Babel to Byzantium* 5). Dickey contrasted Simmons's writing likewise with that of the confessional school, incarnated best by Robert Lowell and his circle, "ghoulish norns, displaying professional wounds" (*Osiris at the Roller Derby* vii).

Simmons, known as Joe, was born in Natchez. After schooling in Mississippi and, it seems, service in the army, as reflected in his writing, he attended Columbia University (BA, 1947, MA, 1948). He pursued his studies at the Sorbonne, then returned to America and entered the teaching profession, moving frequently, with appointments, among other campuses, at the University of William and Mary, Mississippi College, where two of his students were Barry Hannah and Noel Polk, and the University of Texas at El Paso, where he directed the creative writing program between 1967 and 1969. He was married and had a son. He published three volumes of poetry: *Pocahontas and Other Poems* (1957), *Driving to Biloxi* (1968), and the posthumous *Osiris at the Roller Derby* (1983). Poems of his appeared in the *Atlantic Monthly, Chicago Review, Harper's*, the *Nation*, the *New Republic*, and many anthologies. He contributed columns to the New Orleans *Times-Picayune* and the *Dublin Irish Press*.

Among his honors were the Bellamann Literary Award for Poetry (1964) and the Texas Institute of Letters Vortman Poetry Award (1968). It may have been ill health that led him to resign his position in El Paso; he died in a Veterans' Administration hospital in Mississippi. He corresponded with John Crowe Ransom and Dickey, who read from his work at UTEP.

Pocahontas and Other Poems came out when Simmons was in his mid-thirties. It is an honorable beginner's book, although the poems treating Pocahontas, roughly a half-dozen, are uneven. Part of the weakness is connected to voice. "The Dream of John Smith," spoken ostensibly by Smith, begins with rhymed lines marked by inversions and sing-song beats, meant to imitate, one supposes, usage of the time. The remainder is in unrhymed verse, somewhat easier for the modern ear. "Powhatan's Curse" is marred by anachronisms and awkward phrasing: "bathrooms," "night nurse," "brush the smoke from their faces." In "Ressurection" [sic], the archaic S (like an F) replaces the standard character; the words *wyffe*, *liveth*, and *ye chauncelle* (chancel), as well as the echo "Died Matoax . . . / Died Pocahontas," impart their obsolescence. Yet the lines on mortality are moving. The following poems deal with survival in early Jamestown. The last poems are very unequal. Wordplay marks some, in the spirit of Wallace Stevens.

Published eleven years later, *Driving to Biloxi* attests to Simmons's increased command of verse, and his cosmopolitanism and wide reading are visible. Machiavelli, Leonardo, Rousseau, Keats, Whitman, Yeats, and Faulkner all figure in the text. The free verse is generally stanzaic, sometimes with variable left margins, little capitalization, and spaces within lines serving as punctuation—traits he may have studied in modern French poetry. Again, wordplay ("Babbit Rabbit") and incongruity call attention to themselves. In that poem, featuring "the bunch-backed turtle" and "the denotufted rabbit," "The stones chill, ague the web / Sun glare nips the nose / But always glass greenly mirrored / In his watery eyes, the finish line."

Culturally contrasted to such fanciful and wide-ranging evocations, the title poem and others give evidence of southern experience. "Early Passion in a Puritan World" sketches a "strange . . . enveloping and / weirdly enervating world of sex in one / girl" as a music group rides the train to New Orleans for the Mardi Gras. In "A Southerner's Lament for Lincoln," the speaker admits that "we can never love you completely" but acknowledges that Lincoln is "the beautiful razor rock / That cuts our sides / . . . / Yours is the blood that cuts." In jagged lines with interior spaces, "Music from a Southern Town" evokes jazz as performed by a mixed-race combo ("verboten"), recorded in a two-bit Louisiana town and taken back to Mississippi to be played in a grocery store and amplified into the street and the tavern next door.

"Dylan Thomas in Indiana," an excellent elegy, pays homage to the deceased Welshman, recognizing both abilities and flaws and, above all, the refusal by Death, personified as a "maiden pouting," to consider him exceptional. "An American Abroad" rehearses ways of grasping a foreign experience. Likewise well structured, "Begin and End with Water Music in Ireland," which is set on an island at haying time, moves, impressionistically, to childhood and a paddle ferry, then back to the Irish setting. The multipart and wide-ranging "Child at the Riverbed (an anatomy of metaphor)" points discreetly to Simmons's poetics and its "scheme of relatedness" (pt. I). "Man himself is metaphor in his spiritual reflection / The penetration of the self by the self / The spirit grasping himself by means of itself . . ." (pt. II). The title "Implication as Absolute" reinforces the vision of metaphor as truth. Similarly, "The Magnetic Field" shows how the difference between things, called distance, is "the night-lighting of poetry." "Stars are stars to us / Because of distance . . ." and the nothingness that "clings to them."

Osiris at the Roller Derby can be called a long poem, though its contents bear individual titles. It has the artistic unity of collages, provided by the style, freewheeling, explosive. Free verse is used throughout; some lines are short, some very long. In certain poems, syntax and phrases are, again, organized by the use of spaces within lines (substituting for commas and periods) as well as between groups of lines. Elsewhere there is simply no punctuation. Margins vary; in one poem half the letters of the word *juxtaposition* are printed immediately above the others, like superscripts (20). The poet takes other liberties, for instance, *hisfaulted* as a past participle (55). Rationality is precarious: "her curls demand doomsday" (56). Settings can be identified sometimes: Mississippi, Paris, New York (an illustration shows the Brooklyn Bridge), and such sites as a skating rink, an asylum, bars, a prostitute's quarters, a tenement stairwell, and the New York automat. The atmosphere is usually urban, rendering its own local color. But everything is subject to metamorphosis by the poet's word.

Recurring characters include a semimythic hero, Osiris; "Pop," presumably a father, and other old men; "Silone," the queen of the roller derby; a psychiatrist. To these are added countless others, generally shadowy, the passing figures of a city. Among themes and motifs, scrambled together often, are war, sexuality, an apparently miserable marriage, and death, one version of which is "soft suicide," that is, pointless, meaningless lives (46). What, beyond these underlying themes, drives the choice of form and material? Wordplay dictated by sounds, for one thing. "Power cats and power rats" (22); free association—the term appears (42)—with stray bits of culture (Dante, Cézanne, Amos and Andy, Pavlov's dog, Don Quixote, Swift and Stella), all added to presumably random recollected scenes, or snatches thereof. This is the stuff of dreams, delirium tremens, and much modern painting. It is, however, also the stuff of hope, under Simmons's pen. Even though "the time . . . is out of joint," "man is not yet" (46, 48). Osiris will live again.

The "quintessence" of the 1950s—in Paris, in America—is in "the best of Joe Simmons's jagged, searing strokes," wrote Dickey; "his poems will last, for they are better than the materials they come from" (*Osiris at the Roller Derby* vii). Poetry, Simmons told Dickey, had, with the help of his wife and son, enabled him to make "a real life out of the wreck of a life" (vi–vii).

JOHN STONE

The career of John Henry Stone (1936–2008) has been likened to that of William Carlos Williams, since both were physicians as well as poets. Stone, a cardiologist, was born in Jackson. His family lived for some years in Palestine (East Texas) during his boyhood but, when he was fifteen, returned to Jackson, where he graduated from Central High School, then from Millsaps College. He studied medicine at Washington University (St. Louis). He married as a young man and had two boys. (His wife died in the 1990s.) He pursued his training at the University of Rochester and Emory and also served in the US Public Health Service. As a member of the Emory faculty, which he joined in 1969, he created one of the first medical school courses in literature and medicine, viewed now as an important field, enlarging students' experience with human behavior and character. He had extensive experience with emergency medicine; at Grady Memorial Hospital in Atlanta, he established the Emergency Medicine Residential Program.

His interest in literature dated from his high school years, when he also acquired skill on the clarinet and developed what became a lifelong interest in classical music. He was the author of five collections of verse and a prose work, *In the Country of Hearts: Journeys in the Art of Medicine*. He received numerous honorary degrees and other awards, including Georgia Writer of the Year on four occasions and, twice, the Literature Award from the Mississippi Institute of Arts and Letters. He maintained close connections with Mississippi; a hall at Millsaps bears his name.

In *The Smell of Matches* (1972) Stone, using short lines, well-shaped stanzas, and some loose rhymes, proved that he could enter the poetic lists. The doctor likewise is on display, though not ostentatiously. The body is a significant presence, thought Stone's concern with it and way of spotlighting it differ greatly from those of women poets such as Ann Fisher-Wirth. Poems treat such topics as an autopsy, a fourteen-year-old giving birth, dissection of a cadaver, a fetus preserved in a formaldehyde mixture, and what appears to be death in childbirth. The perceptions are not misused; Stone is no leering sadist. The language is not raw, the experience is. "Getting to Sleep in New Jersey," in rhymed couplets, commends his fellow-poet Williams, as it compares his two crafts, obstetrics and poetry. "He tested the general question whether / feet or butt or head-first ever // determines as well the length of labor / of a poem...." Poems concerning a boy suggest, without sentimentality, the value of life, and why physicians strive to preserve it. Boys in the poems can be identified, loosely, with Stone's sons; but other boys have roles from time to time, as when the poet and his brother, apparently, go on a long car journey with their parents ("Coming Home"). Dedicated to Stone's friend the composer Samuel Jones, "da capo" looks back at living in a fraternity house and Jones's habit of conducting recorded music, razor in hand.

In All This Rain (1980) likewise underlines the body, aging, and dying. The book is divided into three parts: "The Man at Second," "The Self-Contained Woman," and "Now What." Among the poems are several short lyrics in rhyme. "Epithalamium Beginning with the Letter W" plays on the sound double u = double you. A doctor figure deals, for instance, with the amputation of a leg ("The Girl in the Hall") and increases his professional credentials ("He Takes the Course in Advanced Cardial Life Support"). "Mr. G.," an anecdote in prose, shows the conscientious and tactful physician, helping God (as he explains to the patient, wary of interventions in what seems divine business).

The title poem conveys lack of religious belief, which might otherwise offset the physical and metaphysical scandal of extinction, even that of a dog—"the brown fact / of your passing." In the eight short, unpunctuated lines of "Death," one sentence and three metaphors suggest how the end arrives. "Losing a Voice in Summer" expresses the well-known experience of being unable to imagine an absent voice—in this case, a father's. Not all is dreary, however; death can be droll. In short, fast-moving lines, the delightful "How I'd Have It" outlines desired funeral arrangements, then imagines the scene, with mourners entering, pausing and peering, saying "What / A Pity A Pity // And So Old, Too." In a different register, but not without connection, the persona, a Walter Mitty, imagines his deceased father watching as he plays baseball, reaching second on a stand-up double. Stone varies the tone again in "The Truck"; the vehicle in question is marked PROGRESS CASKETS. The speaker wishes to find out from the driver what his usual run is, "so I could keep off it."

Renaming the Streets (1985), which demonstrates once more Stone's art, could serve as a young physician's manual, underlining the inevitable failure of some interventions, the manner of dealing with death, and the value of poetry to the human spirit. Besides medicine, themes and motifs include music (Bach), mornings, and paintings (brief lines related to the "Mona Lisa" and Edward Hopper). "Gaudeamus Igitur," an outstanding poem, composed as a commencement address, echoes not only the medieval drinking song used by Brahms in his "Academic Overture" but also, in structure, Christopher Smart's verses on his cat, each beginning "For." Few medical graduates can have heard such wise observations so well couched. "For you can be trained to listen only for the oboe / out of the whole orchestra / For you may need to strain to hear the voice of the patient / in the thin reed of his crying." Prose narratives describe cases of congenital deformity and heart failure, leading to death. Birds are the centerpiece of a series, "The Pigeon Sonnets," mostly Shakespearean. Birds appear likewise in section 2 of "November," preceded by an epigraph from Dickinson on hope, "the thing with feathers." "The Bass" reintroduces the theme of boyhood by means of a charming fishing scene and its lesson.

Where Water Begins (1998) combines skillfully crafted poems with five short prose essays (they do not masquerade as poetry). Frankly autobiographical, they combine narratives with reflection. Key moments from the poet's life take on meaning within these accounts, which are connected to the verse poems. Free verse and traditional forms such as rhymed quatrains and couplets evince equal skill. In "He Attends Exercise Class—Once," "the veterans contort and bend with ease, / even those weighed down with many stone. / I sweat and write, in vivid fantasies, / a book called Some Positions I Have Known." Most poems are in short stanzas, often with short lines; a few are centered. Punctuation may be minimal, with no harm done to understanding. Occasional phrasing suggests acquaintance with the Book of Common Prayer. The poet has lyric gifts, delicately demonstrated in "October," but does fine narratives too. The title poem, which opens the collection, recounts with charm what friends do when the water in their weekend cabin is cut off. Everyday scenes, especially those inspired, apparently, by the death of Stone's wife, find simple expressions to suggest their deep importance. The world of illness and its remedies is visible, though not intrusive; "Transplant," a sonnet, is set in an operating room. The brief "Elegy and Affirmation" intertwines science and love; by both, "we touch the body of the world."

A short series centered around Merton College, Oxford, where the poet resided at one time, includes an ekphrastic poem, "The Forest Fire," inspired by Piero di Cosimo's canvas in the Ashmolean; Stone composed his verses as a counterpart to lines by Derek Mahon on a painting displayed opposite. Music has its place in the series "Canticles of Time," commissioned for the centennial celebration (1990) of Millsaps and set to music by Jones as a choral symphony.

The work consists of a prologue and three parts bearing Latin names, "Scio," "Credo," "Gaudeado," the latter again recalling Brahms. Poetry itself receives attention in the "Trenta-Sei for John Ciardi," which pays homage to art and practitioner alike by illustrating gracefully a form Ciardi developed.

Music from Apartment 8: New and Selected Poems (2004) presents forty pages of new poetry and generous selections from previous books. Like Stone's earlier poems, the new work is amiable. It reflects the activities, habits, and beliefs of the poet in his sixties. Seven poems, set in "Serenity Gardens," an assisted-living establishment, depict the life there of an old woman (clearly his mother) who lives in unit 8 and her interactions with her son—a particular kind of domesticity. A bit of plot line offers interest. Those who visit the elderly recognize the setting. A second group of poems consists of poetic reports from a journey to the Near East. As a physician, the speaker assists fellow-travelers ill and injured; as a poet, he attempts to grasp what time and history may mean. Without heavy-handed exoticism, the poems suggest well how the ruins of Baalbek and Petra may strike a Westerner. In "Mount Sinai Chasing the Sun," "Already, camels are kneeling in the courtyard / like islands surfaced from the sand." In "Looking for the Pal Theater," from the third group of poems, the writer speaks directly of his art: "Poetry consists less of finding / what you set out to find, than in learning to live / with what you've stumbled across."

This observation sheds light on Stone's work, as it confronts clearly both body and mind, viewed as accidents of fate, in the world. His intelligent and imaginative renderings of experience are a significant contribution to poetry in Mississippi and America.

NATASHA TRETHEWEY

Natasha Trethewey, born in Gulfport in 1966, has had an important impact on poetry in the United States. From *Domestic Work* (2000) to *Thrall* (2015), she has created not only individual poems of high quality but also organically unified collections. "Each poem is trying to connect to the others to create a whole. Each is like a separate answer and they're all necessary. And if you take out one of them, there's going to be a blank space" (Kaplan 69).

Trethewey's art derives from suffering and hardship, including living on the margins as biracial. Her father, Eric Trethewey (1943–2014), a Canadian, and her mother, Gwendolyn Turnbough, who met in Kentucky, married in Ohio when interracial marriage was still illegal in the South. They settled in Gulfport, Gwendolyn's home city. Before Natasha started school, her parents divorced, and she was taken by her mother to Decatur, Georgia. She spent her summers with her grandmother in Gulfport, or in New Orleans with her father, who was studying for his MA in English at the University of New Orleans and then his PhD at Tulane. Following his studies, he joined the faculty of Hollins University, where he had a distinguished career as a teacher and poet.

In 1985, when Trethewey was nineteen years old, her mother was murdered by Joel Grimmette, her second husband, whom she had divorced. Her step-brother was imprisoned for cocaine trafficking. After the murder she began writing poetry. "I had some things to make sense of—experiences from my past, as well as a collective past, that I needed to grapple with" (Rowell 405). She did not turn to religion; as a girl, she had spent little time in church. "I am not a religious woman," she remarked, conceding, however, that "much of my thinking comes to me in the language of ceremony . . ." (*Beyond Katrina* 64).

After earning a bachelor's degree in social work (her mother's field) from the University of Georgia, Trethewey chose literature, earning a master's in English from Hollins, where among her teachers were her father and her stepmother, poet Katherine Soniat. She subsequently took an MFA from the University of Massachusetts (1995). She was hired by Auburn University in 1997, then became director of the Creative Writing Program at Emory University. Currently, she teaches at Northwestern University, where her husband, Brett Gadsden, is associate professor in the Department of History. She has given courses also at the Breadloaf Writers' Conference.

Domestic Work was chosen by then US poet laureate Rita Dove for the initial Cave Canem Poetry Prize, given for the best first collection of poems by an African American. It also received an award from the Southern Regional Council and University of Georgia Libraries. *Bellocq's Ophelia* was named a 2003 Notable Book by the American Library Association and was a finalist for the Academy of American Poets' James Laughlin and Lenore Marshall prizes. In 2007 Trethewey won the Pulitzer Prize for *Native Guard* (2006). Her three first books all won the Poetry Prize from the Mississippi Institute of Arts and Letters. In 2012 she was appointed US poet laureate (two terms) and simultaneously Mississippi's poet laureate. The librarian of Congress, James H. Billington, commented, "Her poems dig beneath the surface of history—personal or communal, from childhood or from a century ago—to explore the human struggles that we all face." Although race enters into Trethewey's work, she "asserts that she is not a race poet; rather she is a poet of history" (McHaney 153). "People say I'm writing about race. But, no. I'm writing about loss, history, and what's forgotten.... If I didn't have blackness, people would go to the next thing ... to focus on, but blackness just stands out here like the eight-foot gorilla in the room" (Kaplan 74). She sees herself as "the quintessential southern writer! Quintessentially American too! Geography is fate. Of all the kinds of fate swirling around my very being, this place in which I was born and this particular historical moment matter deeply" (Turner, "Southern Crossings"). She writes, she said, with *sangfroid*; others agree. It is this unflinching look at her own life and American history that has brought her high honors.

Katherine Henninger, for instance, observed that the "domestic work" performed by Trethewey's book of that title established a "familial and African American communal base" to undergird her writing (59). Not that Trethewey planned it all ahead, but "each collection builds and reflects back upon the others in terms of structure, theme, and imagery." While dedicated to her father, *Domestic Work* speaks especially to the lives of her African American grandmother, Leretta Dixon Turnbough, and many other black women. As Dove says in her introduction, "The world of Natasha Trethewey's poetry is peopled with working-class African Americans. Although family members put in an appearance here and there, Trethewey resists the lure of autobiography and is careful to avoid such a narrow identification, weaving no less than a tapestry of ancestors" (xi).

All Trethewey's poetry collections include ekphrastic poems. Part I of *Domestic Work*, in four parts, references photographs in nearly every poem, primarily in free verse, excepting sonnets, one Shakespearean, two unrhymed. "Gesture of a Woman-in-Process" is labeled *"from a photograph, 1902."* In five free-verse tercets, Trethewey describes "clotheslines sagged with linens, / a patch of greens and yam, / buckets of peas for shelling"—all suggestive of the seemingly endless labor of domestics. The title figure stands out because even in the photograph she "won't be still," "her hands circling, / the white blur of her apron still in motion."

Part I ends with "Three Photographs," poems based on work by Clifton Johnson, a white Massachusetts photographer who worked in the South in the early twentieth century. Trethewey likes to take the "negative aspect" from photographs—what is hinted at but not captured, for instance, the "white blur." In *"Daybook April 1901,"* there's a suggestion of the deft, condescending manipulation of black subjects, another negative vein. "And yet, / they make such good subjects. / Always easy to pose...." Furthermore, although the blacks are pictured in an idyllic setting with an arbor, flowers, and trees, the poem ends sarcastically: "How fortunate still / to have found them here / instead of farther along." She adds that the old cemetery has neither new graves—it is full already—nor, consequently, flowers.

Part II, "Domestic Work" is dedicated to her grandmother Turnbough. The title poem bears the date 1937. Dates, Trethewey observed, "provide a very important context for the poem that should point readers to that historical moment that exists outside of the poem" (Kaplan 68). The poem contrasts the work of a domestic cleaning others' houses with her time at home on Sunday mornings, joyously *hers*. She has her church clothes starched and a record going while there are rhythmic "neck bones / bumping in the pot, a choir / of clothes clapping on the line." "This free-verse poem dances with rhythm and refrain" (Warren 78).

Part III includes "Cameo," the title of which refers both to a mother's cameo necklace and the cameo appearance that she makes as she watches her own mother dress. Not all is lovely. "My mother would tie on a black velvet ribbon / at the back of her neck, so tight it seemed to hold / her together, the fine bones of her neck in place." The poem ends with a suggestion of violence: "In the front, a cameo pressing into the hollow / of her throat, hard enough to bruise."

Trethewey examines her double racial identity in "Flounder" and "White Lies." In "Flounder," the persona and her Aunt Sugar are out fishing. *"A flounder, she said, and you can tell / 'cause one of its sides is black / The other side is white."*

The poem ends as the fish "flip-flop, / switch sides with every jump." "White Lies" concerns "passing" (as white). The first stanza summarizes the deception: "The lies I could tell, / when I was growing up / light-bright, near-white / high-yellow, red-boned / in a *black* place, / were just *white* lies [italics added]." A mother, learning what her daughter has done, washes out her mouth with Ivory soap. Her point is not understood. "Believing her, I swallowed suds / thinking they'd work / from the inside out."

Part IV includes several poems about memory. The last, "Limen," which Warren calls an "elegy for the deceased mother" (80), features a woodpecker's persistent hammering. The woodpecker is "hard at his task"; his body is "a hinge, a door knocker / to the cluttered house of memory in which / I can almost see my mother's face." Although the persona "almost" sees her mother "hanging wet sheets on the line," the next stanza discloses "a thin white screen between us." That is the limen, the threshold between the living and the dead.

Bellocq's Ophelia, like *Domestic Work*, centers on women with few choices. The voices are those of biracial prostitutes whom E. J. Bellocq photographed between 1910 and 1912 in Storyville, New Orleans. (The figure of Bellocq appears in several novels and Louis Malle's 1978 motion picture, *Pretty Baby*, filmed in New Orleans.) Trethewey said, "I learned a lot about the balance of historical facts and prosody during that time. I read not only history . . . but also theory. This got me into trouble. . . . When revising, I . . . focused on the imagery . . ." (quoted in Kaplan 67). The poems are couched as letters, diary entries, conversations, portraits, and vignettes. They are organized in three parts and an opening poem, separate, based on a photograph circa 1912.

This initial poem contrasts John Everett Millais's painting of Shakespeare's Ophelia with one of Bellocq's photographs. Millais's figure is face upward in a pond, "her palms curling open / as if she's just said, *Take me*." Bellocq's version has "this other / Ophelia, nameless inmate in Storyville, / naked, her nipples offered up hard with cold." Bellocq's figure expresses a dare, "her body limp as dead Ophelia's, / her lips poised to open, to speak." Both express the vulnerability captured in Toni Morrison's quotation used as an epigraph: "She had nothing to fall back on; not maleness, not whiteness, not ladyhood, not anything. And out of the profound desolation of her reality she may well have invented herself." Trethewey conjectures that Millais's Ophelia—or at least the model—"imagin[es] fish / tangling in her hair or nibbling a dark mole / raised upon her white skin." The hard nipples of Bellocq's woman echo this image. The greatest contrast between the two is, of course, that Bellocq's model is real, not invented, and is spunkier. A second epigraph, from Susan Sontag, reads: "Nevertheless, the camera's rendering of reality must always hide more than it discloses."

Part I is a single poem, epistolary. The second poem of part II, likewise epistolary, is a letter from Ophelia to a friend, "Constance Wright"—not a prostitute, but a woman living appropriately on "Schoolhouse Road," both *constant* and *right* in behavior. The letter explains why she has resorted to prostitution—she was broke and hungry when "Countess P—, / an elegant businesswoman . . . offered / me a place in her house." Redesigned by the madam, trained how to walk, how to behave, and what to say, Ophelia ultimately becomes a piece of furniture: "I could, / if so desired, pose still as a statue for hours, / a glass or a pair of boots propped upon my back." Trethewey emphasizes the sexuality and sensuousness that Ophelia must cultivate, whereas she would like to erase herself and become nothing—"free in the white space of forgetting" (a characteristic image for the poet) (24). Ophelia has become interested in photography, owing to the visits of Bellocq, who appears as a character. It is the only venture that allows her to be actively creative. In "September 1911" she learns "the way the camera can dissect / the body"; "it can also make the flesh glow / as if the soul's been caught." The poem captures the reflecting light of the images in the terms *shimmering, shines, iridescent, glittering, sparkle,* and *glow.* It is one of few hopeful poems, expressing Ophelia's creativity and independence.

The closing poem of part II, in couplets, "Photograph of a Bawd Drinking Raleigh Rye," is based on a Bellocq photograph circa 1912. The first couplet captures movement, akin to the "white blur of her apron" in "Gesture of a Woman-in-Process." Here, "the glass in her hand is the only thing moving— / too fast for the camera—caught in the blur of motion." The "bawd" is raising the glass in a toast, but beside her are a clock, an ebony statuette of a woman, the bottle of rye, shaped like a woman's "slender torso / and round hips," and women in paintings, photographs, and carved in relief. "It's easy to see this is all about desire, / how it recurs—each time you look, it's the same moment, / the hands of the clock still locked at high noon." The images suggest the prostitutes' imprisonment in time.

Part III, "Storyville Diary," includes ten unrhymed sonnets and a final ekphrastic "Vignette." They suggest the kinship of photography and life—how the photographic plates are fragile and can be scratched, like a woman's chest. As Sontag's phrase quoted above indicates, photographs may miss interior, subtle dimensions. The first sonnet, "Naming," concerns a journey. The speaker needs "new words to mark this journey / like the naming of a child." Any optimism vanishes abruptly: "Once, my mother pushed me toward / a white man in our front room. *Your father,* / she whispered. *He's the one that name you, girl.*" The next sonnet, "Father," indicates a poisoned relationship. The persona fears the man even though he brings gifts, because he examines her fingernails, ears, and teeth as if she were an animal. She recites her lessons for him, and when she makes errors, he stops her. She wants him to believe that she is smart, "not the wild / pickaninny roaming the fields, barefoot." Moreover, she fears that there will be a "day a man / enters my room both customer and father." In "Bellocq," the speaker calls the photographer "Papá Bellocq," and notes how he is in charge: "In my room / everything's a prop for his composition." The final sonnet shows that Ophelia recognizes Bellocq's dominance: "I'm not so foolish / that I don't know this photograph *we* make / will bear the stamp of his name, not mine."

"Vignette" refers to the cover photograph of *Bellocq's Ophelia*, a pose: "She wears / white, a rhinestone choker, fur, / her dark crown of hair—an elegant image, / one she might send her mother." Her eyes give her away, however; mentally, she is far removed from the scene. She pictures a sideshow contortionist seen in childhood as well as her own "shallow breath." And "now as she realizes / that it must have been harder every year, / that the contortionist, too, must have ached / each night in his tent." Her brow is furrowed "as she looks out to the left, past all of them," removing herself from objectification. "Imagine her a moment later—after the flash / blinded—stepping out / of the frame, wide-eyed, into her life."

Native Guard, Trethewey's Pulitzer-winning collection, is a rich mixture of history, concerned with correcting historical omissions, and personal record, concerned with recalling her murdered mother, to whose memory the book is dedicated. "Theories of Time and Space," the opening poem, looks at the two dimensions in connection with remembrance. "You can get there from here though / there's no going home." Each moment one is transformed into someone new, someplace new. As a person defined by Mississippi in many ways, Trethewey asks readers to "head south on Mississippi 49": "Follow this / to its natural conclusion—dead end." Then one is "at the coast, the pier at Gulfport," to "board the boat for Ship Island." At boarding, one's photograph is taken. "The photograph—who you *were*— / will be waiting when you return" (italics added)—revealing presumably a changed character. Time and space shift momentarily, but people change quickly and emphatically.

The following poems, autobiographic, explore through the persona a mother's life and murder. "The Southern Crescent" recounts three train rides. The first is the mother's trip in 1959 to see her own father, who does not appear. The second is the poet's own, east from Gulfport, to see *her* father—"that trip, too, gone wrong." In the third, mother and daughter are "sure we can leave home, bound only / for whatever awaits us." The poem ends ominously as "my mother's face appears, clearer now / as evening comes on, dark and certain." "Photograph: Ice Storm, 1971" captures the cold brutality of the mother's second husband. The fierceness of the storm and its "rough edge of beauty" drive people inside. The back of the photograph bears purportedly the names of those pictured and the date; however, why is there "nothing / of what's inside—mother, stepfather's fist?" The marriage, like the icy scene, is fraught with danger: "power lines down, food rotting / in the refrigerator, while outside / the landscape glistens beneath a glaze / of ice."

Among the most brutal poems is the unrhymed sonnet "What Is Evidence?" which reveals unflinchingly the stepfather's cruelty, seen in the woman's "fleeting bruises she'd cover / with makeup, a dark patch as if imprint / of a scope she'd pressed her eye too close to, / looking for a way out." Either "the teeth she wore in place of her own, or / the official document" is evidence of mistreatment. The document could be a medical report of injuries or the death certificate. The "evidence" finally becomes "only the landscape of her body—splintered / clavicle, pierced temporal—her thin bones / settling a bit each day, the way all things do." "Myth," the penultimate poem of Part I, is clever, with palindromic features. It returns to the persona's painful memories—"I was asleep while you were dying"—and perpetuates the mother's existence: "The Erebus I keep you in, still trying / not to let go. You'll be dead again tomorrow, / but in dreams you live." Facing "again and again, this constant forsaking" and trying to accept the loss—"as if you slipped through some rift"—the persona mythologizes her mother.

Part II shifts to recognition of what Mississippi means. In "Pilgrimage" the persona has traveled to Vicksburg for the spring pilgrimage. On Confederate Avenue, the dead Confederates stand in marble, but the ground is "hollowed by a web of caves." Indeed, "this whole city is a grave," but every spring the "living come to mingle / with the dead." Trethewey adds, "The ghost of history lies down beside me, / rolls over, pins me beneath a heavy arm." "Scenes from a Documentary History of Mississippi" comprises "King Cotton, 1907," "Flood of 1927," and two other poems.

An irregular corona sonnet sequence, "Native Guard," follows. The speaker is a fictional slave from Ascension Parish, Louisiana, who keeps a journal, starting November 1862. Former slaves in the Union Army are in "supply units ... *nigger work*," he notes ("December 1862"). "January 1863" describes a man's back, "the scars, crosshatched / like the lines in this journal." Ironically, the duty of these "Native Guards" is to "keep / white men as prisoners—rebel soldiers, / would-be masters." The blacks write letters for illiterate white Confederates. In "June 1863" word comes of the "colored troops, dead / on the battlefield at Port Hudson," abandoned by General Banks, who "was heard to say *I have / no dead there*," leaving bodies unclaimed and rotting on the field. The final section, "1865," notes what "must be accounted for": slaughter under a white flag, a black massacre at Fort Pillow, and the name "Corps d'Afrique, taking the word *native* from our claim." The conclusion reemphasizes Trethewey's mission: making sure that the past is remembered, that "truth be told."

A series of later poems synthesizes the personal and historical themes in *Native Guard*. "Miscegenation" deals, through a persona, with Trethewey's identity. "In 1965 my parents broke two laws of Mississippi; / they went to Ohio to marry, returned to Mississippi." She compares herself with Faulkner's biracial Joe Christmas, but says, "I know more than Joe Christmas did." *Natasha*, for instance, "means *Christmas child*, even in Mississippi." "Southern History" depicts a high school history teacher who says blacks were happier as slaves, since they were cared for; *Gone with the Wind* is accurate. "No one / raised a hand, disagreed. Not even me," says the speaker. The leitmotiv of silence, which runs through Trethewey's poetry, reappears in "Southern Gothic." The persona pictures herself and her parents in 1970, "quiet / in the language of blood." She's the precocious child, always asking, "Why?" Other children call her names: "peckerwood," "nigger lover," "half-breed," "zebra"—"words that take shape / outside us." But "my mother cannot answer, her mouth closed, a gesture / toward her future: cold lips stitched shut." In "Elegy for the Native Guards," on a plaque placed by the Daughters of the Confederacy there are "no names carved for the Native Guards— / 2nd Regiment, Union men, black phalanx."

In the final poem "South," the persona returns to the "dialectic of dark / and light" that is Mississippi. Visiting the "country battlefield / where colored troops fought and died," she sees "roads, buildings, and monuments / . . . named to honor the Confederacy," and acknowledges her identity, given by the state: "I return / to Mississippi, state that made a crime / of me—mulatto, half-breed—native / in my native land, this place they'll bury me." She acts as a "Native Guard," preserving that truth in the state where she was born, where her mother died, and where the "Native Guard" was not properly honored.

Trethewey's fourth collection, *Thrall*, reintroduces her central themes, including paternity. While her mother is present—"a dark Madonna" ("Calling")—the book is dedicated *to* her father (not *for*, unlike *Domestic Work*). Despite that dedication, the readings they gave together, and photographs showing her smiling at him, the book bespeaks a fraught relationship (less awful, perhaps, than Sylvia Plath's with her father, but not serene). Two epigraphs point to Trethewey's struggle to achieve forgiveness. "What is love? One name for it is knowledge" (Robert Penn Warren); "After such knowledge, what forgiveness?" (T. S. Eliot). The opening poem, "Elegy," is inscribed "For my father." The persona pictures a salmon-fishing expedition. Her father wades into deep water, growing "heavier with that defeat." First, he imitates the guide's casting; then he tries "to find / that perfect arc, flight of an insect." In contrast, she reels in "two small trout we could not keep." She observes, "Your daughter. / I was that ruthless. What does it matter / if I tell you I *learned* to be?" The next lines reveal much: "You kept casting / your line, and when it did not come back / empty, it was tangled with mine."

"Miracle of the Black Leg" is based on a painting of the physician-saints Cosmas and Damian and the miracle transplant—black donor, white recipient—that they performed, according to legend. The poem emphasizes the subservience of black to white: "One man rendered expendable, the other worthy / of this sacrifice." "Taxonomy" examines various terms for racial distinctions. Trethewey plays with the word *taint*: "Call it the *taint*—as in / T'aint one and t'aint the other." The triptych of mother, father, and child is "in thrall to a word." In "Knowledge," labeled "After a chalk drawing by J. H. Hasselhorst, 1864," four men examine "the ideal female body." One "peers down as if / enthralled, his fist on a stack of books." Another makes an incision on the dead woman, "the first cut, / a delicate wounding; and yet how easily / the anatomist's blade opens a place in me." In these lines the speaker quotes Eric Trethewey, "Each learned man is my father / and I hear, again, his words—*I study / my crossbreed child*—misnomer." The poem ends as "his scalpel in hand like a pen / [is] poised above me, aimed straight for my heart."

"Siren" clarifies the persona's situation. She is in a dream, strapped to her seat, while her father (masked as Odysseus) is "luring me / to a past that never was." That is the "treachery of nostalgia." Listening to her father's voice, she says, "I must be the captive listener / cleaving to his words. I must be / singing this song to myself." In "Geography" and "*Torna Atrás*" the persona intimates the great harm her father has done. Finally, in "Bird in the House," she notes, "Forgive me, Father, that I brought to that house / my grief. You will not recall telling me / you could not understand my loss, not until / your own mother died." He is shown turning his back on a grave; "I saw you / flatten the mound, erasing it into the dirt."

By an analogy with painting, the title poem (placed late) suggests again the emotional relationship between father and daughter. "I kept my canvases secret / hidden"—until the example of Velázquez liberates the subject, decreeing "unto me / myself." In "Enlightenment," the persona and her father consider Jefferson's relationship with his slave Sally Hemings. Someone asks, "*How white was she? . . .* / as if to name what made her worthy / of Jefferson's attentions: a near-white, / quadroon mistress, not a plain black slave." Uncomfortable with this reply, the poet-persona whispers to her father that she'll go elsewhere, summing up their relationship: "When he laughs, I know he's grateful / I've made a joke of it, this history / that links us—white father, black daughter— / even as it renders us other to each other."

Can there be, she had asked obliquely, forgiveness and love? It seems not. Moving toward independence in her art, she has lost a great deal; but the "elegy" to her father puts an end to her enthrallment.

MARGARET WALKER

Margaret Walker (1915–98), known sometimes by her married name, Alexander, is an important figure in the African American poetry of what she called "My Century." While, appropriately, she entitled her first book *For My People*—following a cultural instinct that many other writers have obeyed—she is not a poet merely for a group, however important it is. Her work belongs to American literature as a whole, and particularly southern literature. "My roots are deep in southern life. . . . I was sired and weaned in a tropic world" ("Sorrow Home," *This Is My Century: New and Collected Poems* 12). (All Walker quotations here are from that volume, containing "one hundred of my best poems selected from a possible thousand" [xi].) "The South is my home, and my accommodation to this South—whether real or imagined (mythic and legendary), violent or non-violent—is the subject and source of all my poetry" (xvii). Among Walker's honors were a National Endowment for the Humanities fellowship (1972), a three-year fellowship from the Lyndhurst Foundation (1989–92), and the National Book Award for Lifetime Achievement. In addition, she was honored locally and received several honorary degrees.

Walker was born in Birmingham, Alabama. When she was five years of age her family moved to Meridian, Mississippi. After returning to Birmingham, the family subsequently went to New Orleans, where she spent her girlhood from age ten. When later she went north, she did not feel at home, despite academic success and friendships. She settled in Mississippi in 1949 and identified herself most closely with that state. She died of cancer, having undergone radiation but rejecting surgery; she was in Chicago, with a daughter.

Walker was the first child of an enterprising Jamaican—teacher, Methodist minister, tailor—and a music teacher. If one reads "Epitaph for My Father" as factual, he came from a family of learning, where books were honored. As a young man, he aspired to study in England; the best he could do was reach Mobile on a visitor's visa. He found the South, with its Jim Crow laws and associated mores, unpleasantly foreign. But he remained, met and married the woman who became Walker's mother, and was nationalized. Both parents taught at small colleges. Money was often in short supply; yet the husband wanted his wife and children to have goods of high quality, and he bought books.

Walker's parents influenced her in productive ways, promoting a solid acquaintance with the Bible, appreciation of rhythm, and poetry, to which she was attracted from an early age. Her liking for the Bible and her religious beliefs (including that in the afterlife) remained with her. While her father called her girlish enthusiasm for verse an urge of puberty, he must have recognized her intellect, which was close to his. She called herself "a strange creature with ... a man's mind in a woman's body" (Graham, *Conversations* vii). He gave her a datebook in which to record her writing. She did so, meticulously. His good advice on images, rhythm, and meaning had lasting results. Later, he expressed the wish that her poetry were more religious; she replied, "It can't be what I'm not" ("Epitaph for My Father").

In New Orleans, Walker attended the segregated Gilbert Academy, where a white teacher she calls Miss Fluke encouraged her. She matriculated at New Orleans University, where both her parents taught (since absorbed into Dillard). Langston Hughes, a visitor, said that the girl should get out of the South so that she could develop into a writer. Her first essay, "What Is to Become of Us?" appeared in 1932 in *Our Youth*, a New Orleans magazine. That year, at age seventeen, she enrolled in Northwestern University, from which both Miss Fluke and her father had graduated. There she had two influential teachers, W. E. B. Du Bois and Edward Buell Hungerford. In Hungerford's writing class, during her senior year, she worked on poetry (including a long poem about Jean Lafitte) and short fiction and also began the novel that became *Jubilee* (1966), which won a Houghton Mifflin literary award and had enormous sales. It is an imaginative account of her great-grandmother's life from the antebellum period, through the war, to Reconstruction. Hungerford's thorough instruction in prosody gave her a solid foundation for writing verse. Arguing on her behalf against those opposed to admitting a black woman into the Poetry Society of America, he persuaded the Northwestern chapter to elect her to membership.

Following graduation (1935) with a BA in English, and some months of unemployment, Walker was hired by the WPA Chicago Writers' Project, with which Gwendolyn Brooks, Frank Yerby, and Richard Wright were involved. Wright's talent and discipline made a favorable impression on her. Their friendship did not last long, however; the differences in their background were, it seems from his statements, too great. While some later commentators asserted she was in love with him, she denied it vigorously. She was among those who constituted the South Side Writers' Group. Having heard Harriet Monroe read, she visited the office of *Poetry*, where she met the editor, George Dillon. He published her poem "For My People." Walker had done translations from German Romantic poets and knew French also. Dillon urged her to read the French symbolists and postsymbolists, such as Paul Valéry, whose works furnished an important complement to her wide reading of English Romantics and American writers, particularly women and blacks.

In 1939 Walker enrolled in the University of Iowa, where she studied with Paul Engle, who encouraged her to try the ballad form. In 1940 she received her MA degree there. (Much later she returned to Iowa and earned her doctorate, in 1965.) Her MA thesis, consisting of twenty-six poems, became *For My People*. On the third submission, having been rejected previously, it won the Yale Younger Poets Award and was published by Yale. Stephen Vincent Benét, with whom Walker had corresponded, furnished the foreword. From 1941 until 1949 she taught at colleges in West Virginia and North Carolina. In 1943 she was invited to the Yaddo colony. That year she met her husband, a disabled veteran in poor health. They were married for thirty-seven years and had four children. She joined the faculty of Jackson State in 1949 and remained until her early retirement in 1968. To judge from *How I Wrote Jubilee*, she was miserable there, mistreated, as she viewed it, by male administrators. Her life "had not been pleasant for a single day" (quoted in Watkins 183). Nonetheless, after retiring she was able to create there an institute for the study of the history, life and culture of black people, now the Margaret Walker Alexander National Research Center.

Thenceforth her time and efforts were devoted to writing, publishing, speaking, and organizing on behalf of African Americans. Trudier Harris pointed out, however, that she had never been able to inspire young writers as Gwendolyn Brooks could, and that, by the late 1960s and 1970s "she was looked upon as one whose achievements were in the past, someone who had earned respect but to whom no undue attention need be given" (Rubin et al. 567). She carried on many projects even though she suffered from diabetes and its debilitating effects. Year after year she went on lecture tours, addressed college audiences, and appeared at dinners, meetings, dedications, and symposia. At the 1984 NAACP convention, she stated that "America is racist to the core." She viewed her race as naturally sensitive, "a feeling people, a people of soul, numinous." Michael Jackson she viewed as a genius. "Most black people are creative" (quoted in Yates 124–25).

Walker became embroiled in two controversies involving well known figures. In 1977, she filed suit against Alex Haley, the author of *Roots*, for plagiarizing her novel *Jubilee*; the judgment went against her. In the 1980s she carried on a lengthy battle with Wright's widow, Ellen, who, having seen an early announcement of Walker's biography *Richard Wright: Daemonic Genius* (1988), objected to Walker's plan to use excerpts from her own diary and letters Wright had sent her in the 1930s. Ellen demanded, futilely, to review the manuscript. When, after the book appeared, the widow sued, the US Court of Appeals ruled in Wright's favor.

Characteristics of Walker's writing have invited comparison with that of Whitman, Carl Sandburg, Edgar Lee Masters, and Robinson Jeffers. But the features were, she said, "not derived from these poets but rather from a lifetime of reading"—the Bible, which she taught at her church and as literature at Jackson State; Eastern works such as *Gilgamesh*, the *Bhagavad-Gītā*; and the African epic *Sundiata*, based on oral tradition and recorded by the French in the late nineteenth and early twentieth century (*This Is My Century* xvi–xvii). She uses a long line like Whitman's, contrasted with a shorter one. Despite the models of French symbolists and postsymbolists, she does not work by implication or suggestion; everything is stated directly, intended to catch, and hold, attention.

Walker uses both free verse and conventional forms such as ballads and unrhymed or rhymed sonnets (examples are "Childhood" and "Whores"). Striking ballads are "Poppa Chicken" and "Molly Means"; the latter conveys popular black speech by means of rough phonetic spellings. Her poems display oddities of capitalization ("DEAR Are the Names That Charmed Me in My Youth"—note also the inversion) and irregular left-hand margins ("For Owen Dodson, 1983"). Numerous poems, in sections, extend over three, four, or five pages. Frequently, as in "Money, Honey, Money," the verse includes echoing sounds, words, or whole lines. The two poems bearing the word *litany* in their titles are not the only ones built on repetition. Always her lines have good beat. "Ode on the Occasion of the Inauguration of the Sixth President of Jackson State College" begins in blank verse: "Give me again the flaming torch of truth / that burned before the altars of our gods; / the spirit nascent, sleeping on the breasts / of black men born to die on foreign shores." The following lines give way to looser verse, though not uncontrolled: "Dark were the years / that spawned three centuries of toil and trouble / deep in this southern land. . . ."

A favorite form is a long poem constituted by multiphrase, sometimes multisentence units, where lines wrap around, recalling Bible verses. Printed, such lines look like stanzas. They invite lyrical expansion: "I want my rest unbroken in the fields of southern earth, freedom to watch the corn wave silver in the sun" ("Southern Song"). A beautiful lyric is "October Journey": "I want to tell you what hills are like in October / when colors gush down mountainsides / and little streams are freighted with a caravan of leaves. / I want to tell you how they blush and turn in fiery shame and joy." Sometimes Walker uses rhyme, as in "Harriet Tubman." The voice of an abusive overseer observes. "This is slavery, Harriet, / Bend beneath the lash; / This is Maryland, Harriet, / Bow to poor white trash."

Walker viewed poetry as a tool for change, even as she loved the genre for itself. She reminded her "people" that "mills of oppression grind songs of the poor" ("The Spirituals"). "We Have Been Believers" begins by rehearsing, in quasi-biblical language, blacks' goodwill, even their good-natured naiveté, and their contributions to the white world. "We have been believers believing in the mercy of our masters and the beauty of our brothers. . . . // Neither the slaves' whip nor the lynchers' rope nor the bayonet could kill our black belief. // We have been believers yielding substance for the world." Changing tone and temporal orientation, the poem then pivots: "We have been believers believing in our burdens and our demigods too long. . . . The long-suffering arise, and our fists bleed against the bars with a strange insistency." As in spirituals, the bondage of blacks in America is assimilated to the Egyptian and Babylonian captivity of the Israelites; Israel's freeing through divine agency parallels the changes issuing from the Emancipation Proclamation and the southern defeat.

Yet the *Plessy v. Ferguson* decision, with its unforeseen and unfortunate consequences, created disappointments that endured well into the twentieth century. Following World War II, Walker's indignation grew and her poetry acquired a sense of urgency. *Prophets for a New Day* (1970), her second book, deals, often using biblical rhetoric, with sit-ins and marches and African American heroes and martyrs of the 1960s. Old Testament prophets join historical and contemporary figures. "The Ballad of the Free" picks out Toussaint L'Ouverture, Nat Turner, and John Brown. "On Police Brutality," "For Malcolm X," and "Micah (In Memory of Medgar Evers of Mississippi)," as well as the title poem, indicate clearly the reforming intention of Walker's collection, marked also by a strong vein of lamentation. "Hosea," a companion piece of "Micah," celebrates, even as it laments, a prisoner in jail "among the bayous and secretly sinister houses of Plaquemine" (Louisiana).

Later poems collected in *This Is My Century* pursue these veins. In "I Hear a Rumbling," built on sound and thematic echoes, *earthquake* stands for human dissatisfaction and the unrest of Native Americans, Chicanos, blacks, and other oppressed. From anticipating such a quake—called "Dies Irae" in the following poem—to inviting it, is a very small step. "Giants of My Century" consists of stanzas on Einstein, Freud, Marx, Kierkegaard, and Du Bois. "Five Black Men" retraces by light touches the impact of Douglass, Du Bois, Martin Luther King Jr., Marcus Garvey, and Malcolm X.

Few poems in *Prophets for a New Day* have memorable stanzas, but they are, as wholes, coherent and striking. Diction such as "crying," "hear the words of ...," "they are full of deceit" remains in the listener's ear and the reader's eye. Biblical figures and motifs from Moses to the Book of Revelation enrich the verse. Abstract nouns, frequent, may be capitalized, as in this characterization of the Beast: "He is War and Famine and Pestilence / He is Death and Destruction and Trouble" ("Prophets for a New Day"). Although clearly pertinent to the oppression of the black race in modern times, these substantives acquire by the majuscule and the context a timeless character; they seem to be *beside* history, not a part of it, and expectations of remedy are feeble. The "Word of the Lord," as spoken by Amos, does include a vision of deliverance, but not the particular message of the New Testament.

Walker's example, as an African American woman poet, is important. "I am a Black woman / and I hold my head up high" ("My Truth and My Flame"). Yet she cannot be taken as a radical feminist; she admired her father too much for her to turn against men. Had she been a man, she wrote, she might have been a preacher, and autonomous, like him ("Epitaph for My Father"). Instead, she was connected to others; "I belong to all the people I have met, / Am part of them, am molded by the throng...." The phrasing reminds one of Tennyson's "Ulysses" (except he emphasized all that he had *seen*) as well as Whitman. She, like him, put her convictions into poetry.

JERRY W. WARD JR.

Born in 1943, Jerry W. (Washington) Ward Jr. is known widely as an activist and a scholar on Richard Wright and African American topics. But he is also a poet; and his poetry is connected to his activism. *Fractal Song: Poems* appeared in 2016. He has edited several important anthologies, including *Black Southern Voices* (1992), and has been an important figure in letters in both Mississippi and Louisiana.

Ward was born in Washington, DC, but when he was six his family moved to Mississippi. "Son to Father, with Love / Graveside Prayer" complains of lack of affection and abandon, when the father-figure dies, but acknowledges resemblance between him and the speaker. Ward attended high schools in Biloxi and Moss Point. Following his junior year, he was able to enroll in Tougaloo College, where he earned a BA in mathematics (1964). That year, he published poems in two Tougaloo publications; his literary career had begun. Two years later he received a master's degree from the Illinois Institute of Technology. He joined the faculty at Tougaloo, where he became the Lawrence Durgin Professor of Literature. There, he mentored numerous students who now belong to the Mississippi literary community. From 1973 on his poems appeared in national publications. In 1978 he received his PhD in English at the University of Virginia. In 2003 he moved to New Orleans as distinguished professor of English and African American world studies at Dillard University. A refugee from Katrina, he published *The Katrina Papers: A Journal of Trauma and Recovery*. In 2011 the Chinese Ministry of Education selected him to participate in a teaching program at Central China Normal University in Wuhan.

Ward was associated with BLKARTSSOUTH in New Orleans, an outgrowth of the Free Southern Theater, the aim of which was to develop theatrical arts in the South and use drama as a tool for social reform. Founded at Tougaloo in 1963, it moved to New Orleans in 1965. Originally including white members, it shortly became exclusively black. Among Ward's BLKARTSSOUTH colleagues were Tom Dent, Kalamu ya Salaam, and Quo Vadis Gex Breaux, to whom he dedicated a poem. He was also a founding member of Jackson Writers' Workshop. He wrote the introduction to a new edition of Wright's *Black Boy* (1992) and coedited *The Richard Wright Encyclopedia* and *The Cambridge History of African American Literature* (2011). Earlier, he cofounded the *Richard Wright Newsletter*. He was an early member of the Mississippi Cultural Arts Coalition and served on the Mississippi Humanities Council and the state Advisory Committee for the US Commission on Civil Rights. He also worked with John Reese's Black Arts Music Society. From that collaboration came "Jazz to Jackson to John," one of Ward's most noted poems, along with "Don't Be Fourteen (in Mississippi)."

Fractal Song belongs to the literature of commitment and testimony. Shadows of other African American poets appear in allusions and dedications. It is in three parts, "Starts," "Middles," "Ends." They are preceded by "To Those Who Grieve the Death of a Poet," which urges its audience to "struggle." Salaam contributed a prose "postscript," which is followed by a final poem, "Fusion." In slightly unusual language, the postscript echoes preceding expressions of racial commitment, specifying that "there's holiness / in speech, in song." Salaam calls Ward "a striking poet hammering syllables and sounds into graceful lyrics and odes." The title *fractals* (recursive geometric patterns), he says, shows that Ward "is not content with the anecdote or individual achievement; he seeks the truly universal—he wants to understand the cycles of life and the import and impact of collective activity." The postscript properly acknowledges that on a local level Ward has dedicated his life to improving his people's lot. (In a blog, Ward acknowledged Salaam's generosity and brotherliness.)

"Love in a Foreign House," a brief lyric, shows why Salaam is not entirely wrong to call the poems "songs, or perhaps even psalms." They are in free verse, varying from unexceptional lines, often short and in stanzas, to lines cascading down the page, with boldface, all capitals or no capitals. The language is standard or sometimes black vernacular; scattered (and pointed) neologisms include "mississippied." The vocabulary of jazz and blues, and allusions to Billie (Holiday), (Thelonious) Monk, and (Charlie) Parker, pay tribute to the genres. Such devices as word and line repetition, with slashes between words (as Sterling D. Plumpp uses them), and what Salaam calls "syllabled beats of a rhythm master" suggest musical analogies. Rhyme appears in "An April Observation" and elsewhere. Wordplay gives rise to developments such as Kafka / Kaddish / Kaffir and portfolio words such as "troublems" ("Fragility"). Loose connections among semantic elements and images mark some poems, but Ward does not indulge in the surrealists' free association. African American cultures furnish tag lines and references, especially from spirituals, always evocative of the faith and community cohesion of the past, but used antiphrastically, as attacks on white society, as in "All God's people got sold" ("Jazz to Jackson to John," ii).

The mood is that of anger and resentment, both particular and generalized. "Injustice is all" is the refrain in "Footnote 666." "This is not a poem," Ward writes in "Blood and Black Fires." "This is a eulogy for a dead rainbow. . . . // I smell black / blood and fire. . . . // And will the furious flower bloom on / the grave of Michael Brown?" (Furious Flower is a center for black poetry at James Madison University.) Among other key names are those of Trayvon Martin, Bob Kaufman, and Amiri Baraka (LeRoi Jones). Enslavement, from the time of the Pharaohs to America, is always the background. Oil (presumably huge corporations) receives much blame. "Don't Be Fourteen" (and black and male) enumerates the risks young African Americans have run, including, for a first offense, forty-eight years in Parchman (the state prison for men) and castration, torture, and death in the river "as guilt offering to blue-eyed susans." As a response, Ward tells boys to be men; "when white boys ask / why you don't like them, / spit on them / with your mouth closed." "Jazz to Jackson to John" imagines the "genesis" of jazz: "it must have been something like / sheets of sound wrinkled / with riffs and scats, / the aftermath of a fierce night. . . ."

JAMES WHITEHEAD

James (Tillotson) Whitehead (1936–2003), known as Jim, was, according to John Freeman, a former student, "as Mississippi as cornbread and cotton" (Interview). Although born in St. Louis, Missouri, and a longtime resident of Arkansas, he was reared in Jackson, where his parents settled, and viewed himself as a Mississippian. His father served in World War II (see "For My Father at Eighty," *Local Men; and, Domains*). A tall man (six feet five), Jim was chosen All-State at Central High School and was awarded a football scholarship to Vanderbilt. An injury put an end to his athletic career. After taking a BA degree there with a major in philosophy (1959) and an MA in English (1960), he taught at Millsaps College for three years, then enrolled in the University of Iowa Writers' Workshop, where he completed his MFA degree in 1965. He joined the faculty at the University of Arkansas and remained there thirty-four years. With William Harrison, who taught fiction, he developed the creative writing program; poet Miller Williams soon joined the faculty. Among Whitehead's students over the years were Barry Hannah, Ellen Gilchrist, Jack Butler, Larry Johnson, John Freeman, and several Louisiana poets. (See Whitehead's "For Ellen After the Publication of Her Stories," from *Near at Hand*.)

Whitehead was praised as an effective teacher; he inspired loyalty and admiration in his students. "He shook the world he walked through. . . . [He] seemed larger than life [and] ultimately made life larger through his voice," wrote Michael Burns, a former student (*The Panther*, introduction). Whitehead married Guendaline Graeber; the couple had seven children. During his lifetime he published a sports novel, *Joiner* (1971), among the *New York Times* Noteworthy Books of the Year, and three collections of verse, in addition to a chapbook, *Actual Size* (1985). His poetry won praise from Howard Nemerov and George Garrett. Poems of his appeared in the *Southern Review, Mississippi*

Review, New Orleans Review, and elsewhere. His first book, *Domains* (1966), earned him a Bread Loaf Writers' Conference Robert Frost Fellowship. In 1972 he was awarded a Guggenheim Fellowship. *Local Men* appeared in 1979 and *Near at Hand* in 1993. *The Panther: Posthumous Poems,* edited by Burns, appeared in 2008. Whitehead and Williams were supporters of James Earl Carter and presented poems to him on the occasion of his return to Georgia from the White House. (Whitehead's can be found in *Near at Hand*). They were invited to Plains, and Carter sought their advice on his own poetry. Whitehead also dedicated to Carter "Some Local Men After Their Election" (*Local Men*). He helped Carter with his book *Always a Reckoning* (1995).

When Whitehead republished *Local Men* and *Domains* together, in 1987, *Domains,* the earlier, came second, suggesting a preference, or the need to read backwards in time. The two works can be considered together while contrasted. The poems are short, fitting usually on one page, at most two or a rare three, and are in free verse. The initial words of lines are capitalized. Stanzaic construction is dominant. Some stanzas are, in fact, short prose paragraphs (a sentence or so), with no capitalization after the initial line, flush with the left-hand margin, and the remainder of the paragraph indented. Loose rhythms outnumber fixed beats; rhyme, half-rhyme, consonance, and assonance appear frequently—binders but not too tight—as in "The Wreck" (*Domains*). The ruined car is "upside down / The wheels still turning around"; then, after two intervening lines, a rhyme: the driver "still seemed sound." "Swimming" (*Domains*) is a Shakespearean sonnet. A sestina in *Local Men* illustrates Whitehead's skill. As a way of ending poems neatly, he often constructs a short concluding observation of one or two lines. "Good Linemen Live in a Closed World," one of several irregular iambic pentameter sonnets (*Local Men*), furnishes an illustration: "Inside their fears / At the closed center of one fear they move / Quickly against themselves with a massive love." Rhetoric, some with a soupçon of outmoded phrasing, is more striking than images, but fine metaphors, such as "the torn rigging of his heart" have their role ("Having Gained Some Spiritual Ruthlessness . . . ," *Local Men*). Titles in *Local Men,* long, in small caps, and resembling each other, recall the cumbersome titles of past centuries—one begins by *Wherein*—but the diction is modern.

The title poem of *Domains* ends the collection but can serve as an introduction to Whitehead's oeuvre. In five short parts, it sets out a political and social stance that sheds light on many poems and underlines a southern preoccupation. "Sometimes I find it hard to concentrate / On politics / And the rugged Brotherhood of Man / I mean to be a Populist." (The concern for the brotherhood of man runs throughout *Domains* and *Local Men*.) Tracts and speeches depress him, says the speaker. He reflects on the Civil War, with one great-great-grandfather dying for the Union, the other surviving Vicksburg and living to write. "It is all death in time I would obliterate / And rigorous confusions of the noble dead. . . ." Whether flesh or memory, he realizes the burden of telling: "I am not fit / To serve at once / Two dying bodies with equal wit." "A Local Man Goes to the Killing Ground" (a title phrasing used in *Local Men*) revisits a place of murder. All in this first Whitehead collection is not social, however; there are short personal lyrics, such as "On the Lady's Clothes" and "For the Lady at Her Mirror," in which features of an aging woman (lines near the eyes, varicose veins), though noted, yield to "every cunning cover" and to the speaker's love.

In both books, characters, settings, dramas small and large, are often topically set. Whether explicitly or not, the territory is generally the South, and, even short, the poems often bear the mark of the southern raconteur. McComb, Jackson, George and Neshoba counties, the Memphis road, the Delta serve as scenes or subjects, and such events as flood, a hurricane, a horrible murder speak clearly of their setting. *Local Men* offers brief vignettes of men and women, many sad, many failures. The voice in these sketches is much the same throughout, a consistency that, with the similarity of titles, ties the poems together. It cannot surprise readers that southern hyperbole plays a role, as in "Long Tour: The Country Music Star Explains Why He Put Off the Bus and Fired a Good Lead Guitar in West Texas." A frequent theme is crime, with the law in the wings. The poems are full of hurt; human beings go through innumerable sufferings. Madness is one ("First Lecture" and "A Local Man Remembers Betty Fuller"); a child's death another ("For a Neighbor Child"). Though men are singled out, women's fate is not overlooked; witness "Cul-de-sac," on a stillbirth. "My Elderly Cousin (For F. S.)" is a touching homage to a woman, a painter, from the 1930s, who can be described as a survivor. Whitehead shows sensitivity to historical wrongs committed by whites against blacks ("Killing Ground" and "Eden's Threat," with its hounds pursuing men).

The title of *Near at Hand*, his last poetry collection before his death, parallels that of *Local Men*, and poem titles tend similarly to be long and suggestive of folkways and popular culture, juxtaposed sometimes with high culture—a feature of Whitehead's poetic character. "Sestina in Celebration of the Voice of Johnny Cash" illustrates the blend. Figures such as Jerry Lee Lewis and Tom T. Hall appear in poems or dedications. Section two (of three) consists of poems on "Coldstream Taggart," "Travis Belfontaine," a country singer, a "Four-County D.A.," and other characters. Although a few poems run to two or four pages, most are short; irregular sonnets are numerous, in various line arrangements. Many technical features of the earlier collections reappear.

The goodness of people radiates often from these poems, as well as the goodness of God ("This Is an Elegy for Charlie Harry . . ."). Modern sadness, even terror are not absent, though, illustrated by cancer of the jaw and a premature infant, severely malformed, without a brain ("We're Listening to the Features Editor"). Garrett, dying of cancer, appears in one poem. A few travel poems featuring Bolivia and Brazil are welcome variations among the local figures and topics. Whitehead evokes scenes wonderfully while being plain and direct, as in "The Mobile Lawyer's Life of Desire." Nostalgically, the speaker recalls driving to Baton Rouge, "with no plan," "on the run" (apparently because of the wrong girl, the wrong marriage), but at peace with himself and his surroundings. He eats oysters purchased in Biloxi, stops to smoke, gets lost in the Felicianas, but doesn't mind; he imagines a woman, perfumed, in a summer dress. "Lord, that time again."

The Panther is Whitehead's most distinctive work, perhaps his best. While certain technical features (long titles, irregular rhymes) are consistent with earlier usage, the twenty-five pages of poems stand out by their topic, consistent tone, and homogeneous poetics, which include stanzaic arrangement. The poems were complete at the time of his sudden death. Burns gathered them together and wrote a brief introduction. James D. Tabor, professor of religious studies at Duke University, contributed an invaluable discussion of the historical background.

The poems, mostly narrative, are centered on Tiberius Julius Abdes Pantera (Greek for *panther*), a Roman soldier of the first archers cohort. Originally from Sidon, he died at age sixty-two and was buried on the German frontier. Whitehead discovered his existence and previous research concerning him and visited his tomb, unearthed in the nineteenth century. (There is no indication that Whitehead knew Thomas Hardy's long poem on him.) Independently, Tabor investigated ascertainable facts and scraps of supporting evidence surrounding the speculation, which dates from the second century AD, that Pantera was a lover or rapist of Mary and thus the father of Jesus of Nazareth. Tabor considers this paternity quite possible, but by no means certain. (The two authors neither met nor corresponded.) Whitehead was, as contributors to the book attest, fascinated with the figure of Pantera and possible connection to Jesus.

The Panther does not begin, however, with the legionnaire but with the 1916 Battle of the Somme, as Whitehead meditated on it during a visit to a British cemetery in Picardy. (Editing may be responsible for this arrangement.) One gravestone inscription disturbed him especially: "Lord, help us bear our loss." The poem recounting the visit is strikingly fresh and convincing. A note supplied by Thomas Kennedy, who accompanied the poet to France and thence to Germany on the Panther's traces, relates the two visits, nearly contemporaneous and obliquely connected by the theme of sacrifice. A later poem relating the visit to the unearthed tomb is dedicated to Kennedy. The final poem, "Amiens and Chartres and the Last Hat I Ever Wore," brings readers back to the present.

In between, monologues in the third or first person concern Pantera, Mary, Joseph (as a lover, then dying), Paul of Tarsus, and Jesus, the scene of whose crucifixion Pantera visits without realizing that the central figure is his son and the grieving woman in blue was long ago the Galilean girl he loved. The diction is contemporary American, with bits of colloquial usage, and the sentiments expressed are familiar, suggesting the blending of sacred and profane, the down-to-earth quality of love and the Incarnation, the interconnections of history and the divine. One poem recounts, curiously, the Annunciation, not to Mary but to Pantera, who hears, without understanding, that his son is "magical" ("Gabriel Visited Abdes Pantera . . ."). Gabriel appears elsewhere, monologuing (for instance, "Walking with the Poet . . ."). In the poem that bears his name, Paul expresses, not dismay at learning of "gossip" concerning Jesus's birth, but joy; his connection to the Gentiles, his improper origins, the pagan elements in Christian worship merely lend themselves to showing how God's power through Christ can make of anything a new creation.

The slant of *The Panther* poses a problem in literary evaluation. Readers' appreciation will generally be colored by their beliefs and their sense of propriety in religious matters. Tabor's obvious respect for the poet's historical imagination and poetic achievement—as for the textual and other investigations that offer indirect and sketchy supporting evidence—cannot be shared by all. When objections can be put aside, the poems will reward readers greatly, displaying the poet's command of measured verse and intimate embrace of a crucial historical moment and its implications.

CLAUDE WILKINSON

Claude Wilkinson (born 1959) is a highly accomplished poet, one of the finest now writing in Mississippi. An anonymous *Oxford Town* reviewer of *Joy in the Morning* stated that he was "poised to become the state's premier poet" (cover of *Marvelous Light*). His parents were Henry Bridgforth Wilkinson and Lula Montcrief Wilkinson. Born in Memphis, he grew up with his three older sisters on a small De Soto County farm near Nesbit, now suburbanized, where he lives presently. He is also a visual artist. An author's profile for him on the *Image: Art, Faith, Mystery* site ("Claude Wilkinson") emphasizes the connection between his painter's and his poet's aesthetic. "His way of looking at the world seems informed by a long engagement with visual art. He dwells on the natural world in a way that always invites us to look beyond and through it."

Wilkinson took a bachelor's degree in education from the University of Mississippi (1981) and an MA in English from the University of Memphis (1990). He taught at Christian Brothers University and LeMoyne-Owen College in Memphis and for seven years at Mississippi Valley State University, until resigning in 2014 (with tenure). He continues to conduct poetry workshops. His verse has appeared in anthologies and in the *Southern Review* and *Oxford American* as well as *Image*. *Reading the Earth* (1998) received the Naomi Long Madgett Poetry Award. *Joy in the Morning* (2004) was nominated for a Pulitzer Prize. The two collections were favorably reviewed in the *Chattahoochee Review* and *Southern Register*. The Sewanee Writers' Conference awarded him its Walter E. Dakin Fellowship in Poetry (1999), and in 2000 he won a Whiting Writers' Award. In 2000–2001 he was John and Renée Grisham Visiting Writer in Residence at Ole Miss, the first poet to hold that position. *Marvelous Light* appeared in 2018 and *World without End* in 2020.

Wilkinson works in oils, watercolors, charcoal, pencil, pen and ink, and other media. His paintings, many of which are landscape scenes from Mississippi and elsewhere, have been exhibited in solo and group shows in his home state and at the African American Museum, the Carnegie Center for Art and History, and the Harrell Performing Arts Theatre (Collierville, Tennessee). His art work was included in the exhibit "Crossing Boundaries: Visual Art by Writers," alongside work by e. e. cummings, Lawrence Ferlinghetti, Allen Ginsberg, and Clarence Major, at Paterson Museum in Paterson, New Jersey (2006); it was also part of "Poet Jazz Paint," curated by Yusef Komunyakaa in La Jolla, California (2001). Additionally, Wilkinson has published criticism on Chinua Achebe, Italo Calvino, and John Cheever. His recent scholarship focuses on artists of the 1960s Black Arts movement, particularly Etheridge Knight. He is interested likewise in cultural representation in photography.

Reading the Earth is beautifully wrought; the poet exercises admirable control over his subject matter, avoiding sentimentality. The collection received a very favorable review by Jane St. Clair, who wrote, "[Wilkinson] stands inside the moment to divine the mysteries inherent in the visible world" (96). The cover painting, by the poet, showing yellow and orange day lilies, is echoed in the biblical epigraph (Luke 12: 27). The poems are in free verse, with varied stanzaic forms, some centered, some with staggered indentation. Wilkinson can exploit short lines and long ones alike and use alternating patterns. The diction is contemporary and direct, without forcing of syntax or metaphor; the poet's erudition shows in a rich lexicon.

The burden of his verse is essentially theological, including the vein of stewardship. He calls on nature constantly, for topics, settings, metaphors; nature's features are "lively oracles" (a poem title). He calls likewise on the Christian tradition. The title poem, a fine example of contemporary verse, opens simply, as the persona, pruning a willow, finds a bird's nest in which foil gum wrappers are deftly twisted among twigs. The nest becomes, imaginatively, Ezekiel's wheel turning in the air, with its warning. The speaker recalls an environmentalist telling his television audience to leave off the Bible and start "reading the earth." Far from leaving the Bible, the persona reflects on Luke's understanding of grace—illustrated in the sparrow—and then on Noah, "history's ultimate conservationist." The passengers on the ark, and even Darwin's finches, could not have asked "What's in a faith?" The creature in "Slug" serves as means to "prove the philosophy of resisting / sin, be the salt / I'm supposed to be." On a cosmic scale, "Orphic lights / swirl above as if / in a burst of Van Gogh" ("By Night").

Wilkinson is skilled in threading together particular and general elements—both pretexts and texts of his considerations. A wasted, dying mother and a toad stubbornly returning to the highway from which the speaker has shooed him away compose a two-paneled meditation on death ("Knell"). Examining a sculpture of horse and rider, with a snake at the base, leads to reflections on the snake in divine creation and the death of a grandfather, from "pinholes" between his ankle and calf (*"The Rattlesnake*—Contemplations on a Bronze by Frederick Remington"). "Hummingbirds," an exquisite lyric, shows the little creatures "always crying to get deeper and sweeter, / ... / dreaming / nothing but red: the color / of all desire." "Act of God," recalling a watercolor with clouds, gulls, a beach, and schooners in the distance, illuminates the experience of a tornado and its aftermath—the moment when each breath feels like a grace, "in the litter of petals and fallen limbs, / when the first ruffled birds / start whirling and chiming / as if they'd just been born." Many poems are little dramas, natural and human. "Marigolds" begins by sketching a sister and her success at growing flowers. The speaker then remembers his desire to emulate her. Lack of success leaves him indifferent. Animal death, however, revives his desire: he cannot keep alive the young bunnies brought by a retriever, and he yearns to cultivate flowers again, for the creatures' sake—"for my sister's golden seeds of hope / to lavishly strew their tomb / and bloom them back to life."

While Wilkinson's use of local color is subtle, certain poems do suggest scenes in Mississippi or elsewhere in the South. "Juke" depicts skillfully a pooltable establishment and its denizens. "Baptism with Water Moccasin" evokes the crowd and a few colorful characters at a creek-side ceremony during which, just above the "baptizing hole," a snake is poised on a tree limb. Using black vernacular, the preacher says: "Leave him be, chillun. / Long as he up there / we knows where he at." The poem is based on an experience related by the poet's mother from her youth in Newton, Mississippi. All is not gentle, to be sure: "Hernando Point" concerns a drowned boy, and "The Men's Club Hunt" ends as a boy sees his reflection "in the frozen gaze of a quail's eye."

The speaker in *Joy in the Morning* is, like the earlier persona, a man of faith and a painter, a colorist. Versification follows that of the earlier book: free verse, many short lines, stanzaic construction frequently (quatrains, tercets, longer blocks of lines), centering, which does not look stilted, and sometimes staggered left-hand margins. "Idea of Beauty" and "Pastoral" are rhymed sonnets, the latter reflecting the mood created elsewhere—almost, if not quite, idyllic. There is always "some / paradise not faded away" ("Elegy"). Artists figure often in the collection, and graphic work inspires word-paintings. The opening poem refers to a painting by Michael Crespo; "The Grace of Dreams" evokes one by Henri Rousseau. Obliquely, "Imperfect Works" weaves in a mention of Michelangelo, and Edward Hopper appears in "Cape Cod Evening, 1939."

The epigraph, from Psalm 30, provides the book title. Morning furnishes the experience of waking to beauty, a new creation daily. In the title poem, it is also the start of a new year, celebrated quietly as snow falls, making topiary of bare stems. "Morning" means, finally, the day of resurrection, "that great gettin' up morning" ("Words to Live By"). With echoes of colloquial speech, the poet imagines a Sunday service. The mention of funerals with second-liners, "where dirges are jazzed / with resurrection tempo, parasols / and handkerchiefs erupt / in blossoms of paradise," raises happy images ("Words to Live By"). Here, as elsewhere, words bear the weight of faith, but lightly, in both "their grace, their heft." (Words become The Word, in "The Family of Bro. Cliff Phillips.") Flashes of beauty prevail over sadder visions, such as that of the speaker's hospitalized mother surviving on painkillers, his father dying, "when we were almost / father and son" ("Nocturne"), or the tension experienced by a couple hoping "for anything that will keep us // from trying the same miserable lies a new, / innumerable time. . . ." The question of theodicy is inevitably behind many poems. Why does a loving God allow evil? Why does one suffer?

The *Image* commentator quoted earlier observed of Wilkinson: "His pace is unhurried, the observations unwind gracefully, but with gentle pressure, insisting: *look here.*" "Mowing the Lawn" illustrates the poet's appreciation of small things. Crouching before the work of a minute spider that survived the mower blades, the speaker admires each "wisp of cable, / by this time as bright / as cathedral glass" and reflecting the setting sun. A rough patch of woods and briers offers delights worth the pain ("Blackberry Fools").

The cover of *Marvelous Light* displays a painting by Wilkinson, "Winter Light." The book pursues the lines of his previous books, displaying forms seen earlier, such as tercets with staggered margins. Additionally one finds masterly rhymed iambic pentameter sonnets and a villanelle, "Deus ex Machina." Birds are, again, a motif. These artful poems, albeit beautiful, do not convey aestheticism. "Marvelous light" is a *calling*. The title, from I Peter 2:9, invites the "chosen generation" to "show forth the praises of God." The first part is titled "The Thing That Perches in the Soul," that is, hope (the phrase is Dickinson's). Ekphrastic writing constitutes a major vein, displayed in poems connected to a *Saturday Evening Post* cover and paintings by Hopper, George Inness, and Andrew Wyeth. "Summer Nights," a substantial series of prose poems, evokes the photographs of Robert Adams. The sonnets, "Effets de neige," derive from canvasses by nineteenth-century French painters.

"Half Past Autumn," twenty-six poems drawing on photographs by Gordon Parks, records and interprets Parks's visions of black lives in America. Both artists are superb observers, and both evince commitment to the truth—the facts and their significance. The subjects are not limited to the South; they include an old Parisian woman, a Sicilian peasant, and Staten Island Ferry commuters. The poet creates his own word-paintings, as in "Snowy Egret Flies Over Parched Mississippi Field." Most poem titles mention dates, from 1942 to 1963—a period of enormous strain for African Americans. "Drinking Fountains, Birmingham, Alabama" illustrates Wilkinson's craft. He first describes a little girl, black, looking into the window of an ice cream parlor window. The speaker recalls what Sebelius asked his grandchildren concerning their dreams. Then the focus turns to the mother, "lovely, obedient," stooping to drink from the "Colored Only" fountain. Finally, the poet imagines for his readers what the girl's dreams might be, in a wondrous world of sweets, where one could drink from either fount. The entire series demonstrates two arts, two sensibilities, in one—confronting pain, summoning hope. This series, like earlier poems, supports Baudelaire's contention that the best criticism of a picture might be a poem—in this case, by one who is a painter also.

Further mentions of musicians, such as Schubert and Ralph Vaughan Williams, and a strong pastoral vein introduce lines of beauty and calm; wistfulness marks youthful memories. "Release," in contrast, is an antipastoral, emphasizing that "the nature of war is to obliterate the other." British bombs—defensive by way of offense; slave ships and their "noble-sounding names"; the ovens of Auschwitz; and the stillness "before / Hiroshima left in a firestorm from heaven"—all were once thought "good ideas."

While reflecting aspects of the contemporary environment, *World Without End*, like Wilkinson's earlier books, transcends it by looking "beyond and through it." Rejecting simplistic Darwinism, though not all scientific understanding, he underlines the harmony of heaven and earth and, again, insists upon the beauty and the sense of purpose visible in all life. In doing so, he displays mastery of tones, images, and technique, including skillful exploiting of spacing. In a range of forms—free verse, couplets, staggered tercets, rhymed quatrains, a Shakespearean sonnet—he presents gorgeous scenes such as "Winter Field White with Snow Geese," and, in "Thusness," imagines the "soul" of a spider. It is a reminder of the same little creature in a previous collection, representing the micro-world, contrasted with the wide cosmos but all part of a continuum. Wilkinson devotes a series of eight poems to "Vincent's Flowers." Amounting to an artistic biography of Van Gogh, they stand above many trite poetic treatments of the Dutch artist; for high quality, they can be compared to Peter Cooley's *The Van Gogh Notebook* (1987).

Wilkinson's collections give evidence that he deserves recognition as a major poet, whose writing will have lasting value.

RICHARD WRIGHT

The celebrated and influential African American author Richard (Nathaniel) Wright (1908–60) is known chiefly for his novels, memoirs, and journalism; but he wrote poetry also, and because of his stature, it deserves attention. He was born in a sharecropper's cabin on Rucker's Plantation between Roxie, Mississippi, and Natchez. All his grandparents had been slaves. Both grandfathers had served in Union military units. When he was six years old (some sources say five), his father Nathaniel (or Nathan), who was illiterate, and mother Ella, a country schoolteacher, were driven off the land they sharecropped. They settled in Memphis, where they lived in a two-room slum tenement. Wright's father deserted the family and his mother fell ill. Richard and his brother, Alan, were placed in an orphanage.

Recovering enough to have them with her, the mother moved to Elaine, Arkansas, where they lived with Aunt Maggie Hoskins and her husband, Silas, who owned a saloon. He was shot dead by white men, apparently envying his lucrative business. Maggie fled north; Ella and the boys fled to Helena, Arkansas, where she found work with a doctor's family. By 1920, after Ella had a stroke and was partially paralyzed, the family had settled in Jackson with the maternal grandparents. A Seventh Day Adventist, Grandmother Margaret Bolden Wilson imposed long, daily prayer sessions, Bible readings, and harsh dietary restrictions. Believing that fiction was the devil's work, she kept books out of the house. Under these constraining conditions, Wright grew violent, pulling a knife on an aunt and committing other aggressive acts. "Violence was at the very center of his life" at the time (Felgar 22).

Wright attended Lanier High School. At the end of ninth grade—the last in the black public schools—he was named class valedictorian. He lived by doing menial jobs. At sixteen he published his first short story, "The Voodoo of Hell's

Half-Acre" in the *Southern Register*. (There is no extant copy.) He held various jobs, working in a clothing store, at a soda fountain, for an optical company, and as a bell boy. In 1927 he reached Chicago. He found work successively as a delivery boy, dishwasher, and post office employee. By the summer of 1928, he was able to have his mother and his brother Alan join him and his aunt Maggie (Rickels 2).

In Chicago Wright read Hart Crane, Dostoevsky, Proust, T. S. Eliot, and Gertrude Stein, who provided special pleasure for him. Her "Melanctha" was "part of the liberating project of . . . his own adaptation of black vernacular as . . . mass cultural idiom" (Mullen). In the 1930s, as the Great Depression worsened, he became unemployed, and the family lived on government surplus food. Mary Wirth, a caseworker, whose husband was a University of Chicago sociologist, was assigned to the family. Recognizing Wright's exceptional intelligence and talent, she sent him to her husband for guidance; Wright became a serious student of sociology and anthropology.

Owing to his wide reading and the visible poverty and racism around him, Wright, a lifelong atheist, was attracted to Communism, joining the John Reed Club in 1932. He became a party member in 1933 and was active through early 1940s. In left-leaning journals he published Marxist-influenced poems on his southern experience. In 1937 he settled in New York, where he became Harlem editor of the *Daily Worker*. Two years later he married a Russian-Jewish ballet dancer, Dhimah Rose Meadman (Dhima or Rose Dhimah). They divorced the following year. In 1941 he married a Communist Party member, Ellen Poplar, likewise white. According to Ann Rayson, he had been in love with her before he married Dhimah. They had two daughters and lived together until his death. In August 1944 he broke publicly with organized Communism in his *Atlantic Monthly* article "I Tried to Be a Communist." A journey to Africa in 1953 allowed him to analyze firsthand African life; his *Black Power* (1954) was inspired by this trip.

Wright's literary career was launched when *Uncle Tom's Children* (1938) won first prize in a contest open to Federal Writers' Project authors for the best book-length manuscript. The prize brought him to national attention. The collection of novellas concerned the plight of American blacks. *Native Son*, published in 1940, painfully reveals their mistreatment. Orson Welles staged the text as a successful 1941 Broadway play. It sold 215,000 copies in the first three weeks after publication and was the first best-selling novel and the first Book-of-the-Month Club selection by an African American author. Irving Shaw wrote in "Black Boys and Native Sons" (1963) that "the day *Native Sons* appeared the American culture was changed forever. No matter how much qualifying the book might later need, it made impossible a repetition of the old lies ... [and] brought into the open, as no one ever had before, the hatred, fear and violence that have crippled and may yet destroy our culture" (quoted in Rayson).

In 1945 Wright published his memoir *Black Boy*, which depicts the poverty, hunger, and racism he encountered as a youth. It too became a bestseller and Book-of-the-Month Club selection. However, the US Senate denounced the book as "obscene." After World War II, Wright became an expatriate, moving to Paris, where he remained until his death. *The Outsider* (1953) is considered by some as the first American existential novel. Other books of his were poorly received. Among them was *White Man, Listen* (1957), a collection of lectures he had delivered in Europe. *Eight Men*, a book of short stories, appeared in 1961. Posthumously published in 1957, his autobiography, *American Hunger*, recounts his experiences in northern cities in America. Similarly posthumous are the novella *Rite of Passage* (1994) and a crime novel, *A Father's Law* (2008).

Prose notwithstanding, Wright began and ended his literary life with poetry. In his first poems, essentially Communist propaganda, he strove to show the plight of African Americans. Toward the end of his life, he turned to haiku, of which he wrote thousands. Although Robert Felgar was convinced that "both the Communist propaganda and the haiku do not justify extended discussion" (preface, *Richard Wright*), treating the latter is suitable in the present context, especially given the fact that critics have published book-length studies on them.

Felgar justifies his opinion by examining "We of the Streets," published in the April 13, 1937 *New Masses*. Felgar views it and "Between the World and Me" as Wright's best poems, exceptions to his otherwise mediocre verse, "poetry only in its appearance on the page" (preface)—that is, prose set into stanzas, where the poet "dispenses with many devices associated with verse in favor of a Socialist Realism that is sincere but unrefined" (30). "We of the Streets" is characteristically loose in syntax and organization; its only organizing principle is listing or cataloging. (Felgar overlooks here similar enumeration in other modern poetry, including urban poetry, some by honored figures.) It alludes to tenements, sticky-fingered babies, stringy curtains, city noises, and billboards. Melissa Girard shows how the opening lines, quoted here, reveal "power through scent." "Streets are full of the scent of us—odors of onions drifting from doorways, / effluvium of baby new-born downstairs, seeping smells of warm soap- / suds—the streets are lush with the ferment of our living." Wright transforms features of nature into urban images: "billboards blossom with the colors of a billion flowers" and "our strip of sky is a dirty shirt." The poem joins the two worlds in which he lived, the rural South and the urban North, ending with the common need for joint strength that permits the feeling of immortality "when / we rushed along ten thousand strong ... aching to shout the / forbidden word, knowing that we of the streets are deathless." Girard sees this final stanza as enacting "a specific shift toward a vision of political empowerment, transforming the street, the home, into a site of freedom."

In "Between the World and Me," the persona stumbles upon the remains of a body that has been tarred, feathered, and burned. "And through the morning air the sun poured yellow / surprise into the eye sockets of the stony skull." The narrator experiences a transference of emotion as he identifies with this ghastly "thing," as the "sooty details of the scene rose, thrusting / themselves between the world and me." His mind takes him to the scene of the crime, and the narrator becomes the victim: "And then they had me, stripped me, battering my teeth / into my throat till I swallowed my own blood. / My voice was drowned in the roar of their voices." When he is burned, he ultimately becomes "dry bones and my face a stony skull staring in / yellow surprise at the sun." The effective image of the sun and skull begins and ends the poem.

During the summer of 1959 Wright was introduced to haiku by a South African friend who lent him R. H. Blyth's volumes on the form and its relationship to Zen Buddhism. Wright settled down "to rediscover his old dream of oneness with all life" (Hakutani 81). As Dana Gioia observed, to African American writers the form has been "half a refuge from racial politics and half a subtle form of cultural rebellion" (cover comment, Zheng, *African American Haiku*). Wright's daughter Julia testified that at the end of his career he was always busy writing haiku. "He wrote them everywhere, at all hours: in bed as he slowly recovered from a year-long, grueling battle against amebic dysentery; in cafés and restaurants where he counted syllables on napkins" (Introduction to Wright, *Haiku* vii). She believed that his haiku were "self-developed antidotes against illness, and that breaking down words into syllables matched the shortness of his breath, especially on the bad days when his inability to sit up at the typewriter restricted the very breadth of writing" (viii). These poems appeared posthumously, in 1998.

Wright was rigorous in following the 5, 7, 5 syllabic measure of haiku. According to Yoshinobu Hakutani, "only a fraction of [his four thousand], perhaps less than one percent, were composed with anomalous syllabic counts.... Most of the contemporary poets ... do not follow the rule" (9). Robert Hass, US poet laureate from 1995 to 1997, was "deeply impressed" by both the poems and Wright's commentary on them (Hakutani 82). Many are superior to his socialist realism verse; but he did not eliminate from them entirely his political and personal attitudes. "Clearly he was experimenting with his own African American approach to the haiku form" (Hakutani 101). Moreover, while classical haiku poets tried to suppress subjectivity and their own presence in their verse, some of Wright's haiku refer, it seems, to him or his circumstances. Haiku

1 centers on a poet-persona, who notes that he, Emily Dickinson (an obvious reference), is nobody. The red sun going down in that poem could signify the failure of Communism, as Wright saw it. In haiku 722 the voice mentions his own "lighted window." In haiku 459, the persona notes that he is paying rent for both the lice and the moonlight in his room.

Another characteristic of Wright's haiku is the interaction of images. In number 687 the wind reaches out its "tongue" and creates whitecaps as it "licks" the water. Some haiku show humanity emulating nature. In haiku 721 the poet reminds readers of how anger steals affirmation; as anger decreases, stars brighten and wind (breath) returns. Among his interesting juxtapositions is that of a bayonet, barbs of wire, and a "spring moon at dawn" (Haiku 477). Like the two edges of the bayonet, he sees humanity's ugliness and evil juxtaposed to natural beauty and tranquility. He also includes humor, as in poem 175, which sketches a bull with a sprig of lilac "dangling from a horn." Contrasting with such whimsy are instances of man's inhumanity to man, as well as a "sympathetic awareness of the complex relationship between humanity and nature" (Hakutani 107).

Gwendolyn Brooks called Wright's collection of haiku "a clutch of strong flowers" (Hakutani 132). Perhaps such strength and beauty come from the African philosophy of life. "Once Wright saw West Africans' way of life during his travels to the Ashanti kingdom in 1953, the images of nature he recalled from his youth in the South [were] transformed into those of Africans, who had a fundamentally different outlook on life." When Wright visited Africa, he "realized for the first time that African culture was buttressed by universal human values—such as awe of nature, family kinship and love, faith in religion, and a sense of honor. For the purpose of writing haiku, this primal outlook on life . . . had a singular influence on his poetic vision" (Hakutani 133).

Wright's poetry is certainly not as powerful as his prose works; it highlights, however, major themes visible elsewhere and the elements of his life. Although not a religious man, he chose, as his life was ending, to steep himself in haiku, many of which addressed the Zen of life, affording, perhaps, spiritual experience.

AL YOUNG

Even though Al (Albert James) Young is associated chiefly with California, where he was poet laureate (2005–8), he was born (1939) in Ocean Springs, Mississippi. Introducing *Heaven: Collected Poems 1956–1990*, "O. O. Gabugah" called Young "a poet whose roots run all the way back to Mississippi and front-porch storytelling, and to listening to everything. . . . Al is still today the great listener and hearer" (5). (O. O. Gabugah is Young's alter ego. He told Don Lee that he borrowed the name—a joke—from an album by Hugh Masakele, a South African poet, who took it, mockingly, from Tarzan movies.) Young is a jazz performer (guitarist, singer), music critic, novelist, screenplay writer, memoirist, and prolific poet. Like his fellow Mississippi poets Sterling D. Plumpp, T. R. Hummer, and Jerry W. Ward Jr., he has drawn on American music for literary purposes, and he has often read his verse to musical accompaniment.

Young wants his poetry to "make you feel good about being alive." "Upbeat," he called himself. He eschewed "poetry of the modern, right-now persuasion" (*Heaven* 3, 4, 8). From the outset communication was more important to him than indulgent self-expression, "somebody's pitiful little hurt feelings" (4). His position is close to the reception theory of Hans Robert Jauss adumbrated earlier by John Erskine. It proposes that the work always exists in a triangular relationship involving the author, the original context of production, and the reading public. "No piece of writing," Young asserted, "is complete until it's been read and the reader hears what's being said and answers. In a sense, readers are the co-writers of whatever they happen to be reading" (3).

In 1969 Young was named to a chair in creative writing at Stanford, where he remained until 1976. Subsequently he taught, as writer in residence, lecturer, or professor, at the University of California at Santa Cruz, Rice University (as Mellon Professor), the University of Washington, and the University of Michigan, in addition to the Charles University in the Czech Republic. He is an avid traveler; he numbers among his innumerable stops Paris, Madrid, Mexico, Singapore, and Australia. His first poetry book was *Dancing: Poems* (1969). Then came *The Song Turning Back into Itself: Poems* (1971); *Geography of the Near Past* (1976); *The Sound of Dreams Remembered: Poems 1990–2000* (2001); and *Coastal Nights and Inland Afternoons: Poems, 2001–2006* (2006). Some of these collections are gathered together, with additional work, in *The Blues Don't Change* (1982) and *Heaven: Collected Poems 1957–1990* (1992).

Among Young's awards and fellowships are a Guggenheim Fellowship (1974), a Fulbright Fellowship to Yugoslavia (1984), NEA fellowships, two PEN-sponsored awards (including the PEN/Library of Congress Award for Short Fiction), and the Richard Wright Award for Excellence in Literature (2007). Further honors include an honorary doctorate of Humane Letters from Whittier College (2009), two American Book Awards, two *New York Times* Notable Book of the Year citations, and a Wallace Stegner Writing Fellowship (1966). These awards recognize his prose more than his poetry, but his stature as a poet is high. His fiction often features musicians and music, and he has received praise for his use of African American speech, especially in *Seduction by Light* (1975). He collaborated with Ishmael Reed to found the *Yardbird Reader*, succeeded by *Quilt*. Poems by Young have appeared in many magazines and anthologies and have often been translated.

Information about Young's childhood is neither abundant nor entirely clear. His parents were Albert James and Mary Campbell Young (referred to as Mary Campbell Simmons in "Moving, Merging, Fading, Standing Still," from *Heaven: Collected Poems*). He spent his first years (and several summers thereafter) in rural and coastal Mississippi, where his father was stationed with the Navy. He recalls frequent walks with his family down to the Gulf to get crabs and shrimp (D. Lee). He worked some in the fields (see *Heaven* 235). Biographical sketches mention his growing up in "small towns"—perhaps with grandparents, who make shadowy appearances in his work. "Pachuta, Mississippi," subtitled "A Memoir" (*The Song Turning Back into Itself*), sketches the town around 1950. "Birthday Poem" (*Dancing*) portrays a country black girl who knows nothing but work: "Papa pull you outta school bout March / to stay on the place & work the crop"—her own "earliest knowledge" being that "of human hopelessness & waste." The genuineness of the portrait is telling. Certain details appear autobiographical: "She carried me around nine months / inside her fifteen year old self.... // How I got from then to now / is the mystery that could fill a whole library." Suggestive of a manifesto, the next poem, "A Little More Traveling Music," dated 1962–1967, reinforces the autobiographical interpretation, evoking as it does "a country kid in Mississippi," "Mama," "Colored music," and endless work, then northern cities and "the ABC reality."

Young's father, having been discharged, moved the family to Detroit, where he worked in the auto industry and as a professional musician. Later, Al James's death brought grief to his son but also "withinness" and an epiphany of peace ("Dreams of Paradise," *Heaven* 302). The boy took up Islam, apparently, at age fifteen; but by his mid-twenties he no longer practiced it ("Arabia," *Heaven* 306). (The figure of God as a loving deity appears occasionally in his oeuvre.) Like his father, he was enthusiastic about music. Even before he was able to earn money as a radio disk jockey, he and a friend carried on mock broadcasts combining talk with records (*Heaven* 7). Lee described Young's voice as that of a "deejay . . . articulate; engaging; most of all, smooth." Young pursued the musician's trade for years but, like his father, eventually gave it up, sick of the atmosphere of gigs.

On CBC broadcasts from Windsor, Ontario, he heard not only good jazz but also poetry readings. He was familiar with verse; a second-grade teacher in Mississippi had made her pupils memorize and recite poems every two weeks, and in Detroit Young read poetry in the public library. Majoring in Spanish, which he had begun learning in Mississippi, he attended the University of Michigan, where he was coeditor of the campus literary magazine, from 1957 until 1960. In summer that year he went with musician friends to New York City. Shortly thereafter he moved to the San Francisco Bay area and enrolled at the University of California at Berkeley, graduating with honors in 1969. He worked at jobs such as folk singer, medical photographer, warehouseman, and disc jockey. In 1963 he married Arline J. Belch, a technical writer and editor; they have one son, Michael. She is glimpsed in "Berkeley Pome." Other feminine figures slip in and out of the poems.

Young was in his twenties and early thirties during the tumultuous decade marked by ongoing and controversial warfare in Vietnam, James Meredith's admission as the first black student at the University of Mississippi, the federal civil rights legislation, protests and armed struggles in the South, assassinations, campus riots at Berkeley and elsewhere, and countercultural surges—all signs of widespread social unrest. Successful in several ways, Young nevertheless shared the difficulties of being an American black man, illustrated dramatically in Mississippi but not there only. His early poems deal frequently with the vital questions of self-identity, racial history, and skin color. He did not, however, adopt radical poetics, although one of his early idols was Rimbaud, both social rebel and poetic innovator. Other influences came from church— Call-and-Response and the Amen Corner. The list he gives of types of music and writing and figures that have influenced him is long and cosmopolitan:

Hindu philosophy, American Indian poetry and song, Afro-American folk and popular music, Caribbean music of both English- and Spanish-speaking peoples, the Bible, Li Po, Rabinadrath Tagore, the early T. S. Eliot, Blaise Cendrars, Léopold Senghor, Federico García Lorca, LeRoi Jones (Amiri Baraka), and Kenneth Rexroth (*Heaven* 7–8).

Such is the background of *Dancing: Poems* (1969). (That collection and the two discussed just below are republished in *The Blues Don't Change* and *Heaven*.) While vague reminiscences of surrealism surface here and there, and Young uses ampersands and forgoes certain standard uses (capitalization sometimes, apostrophes in words such as *you've*), his free verse is generally rational and well crafted, showing in the line breaks as well as overall structure his sense of composition. This quality is in harmony with his position that poetry by black authors must not follow the trends of the ghetto. In "A Dance for Militant Dilettantes," the initial poem in *Dancing*, a "hip friend" says African Americans must adapt their writing to black expectations—"You got to learn to put in about / stone black fists / coming up against white jaws / & red blood splashing"—adding: "Don't nobody want no nice nigger no more." But the rhetoric of the poem points to irony throughout. Young's own practice supports this interpretation; poetry must be *poetry* first of all. It may be critical but neither programmatic nor cut off from common discourse.

Dancing displays Young's command of free verse. Lines may end with punctuation, but often the construction makes commas and semicolons unnecessary. He favors very short lines. "A potted fern / in a Vine St. apartment / spreads its green delicate tentacles . . ." ("Takes from Love in Los Angeles"). "Dreamily he clings to his favorite memories / . . . / cold implosions in the blue of his heart" ("The Aging Hipster"). Or Young mixes short and longer lines to effect: "Warmblooded & / a little confused / I move toward what I'm hoping is the light. // All my struggles have led me to this moment" ("Dancing," sec. 4). He creates beautiful lyrics and lyrics on beauty, such as "Lemons, Lemons": "Sweet goldenness of light / & life itself / sunny at the core / lasting all day long."

In "Dancing All Alone," an effective short poem, the speaker takes a perspective on himself: "We move thru rooms & down the middle of freeways, / myself and I. / A feeling lumps up in the throat / that says I wont be living forever." Keen comprehension appears when he expresses disaffection with his land and what he calls the "Amurkan problem," a strong current ("The Dancer"). "A Dance for Ma Rainey" connects the poet's enterprise to the suffering that blues artists expressed, "aching to be heard / . . . / that bottomlessness / first felt by some stolen delta nigger / swamped under with redblooded american agony. . . ." His home state is "Richard Wright's / or my own wrong Mississippi" ("Paris"). Accompanying the disaffection is a religious current, the recognition that "love of life is love of God / sustaining all life, sustaining me / when wrong or un-self-righteous / in drunkenness and in peace" ("Myself When I Am Real"). The poetic voice identifies himself with the world in its goodness. "My heart is rain, my brain earth, / but there is only one sun & forever / it shines forth one endless poem." "Dancing in the Street" honors a "gold picture" of African Americans, "the way we looked today / the way we are all the time inside, / healthy black masters / of our own destiny." At the same time the poem attacks America with broad sarcasm, its "trillion dollar mule team / dragging its collective ass / into that nowhere desert / of bleached bones & bomb tests." "Dance of the Infidels" expresses Young's gratitude to Bud Powell, whose music he heard "in those city years when I could / very well have fasted on into oblivion," as he sought beauty "before I was even aware of it."

The Song Turning Back into Itself (1971) displays a wide range of line and stanza arrangements, including lines with staggered margins, long, wrap-around building blocks, and poems in prose. Light and kindness radiate from many poems, among them, "The Song Turning Back into Itself" (3), a por-trait of "Ocean Springs Missippy" and "Ma," with "the ocean lapping up light" and a woman with "the sun in her voice." In "Loneliness," Young writes: "The poet is the dreamer & / the poet is himself the dream / & in this dream / he shares your presence." Elsewhere, "the poet is a prestidigitator"; he walks "thru mirrors to the other side" (perhaps a reminiscence of Jean Cocteau's 1950 film about a poet's destiny, *Orphée*) ("The Prestidigitator" 1 and 2). California scenes, although generic, are not trite. "You look up toward the hills & fog / the familiarity of it after so many years / a resident tourist," the speaker says to himself. "Like distant hills by moonlight / your own dark beauty / brightens / like meanings of remembered places ..."; they include "sand the ocean the untakeable sea breeze / ... / forest of countryside and city"—illuminated "by time & distance."

Geography of the Near Past (1976), similarly varied in versification, begins with poems on a pregnant woman and the birth of "Michael." Their tenderness reappears in "Rediscovered Diary Entry," presenting "an old robed Zen master from Japan / whose head glistened youthfully / like the skin of a new apple / rubbed lovingly against a sleeve." The persona recalls seeing him, "too many Aprils ago," on the bus on Berkeley mornings, the speaker "on his way to work." This day they have shaken hands. "Today I am on my way" (an echo of the Bud-dhist phrase). Jazz greats, making cameo appearances—Charlie Parker, Billie Holiday, Ray Charles—contrast with men in prison, girls in the street, racial misery. "The Old O. O. Blues" and a few following poems, in black vernacular and loose rhyme, have strong tones of revolutionary protest. "What You Seize Is What You Can Git" bears the identifying line "Paris / Dar-es-Salaam 1972."

The Blues Don't Change (the collection comprising the volumes above) closes with additional poems, some of which cannot go unmentioned. Among them is the lovely still life, unpunctuated, "Poem with Orange." "How closely the wet /glistening flesh of / this bright fruit / resembles all galaxies." The painterly motif appears in the previous poem, "How the Rainbow Works": "Think of the dreamer as God, a painter, / a ham, to be sure, but a divine old master / whose medium is light...." Additional poems in this cluster deal with Young's maternal grandmother, married love ("In Marin Again"), a midlife crisis, and the blues, in several poems.

Heaven: Collected Poems, 1956–1990 presents three chronologically grouped "books" of published and unpublished poetry, followed by fifty additional pages of uncollected poems, a few from Young's teens, many from his twenties. The effect of the whole is vigor, solidity, and serious purpose, combined with the lightness of his poetic touch. Among the early poems one finds lines developed later, both formal (free verse and formal verse together) and thematic, such as jazz. Hallucinogenics play a small role, and Vietnam is not absent ("Suicide" 309).

The first group of poems, "By Heart (1982–1985)" reveals a writer in middle age, qualifying or moving away not from his memories but from the raw experience they preserve. Anyway, "you can't tell anything about the actual past / without making it up, really" ("Hoboken Broken Down" 220). Lines, often impressionistic, move fast, like years. The mood is generally cheerful. "Poetry / like a bent ray / of light / returns ..." ("After Visiting Arl at the Hospital" 210). One is "nothing / if not spirit / dreaming its otherness / dreaming bent rays." Dedicated to Young's mother, who died of cancer in 1982, the poem "Moving, Merging, Fading, Standing Still" affords glimpses of a childhood "always on the move & moving on," from "Pachuta, Laurel, Ocean Springs ..." (212). God appears more than once, "holding all of Creation in the most durable / yet delicate of suspensions, letting go / with constellations of bliss" ("Improvisation" 214). Age-old problems present themselves. In "Process," the poet meditates on the assumption, erroneous, he says, that there are such things as fixed objects existing in an external world. "No, perception itself is process. / The thing perceived and the perceiver / are one; everything is in flux.... // And where do we come from?" (218)

"More Clues to the Blues" provides a bitter definition of the mood: "The blues is an encroachment; a mental state of being / the very people upon whom roaches rush in to feed" (220). "Your Basic Black Poet" humorously imagines reactions from audiences: "What can he tell us new / about the racial situation?" and "What's the matter with / his diction man he /sho dont sound that black?" (221). "A Poem for Lena Horne" pays due tribute to the singer's character as well as voice. "The Midnight Special Revisited" sketches the Houston milieu, long gone, that Leadbelly evoked in his song.

"22 Moon Poems (1984–85)," the second cluster of new work in *Heaven: Collected Poems*, came out of stays in Italy, Yugoslavia, New York, and California after several "dark seasons of personal tragedy and heartbreak" (236). The poems sketch the moonlight shining on Belgrade, Dubrovnik, Sarajevo, and other sites. The third cluster, "Sea Level (1986–1990)," comprises poems on cold rain in Milwaukee, "The Lovesong of O. O. Gabugah," Big Sur, and other California sites.

The Sound of Dreams Remembered: Poems 1990–2000 (2001) bears endorsements from Lawrence Ferlinghetti and Yusef Komunyakaa. To the question posed in "The Gold Rush Revisited," "How is the dream connected to real life?" one of the epigraphs (a quotation from Gail Godwin) replies that "dreams say what they mean, / but they don't say it in daytime language." This substantial volume, with charming pen-and-ink drawings, displays a wide range of topics and settings. Young's easily flowing verse is equal to almost any challenge. The diction and forms are generally standard. Free verse has its place, but rhyme and off-rhyme are used frequently, and well, in poems such as "Openings" and "The Real Bird World," a delightful, witty lyric. "An American Champion in Love" is among poems in rhymed quatrains and iambic pentameter. "Filming" and "Córdoba" are sonnets. "Prelude to a Kiss" is a prose poem. "The Gospel Trees, Detroit" is partly in monosyllabic verse. Black vernacular appears in "Conjugal Visits" and additional poems; "How the Flower Flourishes," like various others, is centered.

"April in Paris," in quatrains and labeled "after Yip Harburg and Vernon Duke" (the creators of the song), opens the book. On the Left Bank two Americans find escape "from the loveless edges of that country we'd both fled." Paris becomes "the adopted country of each other's arms." The two are foreigners but less out of place than "back home," where "we knew what it was like to be the other— / displaced, despised, imprisonable." Love appears elsewhere, embodied in a man and woman, or generalized but by precise, concrete images, as in "All bets are off / when love wobbles into the picture" ("Fuzzy Logic") and "The hardest hit to take aims for the heart" ("One Way to Take a Hit"). Aural images feed the charming "Poem for Listeners," where the hearing of elephants and bats and the sounds of John Coltrane, Ravel, and Spanish gypsies provide notes for the theme. In a meditation called "The Skin of Light," the poet advises, "Do not take lightly the miracle / of light; the shiny play of time and time and time." Everything fits, including the fact that light can travel billions of years to reach the earth. "O see / as light the field upon which we earn our blazing points." "Love Poem," in couplets, earns its title, explaining that love is

an "inexhaustible art / that ranks right up there with taxes, death and // time."
"I wade into an ocean-you, pulled and lulled by love."

Music plays a role, as in previous books; subtly or directly, jazz, in particular, insinuates itself into the poem. "Snowy Morning Blues," set in New York and composed in tribute to James P. Johnson and Langston Hughes, advises "Let the blues roll on." The abuses of capitalism—or the system itself—are visible in "Détroit moi," a ranging impressionistic tapestry in tercets and two parts, dealing variously with the title city, the Mississippi River, and Lake Pontchartrain, along with music, classical (Vivaldi) and popular (Diana Ross, Stevie Wonder), and the black exodus from the South to Michigan. (Young may have had such capitalist abuses in mind when he wrote in 1960 of "an evil in this land that hovers / far beyond the economic slums of my childhood" [*Heaven: Collected Poems.*])

The facts of Young's career and his writing indicate his artistic versatility and the range of his interests. He cannot be pigeonholed as a writer, still less as a man. A Mississippian, certainly, by birth and early rearing, and by his continuing identification with the South; but also with roots in Detroit and California. A traveler, too, whose travels have fed his verse. An erudite musician, with wide interests. Serious, yet skilled at identifying humor and conveying it. A quick-sketch artist also, capturing characters and scenes and their individuality so well that the reader wants to be there with him. A critic of his birthplace and homeland, with respect to treatment of the disadvantaged and disdained, including those of his race—himself doubtless, occasionally—and criminals; but without an agenda in his poetry. For it is not programmatic; it demonstrates what even, for all his ranting, the wild, anarchic surrealist Bob Kaufman (another southerner transplanted to California) knew: that a poet's loyalty should go to the art itself, not to a cause.

SELECTED BIBLIOGRAPHY

Primary sources cited in the text and selected additional poetry titles appear here, in addition to certain works in other genres by the respective poets, including anthologies. Pertinent coauthored, edited, and translated books by each poet are listed after individually authored works. Secondary sources include biographical and critical books and articles, interviews, reviews, additional anthologies, and general works. Interviews not otherwise identified are with the present author.

PRIMARY SOURCES

Autry, James A. "How I Got Here." *DSM*. http:/www.dsmmagazine.com/2017/01/09/how-i-got-here-james-a-autry/.

Autry, James A. *Life After Mississippi*. Introduction by Willie Morris. Photography by Lola Mae Autry. Oxford, MS: Yoknapatawpha Press, 1989.

Autry, James A. *Nights Under a Tin Roof: Recollections of a Southern Boyhood*. Introduction by John Mack Carter. Illustrated with photographs. Oxford, MS: Yoknapatawpha Press, 1989.

Autry, James A. *On Paying Attention: New and Selected Poems*. Macon, GA: Peake Road Press / Smyth and Helwys, 2015.

Ball, Angela. *Kneeling Between Parked Cars*. Seattle: Owl Creek Press, 1990.

Ball, Angela. *The Museum of the Revolution: 58 Exhibits*. Pittsburgh: Carnegie Mellon Press, 1999.

Ball, Angela. *Night Clerk at the Hotel of Both Worlds*. Pittsburgh: University of Pittsburgh Press, 2007.

Ball, Angela. *Possession*. Pasadena, CA: Red Hen Press, 1995.

Ball, Angela. *Quartet*. Pittsburgh: Carnegie Mellon Press, 1995.

Ball, Angela. *Talking Pillow*. Pittsburgh: University of Pittsburgh Press, 2017

Bell, Charles Greenleaf. *Delta Return*. Bloomington: Indiana University Press, 1956.

Bell, Charles Greenleaf. *Five Chambered Heart*. New York: Persea Books, 1986.

Bell, Charles Greenleaf. *Millennium Harvest: The Life and Collected Poems of Charles Greenleaf Bell*. Sante Fe, NM: Helen Lane, 2007.

Bell, Charles Greenleaf. *Songs for a New America*. Bloomington: Indiana University Press, 1953. Rpt. Dunwoody, GA: N. S. Berg, 1966.

Bell, Charles Greenleaf. *The Wheel*. Cleveland, OH: American Weave Press, 1952.

Berry, D. C. "Ars pugilistica." Unpublished manuscript.

Berry, D. C. *Divorce Boxing*. Cheney: Eastern Washington University Press, 1998.

Berry, D. C. *Hamlet Off Stage*. Huntsville: Texas Review Press, 2009.

Berry, D. C. Interviews (handwritten and emailed), April–May 2018.

Berry, D. C. *Jawbone: Portraits of Contemporary Poets*. Birmingham, AL: Thunder City Press, 1978.

Berry, D. C. *Saigon Cemetery*. Athens: University of Georgia Press, 1972.

Berry, D. C. *The Vietnam Ecclesiastes: 1945–1975*. Black River, NY: Black Lawrence Press, 2007.

Berry, D. C. *Yes, Cancer French Kisses*. Huntsville: Texas Review Press, 2017.

Berry, D. C. *Zen Cancer Saloon*. *Black Warrior Review* 30, no. 2 (Spring–Summer 2004): 99–119.

Bodenheim, Maxwell. *My Life and Loves in Greenwich Village*. New York: Bridgehead Books, 1954.

Bodenheim, Maxwell. *Selected Poems*. New York: Beechhurst Press / Bernard Ackerman, 1946.

Bodenheim, Maxwell, et al. *Seven Poets in Search of an Answer: A Poetic Symposium*. Ed. Thomas Yoseleff. New York: Bernard Ackerman, 1944.

Brigham, Besmilr. *Agony Dance: death of the (Dancing Dolls*. Portland, OR: Prensa de Lagar, 1969.

Brigham, Besmilr. *Heaved from the Earth*. New York: Knopf, 1971.

Brigham, Besmilr. *Run Through Rock: Selected Short Poems*. Ed. C. D. Wright. Barrington, RI: Lost Roads Press, 2000.

Brigham, Besmilr. *Spring*. [Horatio, AR?]: Victor Coleman, 1969.

Butler, Jack. *Broken Hallelujah: New and Selected Poems*. Huntsville: Texas Review Press, 2013.

Butler, Jack. Interviews (emailed), March and October 2018.

Butler, Jack. *The Kid Who Wanted to Be a Spaceman*. Little Rock, AR: August House, 1984.

Butler, Jack. *West of Hollywood: Poems from a Hermitage*. Little Rock, AR: August House, 1980.

Cassity, Turner. "The Airship Boys in Africa: A Serial in Twelve Chapters." *Poetry* 116, no. 4 (July 1970), 211–55.

Cassity, Turner. *Between the Chains*. Chicago: University of Chicago Press, 1991.

Cassity, Turner. *The Defense of the Sugar Islands: A Recruiting Poster*. Los Angeles: Symposium Press, 1979.

Cassity, Turner. *The Destructive Element: New and Selected Poems*. Athens: Swallow Press / Ohio University Press, 1998.

Cassity, Turner. *Devils & Islands: Poems*. Athens: Swallow Press / Ohio University Press, 2007.

Cassity, Turner. *Hurricane Lamp*. Chicago: University of Chicago Press, 1986.

Cassity, Turner. *No Second Eden*. Athens: Swallow Press / Ohio University Press, 2002.

Cassity, Turner. *Silver out of Shanghai*. Illustrations by Steve Fritz. Atlanta: Planet Mongo, 1973.

Cassity, Turner. *Steeplejacks in Babel*. Boston: David R. Godine, 1973.

Cassity, Turner. *To the Lost City, or the Sins of Ninevah*. Florence, KY: R. L. Barth, 1987.

Cassity, Turner. *Watchboy, What of the Night?* Middletown, CT: Wesleyan University Press, 1966.

Cassity, Turner. *Yellow for Peril, Black for Beautiful*. Preface by Richard Howard. New York: George Braziller, 1975.

Cassity, Turner, R. L. Barth, and Warren Hope. *Mainstreaming: Poems of Military Life*. Florence, KY: R. L. Barth, 1987.

Clay, Adam. *"Caught No Fish Last night."* *Black Warrior Review*, 30, 2 (Spring–Summer 2004): 66.

Clay, Adam. *A Hotel Lobby at the Edge of the World*. Minneapolis: Milkweed Editions, 2012.

Clay, Adam. *Stranger*. Minneapolis: Milkweed Editions, 2016.

Clay, Adam. *The Wash*. Anderson, SC: Parlor Press, 2016.

Cox, Carol. *The Water in the Pearl*. Brooklyn, NY: Hanging Loose, 1982.

Cox, Carol. *Woodworking and Others Nearby*. Brooklyn, NY: Hanging Loose, 1979.

Cox, Carol, Sheree Hightower, and Cathie Stanga, eds. *Mississippi Observed: Photographs from the Photography Collection of the Mississippi Department of Archives and History with Selections from Literary Works by Mississippians*. Jackson: University Press of Mississippi, 1994.

Creekmore, Hubert. *Formula*. Berkeley, CA: Circle Editions / George Leite, 1947.

Creekmore, Hubert. *The Long Reprieve and Other Poems from New Caledonia*. New York: New Directions, 1946.

Creekmore, Hubert. *Personal Sun: The Early Poems of Hubert Creekmore*. Prairie City, IL: Village Press, 1940.

Creekmore, Hubert. *The Stone Ants*. Los Angeles: Ward Ritchie Press, 1943.

Drew, George. *American Cool*. Penns Park, PA: Tamarack Editions, 2009.

Drew, George. *Down & Dirty*. Huntsville: Texas Review Press, 2015.

Drew, George. *Drumming Armageddon*. Dallas, TX: Madville Publishing, 2020.

Drew, George. *Fancy's Orphan*. Rochester, NY: Tiger Bark Press, 2017.

Drew, George. *"Funk."* *Atticus Review*, May 2013. https://atticusreview.org.funk.

Drew, George. *The Hand That Rounded Peter's Dome*. Cincinnati: Turning Point, 2010.

Drew, George. *The Horse's Name Was Physics*. Cincinnati: Turning Point / Word Tech Communications, 2006.

Drew, George. Interview (emailed), February 16, 2019.

Drew, George. *Pastoral Habits: New and Selected Poems*. Huntsville: Texas Review Press, 2016.

Drew, George. *Toads in a Poisoned Tank*. Penns Park, PA: Tamarack Editions, 1986.

Drew, George. *The View from Jackass Hill*. Huntsville: Texas Review Press, 2011.

Estess, Sybil Pittman. *Blue, Candled in January Sun: Poems*. Cincinnati: Cherry Grove Collections, 2005.

Estess, Sybil Pittman. *Labyrinth*. San Antonio: Pecan Grove Press, 2007.

Estess, Sybil Pittman. *Like That: New and Selected Poems*. Austin, TX: Alamo Bay Press, 2014.

Estess, Sybil Pittman. *Maneuvers*. South Portland, ME: Inleaf Press, 2010.

Estess, Sybil Pittman. *"On the Path to Poetry."* *Langdon Review of the Arts in Texas* 3 (2006–2007): 13–17.

Estess, Sybil Pittman. *Seeing the Desert Green*. Mansfield, TX: Latitudes Press, 1987.

Faulkner, William. *Early Prose and Poetry*. Ed. Carvel Collins. Boston: Little, Brown, 1962.

Faulkner, William. *The Faulkner Reader*. New York: Random House, 1954.

Faulkner, William. *A Green Bough*. New York: H. Smith and R. Haas, 1933.

Faulkner, William. *Helen: A Courtship; and Mississippi Poems*. Introductory essays by Carvel Collins and Joseph Blotner. New Orleans: Tulane University (Friends of the Library); Oxford, MS: Yoknapatawpha Press, 1981.

Faulkner, William. *The Marble Faun*. Boston: Four Seas, 1924.

Faulkner, Wlliam. *The Marble Faun; and A Green Bough*. New York: Random House, 1965.

Faulkner, William. *This Earth: A Poem*. Drawings by Albert Heckman. N.p.: Equinox, 1932.

Faulkner, William, and William Spratling. *Sherwood Anderson and Other Famous Creoles*. New Orleans, 1926; enlarged, Austin: Humanities Research Center, University of Texas, 1966.

Fennelly, Beth Ann. *A Different Kind of Hunger: Poems*. Huntsville: Texas Review Press, 1998.

Fennelly, Beth Ann. *Kudzu*. Tuscaloosa, AL: Crown Ring Press, 2005.

Fennelly, Beth Ann. *Open House: Poems*. Lincoln, NE: Zoo Press, 2002.

Fennelly, Beth Ann. *Tender Hooks: Poems*. New York: Norton, 2004.

Fennelly, Beth Ann. *Unmentionables: Poems*. New York: Norton, 2008.

Fisher-Wirth, Ann. *Blue Window: Poems*. Los Angeles: Archer Books, 2003.

Fisher-Wirth, Ann. *The Bones of Winter Birds*. West Caldwell, NJ: Terrapin Books, 2019.

Fisher-Wirth, Ann. *Carta Marina: A Poem in Three Parts*. San Antonio: Wings Press, 2009.

Fisher-Wirth, Ann. *Dream Cabinet*. San Antonio: Wings Press, 2012.

Fisher-Wirth, Ann. *First, earth*. In *The Chapbook*, ed. Alan May, no. 5 (2015): 35–60.

Fisher-Wirth, Ann. *Five Terraces*. Nicholasville, KY: Wind Publications, 2005.

Fisher-Wirth, Ann. Interview (emailed), June 29, 2018.

Fisher-Wirth, Ann. *Mississippi*. Poems by Ann Fisher-Wirth. Photographs by Maude Schuyler Clay. San Antonio: Wings Press, 2018.

Fisher-Wirth, Ann. *Slide Shows*. Georgetown, KY: Finishing Line Press, 2009.

Ford, Charles Henri. *Flag of Ecstasy*. Introduction by Edward B. Germain. Boston: Black Sparrow / David R. Godine, 1972.

Ford, Charles Henri. *The Garden of Disorder*. New York: New Directions, 1938.

Ford, Charles Henri. *Out of the Labyrinth: Selected Poems*. San Francisco: City Lights, 1991.

Ford, Charles Henri. *The Overturned Lake*. Cincinnati: Little Man Press, 1941.

Ford, Charles Henri. *A Pamphlet of Sonnets*. Majorca: Caravel Press, 1936.

Ford, Charles Henri. *Poems for Painters*. New York: View Editions, 1945.

Ford, Charles Henri, and Parker Tyler. *The Young and Evil*. Paris: Obelisk, 1933. Rpt. London: Gay Men's Press, 1989.

Freeman, John. *Illusion on the Louisiana Side*. Albion, CA: Pygmy Forest Press, 1994.

Freeman, John. *In the Place of Singing*. Hammond, LA: Louisiana Literature Press, 2005.

Freeman, John. *Standing on My Father's Grave*. Lewiston, NY: Mellen Poetry Press, 2001.

Freeman, John. Interview (written), October 25, 2016.

Freeman, John, et al. *Quartet: Selected Poems from the Editors of Batture Willow Press*. Marietta, GA: Batture Willow Press, 2012.

Gilchrist, Ellen. *Falling Through Space: The Journals of Ellen Gilchrist*. Updated ed. Jackson: University Press of Mississippi, 2000.

Gilchrist, Ellen. *The Land Surveyor's Daughter: Poems by Ellen Gilchrist*. Fayetteville, AR: Lost Roads, 1979.

Gilchrist, Ellen. *Riding Out the Tropical Depression: Selected Poems 1975–1985*. New Orleans: Faust Publishing, 1986.

Gilchrist, Ellen. *Things like the Truth: Out of My Later Years*. Jackson: University Press of Mississippi, 2016.

Ginsburg, Melissa. *Arbor*. Grand Rapids, MI: New Michigan Press, 2007.

Ginsburg, Melissa. *Dear Weather Ghost*. New York: Four Way Books, 2013.

Ginsburg, Melissa. *Double Blind*. Chicago: Dancing Girl Press, 2015.

Ginsburg, Melissa. "Pastoral." *New Yorker*, June 8 and 15, 2020.

Ginsburg, Melissa. "Séance." *Kenyon Review*, May/June 2016. https://kenyonreview.org/journal/mayjune-2016/selections/melissa-ginsburg/.

Hamblin, Robert W. *Crossroads: Poems of a Mississippi Childhood*. St. Louis, MO: Time Being Books, 2010.

Hamblin, Robert W. *From the Ground Up: Poems of One Southerner's Passage to Adulthood*. St. Louis, MO: Time Being Books, 1992.

Hamblin, Robert W. *Keeping Score: Sports Poems for Every Season.* St. Louis, MO: Tme Being Books, 2008.

Hamblin, Robert W. *Mind the Gap: Poems by an American in London.* Cape Giraudeau: Southeast Missouri State University Press, 2004.

Hamblin, Robert W. *Perpendicular Rain.* Cape Giraudeau, MO: Southeast Missouri State University, 1986.

Hamblin, Robert W. *Poems and Songs.* Victoria, BC, Canada: First Choice Books, 2015.

Harriell, Derrick. *Cotton.* Detroit: Aquarius Press / Willow Books, 2010.

Harriell, Derrick. *Ropes.* Detroit: Aquarius Press / Willow Books, 2013.

Harriell, Derrick. *Stripper in Wonderland.* Baton Rouge: Louisiana State University Press, 2017.

Howell, Elmo. *The Apricot Tree.* Memphis: E. Howell, 1993.

Howell, Elmo. *Mississippi Back-Roads: Notes on Literature and History.* Memphis: Langford and Associates, 1998.

Howell, Elmo. *Mississippi Home-Places: Notes on Literature and History.* Memphis: E. Howell, 1988, 1991.

Howell, Elmo. *Mount Pleasant.* Memphis: Langford and Associates, 2001.

Howell, Elmo. *Mississippi Scenes: Notes on Literature and History.* Memphis: E. Howell, 1992.

Howell, Elmo. *Notes on Southern Literature.* Memphis: Langford and Associates, 2005.

Howell, Elmo. *Tuesday's Letter and Other Poems.* Memphis: Langford and Associates, 2000.

Howell, Elmo. *Winter Verses.* Memphis: E. Howell, 1989.

Haxton, Brooks. *Dead Reckoning.* Santa Cruz, CA: Story Line Press, 1989.

Haxton, Brooks. *Dominion.* New York: Knopf, 1986.

Haxton, Brooks. *The Lay of Eleanor and Irene.* Woodstock, VT: Countryman Press, 1985.

Haxton, Brooks. *Nakedness, Death, and the Number Zero.* New York: Knopf, 2001.

Haxton, Brooks. "Not a Dicey Lover." *New York Times Book Review,* January 27, 2002.

Haxton, Brooks. *The Sun at Night.* New York: Knopf, 1995.

Haxton, Brooks. *They Lift Their Wings to Cry.* New York: Knopf, 2008.

Haxton, Brooks. *Traveling Company.* New York: Knopf, 1989.

Haxton, Brooks. *Uproar: Antiphonies to Psalms.* New York: Knopf, 2004.

Haxton, Brooks, translator. *Selected Poems of Victor Hugo.* New York: Viking Penguin, 2002.

Haxton, Brooks, translator. *My Blue Piano,* by Else Lasker-Schüler. Syracuse, NY: Syracuse University Press, 2015.

Hummer, T. R. *After the Afterlife.* Cincinnati, OH: Acre Books, 2018.

Hummer, T. R *The Angelic Orders.* Baton Rouge: Louisiana State University Press, 1982.

Hummer, T. R. *Available Surfaces: Essays on Poesis.* Ann Arbor: University of Michigan Press, 2012.

Hummer, T. R. *Bluegrass Wasteland: Selected Poems 1978–2003.* Todmorden, Lancashire, UK: Arc Publications, 2005.

Hummer, T. R. *The 18,000-Ton Olympic Dream: Poems.* New York: Quill / Morrow, 1990.

Hummer, T. R. *Eon.* Baton Rouge: Louisiana State University Press, 2018.

Hummer, T. R. *Ephemeron.* Baton Rouge: Louisiana State University Press, 2011.

Hummer, T. R. *The Infinity Sessions.* Baton Rouge: Louisiana State University Press, 2005.

Hummer, T. R. *In These States.* Durham, NC: Jacar Press, forthcoming 2020.

Hummer, T. R. "Louisiana." *New Yorker,* November 4, 2019, 49.

Hummer, T. R. *Lower-Class Heresy.* Urbana: University of Illinois Press, 1987.

Hummer, T. R *The Passion of the Right-Angled Man.* Urbana: University of Illinois Press, 1984.

Hummer, T. R. *Skandalon.* Baton Rouge: Louisiana State University Press, 2014.

Hummer, T. R. *Useless Virtues.* Baton Rouge: Louisiana State University Press, 2001.

Hummer, T. R. *Walt Whitman in Hell*. Baton Rouge: Louisiana State University Press, 1996.

Jackson, Angela. *And All These Roads Be Luminous: Poems Selected and New*. Evanston, IL: TriQuarterly Books, 1998.

Jackson, Angela. *Dark Legs and Silk Kisses: The Beatitudes of the Spinners*. Evanston, IL: TriQuarterly Books, 1993.

Jackson, Angela. *The Greenville Club*. In *Four Black Poets*. Kansas City, MO: BkMk Press, 1977.

Jackson, Angela. *It Seems Like a Mighty Long Time*. Evanston, IL: TriQuarterly Books, 2015.

Jackson, Angela. "Angels and Tricksters: Looking Back at the Black Arts Movement and Measuring Its Impact Now." In "The Black Arts Movement in Chicago." Edited by Andrew Peart, Eric Powell, and Gerónimo Sarmiento Cruz, 12–27. Special issues, *Chicago Review* 62, no. 4 and 63, nos. 1–2 (2019).

Jackson, Angela. *The Man with the White Liver*. New York: Contact II Publications, 1987.

Jackson, Angela. *Solo in the Boxcar Third Floor E*. Chicago: OBA House, 1985.

Jackson, Angela. *A Surprised Queenhood in the New Black Sun: The Life and Legacy of Gwendolyn Brooks*. Boston: Beacon Press, 2017.

Jackson, Angela. *Voo Doo / Love Magic*. Chicago: Third World Press, 1974.

Johnson, Larry. *Alloy*. Cincinnati: David Robert Books, 2014.

Johnson, Larry. "Comments for *Hellas* (Polychromatic Density in Poetry.)" Paper solicited but unpublished, 1988.

Johnson, Larry. Interview (emailed), March 10, 2018.

Johnson, Larry. *Veins*. Cincinnati: David Robert Books, 2009.

Knight, Etheridge. *Belly Song and Other Poems*. Detroit: Broadside Press, 1973.

Knight, Etheridge. *Born of a Woman: New and Selected Poems*. Boston: Houghton Mifflin, 1980.

Knight, Etheridge. *The Essential Etheridge Knight*. Pittsburgh: University of Pittsburgh Press, 1986.

Knight, Etheridge. *Poems from Prison*. Detroit: Broadside Press, 1968.

Knight, Etheridge, and Other Inmates of Indiana State Prison. *Black Voices from Prison*. New York: Pathfinder Press, 1970.

Kolin, Philip C. "At a Civil Rights Museum." *Arkansas Review* 49, no. 3 (December 2018): 194–95.

Kolin, Philip C. *Benedict's Daughter*. Eugene, OR: Resource Publications, 2017.

Kolin, Philip C. *Deep Wonder*. Takoma Park, MD: Grey Owl, 2000.

Kolin, Philip C. *Departures: A Collection of Poems*. Mobile, AL: Negative Capability Press, 2014.

Kolin, Philip C. *Emmett Till in Different States: Poems*. Chicago: Third World Press, 2015.

Kolin, Philip C. Interviews (emailed), March 2018.

Kolin, Philip C. *In the Custody of Words: Poems*. Steubenville, OH: Franciscan University Press, 2013.

Kolin, Philip C. *A Parable of Women: Poems*. Itta Bena, MS: Yazoo River Press, 2009.

Kolin, Philip C. *Pilsen Snow: Poems*. Georgetown, KY: Finishing Line Press, 2015.

Kolin, Philip C. *Reaching Forever: Poems*. Eugene, OR: Cascade/Wipf and Stock, 2019.

Kolin, Philip C. *Reading God's Handwriting*. Saint Simon's Island, GA: Kaufmann, 2012.

Kolin, Philip C. *Wailing Walls: Poems*. Conneaut Lake, PA: Wind and Water Press, 2006.

Kolin, Philip C., and Jack B. Bedell, eds. *Down to the Dark River: An Anthology of Contemporary Poems about the Mississippi River*. Hammond, LA: Louisiana Literature Press, 2016.

Kolin, Philip C., and Susan Swartwout, eds. *Hurricane Blues: Poems about Katrina and Rita*. Cape Girardeau: Southeast Missouri University Press, 2006.

McInnis, C. Liegh. *Confessions: Brainstormin' from Midnight till Dawn*. Clinton, MS: Psyche-delic Literature, 1998.

McInnis, C. Liegh. "Continuing the Analysis of Art as Socio-Political Engagement." *Journal of Ethnic American Literature*, no. 1 (2011): 127–52.

McInnis, C. Liegh. *Da Black Book of Linguistic Liberation*. Clinton, MS: Psychedelic Litera-ture, 2007.

McInnis, C. Liegh. "The Importance of Teaching Cultural Diversity in College World Literature Courses." In Motion Magazine, September 20, 1999. https://www.inmotion-magazine.com/mcinnis.html.

McInnis, C. Liegh. Interview (emailed), January 22, 2019.

McInnis, C. Liegh. *Matters of Reality: Body, Mind and Soul*. Clinton, MS: Psychedelic Litera-ture, 1996.

McInnis, C. Liegh. "The New African American Writers of Mississippi." In Motion Maga-zine. http://www.inmotionmagazine.com//naawm.html.

McInnis, C. Liegh. *Searchin'4 Psychedelica*. Clinton, MS: Psychedelic Literature 1999.

Mills, William. *The Meaning of Coyotes*. Baton Rouge: Louisiana State University Press, 1984.

Mills, William. *Stained Glass*. Baton Rouge: Louisiana State University Press, 1979.

Mills, William. *The Stillness in Moving Things: The World of Howard Nemerov*. Memphis: Memphis State University Press, 1975.

Mills, William. *Watch for the Fox*. Baton Rouge: Louisiana State University Press, 1974.

Morris, Benjamin. *Coronary*. New Orleans: Fitzgerald Letterpress, 2011.

Morris, Benjamin. *Ecotone*. Paintings by Myrtle von Damitz III. New Orleans: Antenna / Press Street Press, 2017.

Morris, Benjamin. *A History of the Hub City*. Charleston, SC: Arcadia / History Press, 2014.

Percy, William Alexander. *The Collected Poems of William Alexander Percy*. Foreword by Roark Bradford. New York: Knopf, 1943.

Percy, William Alexander. *Lanterns on the Levee: Recollections of a Planter's Son*. New York: Knopf, 1941.

Percy, William Alexander. *Selected Poems*. Preface by Llewellyn Jones. New Haven, CT: Yale University Press, 1930.

Plumpp, Sterling D. *Blues Narratives*. Chicago: Tia Chucha Press, 1999.

Plumpp, Sterling D. *Blues: The Story Always Untold*. Chicago: Another Chicago Press, 1989.

Plumpp, Sterling D. *Clinton*. Detroit: Broadside Press, 1976.

Plumpp, Sterling D. [Four poems.] In "The Black Arts Movement in Chicago." Edited by Andrew Peart, Eric Powell, and Gerónimo Sarmiento Cruz, 219–23. Special issues, *Chicago Review* 62, no. 4 and 63, nos. 1–2 (2019).

Plumpp, Sterling D. *Home/Bass: Poems*. Introduction by Reginald Gibbons. Chicago: Third World Press, 2013.

Plumpp, Sterling D. *Horn Man*. Chicago: Third World Press, 1995.

Plumpp, Sterling D. Interview (telephone), October 15, 2018.

Plumpp, Sterling D. *Johannesburg and Other Poems*. Chicago: Another Chicago Press, 1993.

Plumpp, Sterling D. *The Mojo Hands Call, I Must Go*. New York: Thunder's Mouth Press, 1982.

Plumpp, Sterling D. *Ornate with Smoke*. Chicago: Third World Press, 1997.

Plumpp, Sterling D. *Portable Soul*. Chicago: Third World Press, 1969. Revised ed., 1974.

Plumpp, Sterling D. *Steps to Break the Circle*. Chicago: Third World Press, 1974.

Plumpp, Sterling D. *Velvet Bebop Kente Cloth.* Chicago: Third World Press, 2003.

Plumpp, Sterling, ed. *Somehow We Survive: An Anthology of South African Writing.* Illustrated. New York: Thunder's Mouth Press, 1982.

Polk, Noel. *Walking Safari or, The Hippo Highway and Other Poems.* Huntsville: Texas Review Press, 2011.

Ruffin, Paul. *The Book of Boys and Girls.* Hammond, LA: Louisiana Literature Press, 2003.

Ruffin, Paul. *Circling.* Dallas: Browder Springs Press, 1996.

Ruffin, Paul. *Lighting the Furnace Pilot.* Peoria, IL: Spoon River Poetry Press, 1980.

Ruffin, Paul. *New and Selected Poems.* Fort Worth: Texas Christian University Press, 2010.

Sargent, Robert. *Aspects of a Southern Story.* Washington, DC: Word Works, 1983.

Sargent, Robert. *Now Is Always the Miraculous Time.* Washington, DC: Washington Writers' Publishing House, 1977.

Sargent, Robert. *A Woman from Memphis: Poems 1960–1978.* Washington, DC: Word Works, 1979.

Seay, James. Interview (emailed), April 5, 2018.

Seay, James. *Let Not Your Hart.* Middletown, CT: Wesleyan University Press, 1970.

Seay, James. *The Light As They Found It.* New York: Morrow, 1990.

Seay, James. *Open Field, Understory: New and Selected Poems.* Baton Rouge: Louisiana State University Press, 1997.

Seay, James. *Said There Was Somebody Talking to Him through the Air Conditioner.* Winston-Salem, NC: Palaemon Publishers, 1985.

Seay, James. *Water Tables.* Middletown, CT: Wesleyan University Press, 1974.

Seay, James. "The Weight of a Feather." *Oxford American,* 82 (Fall 2013).

Seay, James. *Where Our Voices Broke Off.* Deerfield, MA: Deerfield Press / Dublin: Gallery Press, 1978.

Shirley, Aleda. *Chinese Architecture.* Athens: University of Georgia Press, 1986.

Shirley, Aleda. *Dark Familiar: Poems.* Louisville, KY: Sarabande Books, 2006.

Shirley, Aleda. *Long Distance.* Oxford, OH: Miami University Press, 1996.

Shirley, Aleda. *Silver Ending.* St. Louis. MO: St. Louis Poetry Center, 1991.

Shirley, Aleda, Susan M. Glisson, and Ann J. Abadie, eds. *Mississippi Writers. Directory and Literary Guide.* University, MS: Center for the Study of Southern Culture / University of Mississippi, 1995.

Shirley, Aleda, David Wojahn, et al. *Rilke's Children.* Foreword by Guy Davenport. Frankfort, KY: Frankfort Arts Foundation, 1987.

Simmons, J. Edgar. *Driving to Biloxi.* Baton Rouge: Louisiana State University Press, 1968.

Simmons, J. Edgar. *Osiris at the Roller Derby.* Foreword by James Dickey. Bryan, TX: Cedarshouse Press, 1983.

Simmons, J. Edgar. *Pocahontas and Other Poems.* Privately printed, ©1957.

Stone, John. *In All This Rain.* Baton Rouge: Louisiana State University Press, 1980.

Stone, John. *Music from Apartment 8: New and Selected Poems.* Baton Rouge: Louisiana State University Press, 2004.

Stone, John. *Renaming the Streets.* Baton Rouge: Louisiana State University Press, 1985.

Stone, John. *The Smell of Matches.* New Brunswick, NJ: Rutgers University Press, 1972.

Stone, John. *Where Water Begins.* Baton Rouge: Louisiana State University Press, 1998.

Trethewey, Natasha. *Bellocq's Ophelia: Poems by Natasha Trethewey.* Minneapolis: Graywolf Press, 2002.

Trethewey, Natasha. *Beyond Katrina: A Meditation on the Mississippi Gulf Coast*. Athens: University of Georgia Press, 2012.

Trethewey, Natasha. *Domestic Work: Poems by Natasha Trethewey*. Minneapolis: Graywolf Press, 2000.

Trethewey, Natasha. *Native Guard: Poems*. Boston: Houghton Mifflin, 2006.

Trethewey, Natasha. *Thrall: Poems*. Boston: Houghton Mifflin Harcourt, 2012.

Trethewey, Natasha. Foreword to *Photographs*, by Eudora Welty. New ed. Jackson: University Press of Mississippi, 2019.

Walker, Margaret. *For My People*. Foreword by Stephen Vincent Benét. New Haven, CT: Yale University Press, 1942.

Walker, Margaret. *Jubilee*. New York: Bantam Books, 1967.

Walker, Margaret. *Prophets for a New Day*. Detroit: Broadside Press, 1970.

Walker, Margaret. *This Is My Century: New and Collected Poems*. Athens: University of Georgia Press, 1989.

Ward, Jerry W., Jr. *Fractal Song: Poems*. Boston: Black Widow Press, 2016.

Ward, Jerry W., Jr. *The Katrina Papers: A Journal of Trauma and Recovery*. New Orleans: University of New Orleans Publishing, 2008.

Ward, Jerry W., Jr. "On Fractal Song." http://jerryward.blogspot.com/2016/10/on-fractal -song.html.

Whitehead, James. "For Ellen after the Publication of Her Stories." *Southern Review* 19, no. 4 (October 1983).

Whitehead, James T. *For, From, About James T. Whitehead*. Ed. Michael Burns. Springfield, MO: Moon City Press, 2009.

Whitehead, James T. *Local Men; and, Domains: Two Books of Poetry*. Urbana: University of Illinois Press, 1987.

Whitehead, James T. *Near at Hand*. Columbia, MO: University of Missouri Press, 1993.

Whitehead, James T. *The Panther: Posthumous Poems*. Ed. Michael Burns. Introduction by James Tabor. Springfield, MO: Moon City Press, 2008.

Wilkinson, Claude. "The Good, the Bad, and the Ugly of Black Representation in Works by Three Mississippi Photographers," *Arkansas Review* 49, no. 3 (December 2018): 168–76.

Wilkinson, Claude. *Joy in the Morning*. Baton Rouge: Louisiana State University Press, 2004.

Wilkinson, Claude. *Marvelous Light*. Nacogdoches, TX: Stephen F. Austin University Press, 2018.

Wilkinson, Claude. *Reading the Earth*. East Lansing: Michigan State University Press, 1998.

Wilkinson, Claude. *World Without End*. Eugene, OR: Slant Books/Wipf and Stock, 2020.

Wright, Richard. "Between the World and Me." Poem Hunter. https://www.poemhunter. com/richard-wright.

Wright, Richard. *Haiku: The Last Poems of an American Icon*. Ed. Yoshinobu Hakutani and Robert L. Tener. New York: Arcade Publishing, 2012. First published 1998 by Arcade as *Haiku: This Other World*.

Wright, Richard. "We of the Streets." Undocumented Ohio. http://undocumentedohio. wordpress.com/2012/01/19/we-of-the-streets-by-richard-wright.

Young, Al. *The Blues Don't Change: New and Selected Poems*. Baton Rouge: Louisiana State University Press, 1982.

Young, Al. *Coastal Nights and Inland Afternoons*. Santa Monica, CA: Angel City Press, 2006.

Young, Al. *Dancing: Poems*. New York: Corinth Books, 1969.

Young, Al. *Geography of the Near Past: Poems*. New York: Holt, Rinehart and Winston, 1976.

Young, Al. *Heaven: Collected Poems 1956–1990*. Berkeley: Creative Arts, 1992.

Young, Al. *The Song Turning Back into Itself: Poems*. New York: Holt, Rinehart and Winston, 1971.

Young, Al. *The Sound of Dreams Remembered: Poems 1990–2000*. Berkeley: Creative Arts, 2001.

SECONDARY SOURCES

Abbott, Dorothy, ed. *Mississippi Writers: An Anthology*. Jackson: University Press of Mississippi, 1991.

Abbott, Dorothy, ed. *Mississippi Writers: Reflections of Childhood and Youth*. Vol. 3, *Poetry*. Jackson: University Press of Mississippi, 1988.

Adams, Richard P. *Faulkner: Myth and Motion*. Princeton, NJ: Princeton University Press, 1968.

Anaporte-Easton, Jean. "Etheridge Knight: Poet and Prisoner, An Introduction." *Callaloo* 19, 4 (1996): 941–46. http://www.jstor.org/stable/3299129.

"Angela Jackson." poetryfoundation.org.

Bailey, Tom. "*Coronary* by Benjamin Morris." The Literateur. http://literateur.com/coronary-by-benjamin-morris/.

Bain, Robert, and Joseph M. Flora, eds. *Contemporary Poets, Dramatists, Essayists, and Novelists of the South: A Bio-Bibliographical Sourcebook*. Westport, CT: Greenwood Press, 1994.

Baker, Lewis. *The Percys of Mississippi: Politics and Literature in the New South*. Baton Rouge: Louisiana State University Press, 1983.

Baker, Peter. *Obdurate Brilliance: Exteriority and the Modern Long Poem*. Gainesville: University of Florida Press, 1991.

Barry, John M. *Rising Tide: The Great Mississippi River Flood of 1927 and How It Changed America*. New York: Simon & Schuster, 1997.

Baumgaertner, Jill. Review of *Reaching Forever: Poems*, by Philip C. Kolin. *Christian Century* 136, no. 17 (August 14, 2019): 41, 43.

Beatty, Richmond, Floyd C. Watkins, and Thomas Daniel Young, eds. *The Literature of the South*. Chicago: Scott, Foresman, 1952; revised, 1968.

Bedient, Calvin. *In the Heart's Last Kingdom: Robert Penn Warren's Major Poetry*. Cambridge, MA: Harvard University Press, 1984.

Billington, James H. "Natasha Trethewey Appointed U.S. Poet Laureate." News from the Colby College Libraries, November 19, 2019. http://web/newsfromthelibraries/2012/06/08/natasha-trethewey-appointed-19th-poet-laureate-consultant-in-poetry.

Birdsong, Destiny O. "'Memories That Are(n't) Mine': Matrilineal Trauma and Defiant Reinscription in Natasha Trethewey's *Native Guard*." *African American Review* 48, no. 1–2 (Spring / Summer 2015): 97–110.

Black, Patti Carr, and Marion Barnwell. *Touring Literary Mississippi*. Jackson: University Press of Mississippi, 2002.

Bledsoe, C. L. "Besmilr Moore Brigham." *Encyclopedia of Arkansas*. http://www.encyclopediaofarkansas.net/encyclopedia/entry-detail.aspx?entryID=1026.

Blotner, Joseph. *Faulkner: A Biography*. Vol 1. New York: Random House, 1974.

"Book of the Week: *The Chain in the Heart*, by Hubert Creekmore." (By C. M.) *Jet*, August 6, 1953: 50.

Boozer, William. *William Faulkner's First Book: The Marble Faun, Fifty Years Later*. Memphis: Pigeon Roost Press, 1974.

Brooks, Cleanth. *On the Prejudices, Predilections, and Firm Beliefs of William Faulkner.* Baton Rouge: Louisiana State University Press, 1987.

Browning, Maria. Review of *Mississippi*, by Ann Fisher-Wirth and Maude Schuyler Clay. Chapter 16. https://chapter16.org/mississippi-voices/.

Bryant, J. A., Jr. *Twentieth-Century Southern Literature.* Lexington: University Press of Kentucky, 1997.

Burt, Stephanie. *Don't Read Poetry.* New York: Basic Books, 2019.

Carson, Joelle. Interview with Melissa Ginsburg. Lunar Cougar, September 9, 2016. http://development.uh.edu/lunarcougar/melissa-ginsburg-02/.

Chicago Literary Hall of Fame. *Program of Presentation of the Fuller Award to Sterling Plumpp.* In cosponsorship with the Poetry Foundation. September 19, 2019.

"Claude Wilkinson." *Image: Art, Faith, Mystery.* http://imagejournal.org/artist/claude-wilkinson/.

Cobb, James C. *The Most Southern Place on Earth: The Mississippi Delta and the Roots of Southern Identity.* New York: Oxford University Press, 1991.

Collins, Michael S. *Understanding Etheridge Knight.* Columbia: University of South Carolina Press, 2012.

"Conversation with Melissa Ginsburg." *Kenyon Review.* Accessed August 8, 2019. https://www.kenyonreview.org/conversation/melissa-ginsburg/.

Corrington, John William, and Miller Williams, eds. *Southern Writing in the Sixties.* Vol. 2, *Poetry.* Baton Rouge: Louisiana State University Press, 1967.

Cunningham, James. "Sterling D. Plumpp." *Dictionary of Literary Biography.* Vol. 41, *Afro-American Poets since 1955*, 257–65. Ann Arbor, MI: Gale Research Company, 1985.

Cycholl, Garin. "'a contract with distance': The Epic Shape of Sterling Plumpp's Blues Lyric." In "The Black Arts Movement in Chicago." Edited by Andrew Peart, Eric Powell, and Gerónimo Sarmiento Cruz, 211–18. Special issues, *Chicago Review* 62, no. 4 and 63, nos. 1–2 (2019).

Davie, Donald. "On Turner Cassity." *Chicago Review* 34 (Summer 1983): 22–29.

Deavours, Ernestine Clayton. *The Mississippi Poets.* Memphis: E. H. Clarke & Bro., 1922.

DeFatta, Jeremy. "An Interview with Painter-Poet Claude Wilkinson." *Arkansas Review* 50, no. 1 (April 2019): 43–47.

Dickey, James. *Babel to Byzantium: Poets and Poetry Now.* New York: Farrar, Straus and Giroux, 1968.

Dickinson, Emily. *The Poems of Emily Dickinson.* Ed. R. W. Franklin. Cambridge: Belknap Press of Harvard University Press, 1999.

Donovan, Gregory. Interview with T. R. Hummer. https://blackbird.vcu.edu/v2n2/features/hummer_tr_021404/hummer_tr_text.htm.

"Ellen Gilchrist." Encyclopedia.com.

"Ellen Gilchrist." University of Arkansas website. http://fulbright.uark.edu.

Elliott, Elise. Review of *Labyrinth*, by Sybil Pittman Estess. *Louisiana Literature* 25, no. 2 (Fall–Winter 2008).

Erskine, John. *The Delight of Great Books.* Indianapolis: Bobbs-Merrill, 1928.

"Etheridge Knight." poetryfoundation.org.

"Etheridge Knight." poets.org.

Felgar, Robert. *Richard Wright.* Boston: Twayne, 1980.

Flora, Joseph M. *Fifty Southern Writers after 1900: A Bio-Bibliographic Sourcebook.* Westport, CT: Greenwood Press, 1987.

Flora, Joseph M., and Amber Vogel, eds. *Southern Writers: A New Biographical Dictionary.* Baton Rouge: LSU Press, 2006.

Fried, Daisy. "A Muse for Our Messed-Up World." *New York Times Book Review*, December 16, 2018, 11.

Gardner, Stephen, and William Wright, eds. *The Southern Poetry Anthology*. Vol. 2, *Mississippi*. Huntsville: Texas Review Press, 2011.

Garrett, George P. "An Examination of the Poetry of William Faulkner." *Princeton University Library Chronicle*. 18, no. 3 (Spring 1957), 124–35.

Garrett, George, ed. *The Yellow Shoe Poets: Selected Poems, 1964–1999*. Baton Rouge: Louisiana State University Press, 1999.

Gates, Henry Louis, Jr., and Valerie Smith, eds. *The Norton Anthology of African American Literature*. 3rd ed. New York: Norton, 2014.

Girard, Melissa. "On 'We of the Streets.'" *Modern American Poetry*. http://www.english.illinois.edu/maps/poets/s_z/r_wright/streets.html.

Graham, Maryemma, ed. *Conversations with Margaret Walker*. Jackson: University Press of Mississippi, 2002.

Groult, Benoîte. *Mon évasion: Autobiographie*. Paris: Bernard Grasset, 2008.

Hakutani, Yoshinobu. *Richard Wright and Haiku*. Columbia: University of Missouri Press, 2014.

Hannan, Chris, ed. *Alluvial Cities*. Huntsville: Texas Review Press, 2015.

Hayes, Terrance. *To Float in the Space Between: A Life and Work in Conversation with the Life and Work of Etheridge Knight*. New York: Wave Books, 2018.

Hearne, Dixon. Review of *Emmett Till in Different States*, by Philip C. Kolin. *Louisiana Literature* 35, no. 1 (2018): 207–8.

Henninger, Katherine R. "What Remains: Race, Nation, and the Adult Child in the Poetry of Natasha Trethewey." *Southern Quarterly* 50, no. 4 (Summer 2013): 55–74.

Hobratsch, Jonathan. Interview with T. R. Hummer. HuffPost, March 30, 2015; updated May 30, 2015. https://www.huffpost.com/entry/2015-poetry-month-an-interview-with-t-r-hummer_b_6965884.

Hobson, Geary, Janet McAdams, and Kathryn Walkiewicz, eds. *People Who Stayed: Southeastern Indian Writing after Removal*. Norman: University of Oklahoma Press, 2010.

Hoppenthaler, John. Interview with T. R. Hummer. Connotation Press 10, no. 6 (July 2019). https://connotationpress.com/hoppenthaler-s-congeries/2010/february-2010/300-t-r-hummer-interview-poetry.

Howard, Alexander. *Charles Henri Ford: Between Modernism and Postmodernism*. London and New York: Bloomsbury Academic, 2017.

Howard, John. *Men Like That: A Southern Queer History*. Chicago: University of Chicago Press, 1999.

Hummel, H. K. Review of *Eon*, by T. R. Hummer. *Arkansas Review* 49, no. 3 (December 2018): 214–15.

Humphries, Jefferson, and John Lowe, eds. *The Future of Southern Letters*. New York: Oxford University Press, 1996.

James, Alice, ed. *Mississippi Verse*. Chapel Hill: University of North Carolina Press, 1934.

Jones, John Griffin, ed. *Mississippi Writers Talking*. Jackson: University Press of Mississippi, 1982.

Jones, Roger D. "T. R. Hummer." *Dictionary of Literary Biography*. Vol. 120, 151–56. Ann Arbor, MI: Gale Research Company, 1992.

Kaplan, Sara. "Interview: Natasha Trethewey on Facts, Photographs, and Loss." *Fugue*, no. 32 (Winter–Spring 2007): 66–74.

King, Richard. *A Southern Renaissance: The Cultural Awakening of the American South, 1930–1955*. New York: Oxford, 1980.

Komunyakaa, Yusef. *Blue Notes: Essays, Interviews, and Commentaries*. Ed. Radiclani Clytus. Ann Arbor: University of Michigan Press, 2000.

Komunyakaa, Yusef. *Conversations with Yusef Komunyakaa*. Ed. Shirley A. James Hanshaw. Jackson: University Press of Mississippi, 2010.

Lee, Don. "About Al Young: A Profile." *Ploughshares*, no. 60 (Spring 1993).

Lee, Felicia R. "Like Author, Like Heroine: Blazing a Trail into the World of Elite Education." *New York Times*. October 12, 2009. https://www.nytimes.com/2009/10/13/books/13jackson.html.

Lloyd, James B., ed. *Lives of Mississippi Authors, 1817–1967.* Jackson: University Press of Mississippi, 1981.

Lumpkin, Shirley. "Etheridge Knight." *Dictionary of Literary Biography*. Vol. 41, *Afro-American Poets since 1955*, 202–11. Ann Arbor, MI: Gale Research Company, 1985.

Marshall, Randy. "T. R. Hummer: Visionary Imperfect." *Blackbird: An Online Journal of Literature and the Arts* 15, no. 2 (Fall 2016).

Marx, Leo. *The Machine in the Garden: Technology and the Pastoral Ideal*. New York: Oxford University Press, 1964.

McCay, Mary A. *Ellen Gilchrist*. New York: Twayne, 1997.

McClanahan, Brion. "Stoop, Angels, Hither from the Skies." Podcast, December 8, 2018. https://www.abbevilleinstitute.org/blog/podcast-episode-149/.

McClure, John. "Literature Less and Less." New Orleans *Times-Picayune*, January 25, 1925.

McFee, Michael. *Appointed Rounds: Essays*. Macon: Mercer University Press, 2018.

McHaney, Pearl Amelia. "Natasha Trethewey's Triptych: The Bodies of History in *Bellocq's Ophelia, Native Guard,* and *Thrall.*" *Southern Quarterly* 50, no. 4 (Summer 2013): 153–72.

McNeely. Thomas, Jr., and Peter Buttross, Jr. *Beyond the Bars*. Natchez: Red Dawn Press, 2004.

McNeil, Sophie. "C. Liegh McInnis: Jackson's Renaissance Man." *Jackson Free Press*, December 31, 2008.

Middleton, Billy. Review of *Pilsen Snow*, by Philip C. Kolin. *Louisiana Literature* 33, no. 2 (2016): 135–37.

Millichap, Joseph. "'Love and Knowledge': Daughters and Fathers in Natasha Trethewey's *Thrall.*" *Southern Quarterly* 50, no. 4 (Summer 2013): 189–207.

Mississippi Encyclopedia. Jackson: University Press of Mississippi, 2017.

Mississippi History Now. www.mshistorynow.mdah.ms.gov.

Mississippi Writers and Musicians. http://www.mswritersandmusicians.com.

Mississippi Writers Page. http://mwp.olemiss.edu.

Moore, Jack B. *Maxwell Bodenheim*. New York: Twayne, 1970.

Morris, Willie. *My Mississippi*. Photographs by David Rae Morris. Jackson: University Press of Mississippi, 2000.

Mullen, Bill. "On Richard Wright's Poetry." *Modern American Poetry*. http://www.english.illinois.edu/maps/poets/s_z/r_wright/about.html.

Nesanovich, Stella. Review of *Departures*, by Philip C. Kolin. *Louisiana Literature* 32, (2015): 132–44.

Nesanovich, Stella. Review of *Wailing Walls* by Philip C. Kolin. *Christianity and Literature* 56, no. 1 (2006): 181–84.

Nussbaum, Emily. "High Lyrical, Low Cynical." *New York Times Book Review*, December 30, 2001.

Olson, Ray. Review of *No Second Eden*, by Turner Cassity. *Booklist*, September 15, 2002.

Owen, Guy, and Mary C. Williams, eds. *Contemporary Southern Poetry: An Anthology.* Baton Rouge: Louisiana State University Press, 1979.

Patterson, Tracy J. "Angela Jackson." *The Concise Oxford Companion to African American Literature.* Ed. William L. Andrews, Frances Smith Foster, and Trudier Harris. New York: Oxford University Press, 2001.

Peart, Andrew, Eric Powell, and Gerónimo Sarmiento Cruz, eds. "The Black Arts Movement in Chicago." Special issues, *Chicago Review* 62, no. 4 and 63, nos. 1–2 (2019).

Pence, Amy. Review of *Dear Weather Ghost* by Melissa Ginsberg. The Rumpus, February 26, 2014. https://therumpus.net/2014/02/dear-weather-ghost-by-melissa-ginsburg/.

Perkins, David. *A History of Modern Poetry.* 2 vols. Cambridge: Belknap Press of Harvard University Press, 1976.

Pinsker, Sanford. "A Conversation with Etheridge Knight." *African American Review* 50, no. 4 (Winter 2017): 711–14.

Polk, Noel, and James R. Scafidel, eds. *An Anthology of Mississippi Writers.* Jackson: University Press of Mississippi, 1979.

Pound, Ezra. "A Retrospect." In *Literary Essays of Ezra Pound,* 3–14. 1918. Norfolk, CT: New Directions, 1968.

Powell, Dawn. "A Diamond to Cut New York." *New Yorker,* December 3, 2018, 52.

Rayson, Ann. "Richard Wright's Life." *Modern American Poetry.* http://www.english.illinois .edu/maps/poets/s_z/r_wright_life.html.

Reed, John Shelton. *Dixie Bohemia: A French Quarter Circle in the 1920s.* Baton Rouge: Louisiana State University Press, 2014.

Reed, John Shelton. *The Enduring South: Subcultural Persistence in Mass Society.* Lexington, MA: D. C. Heath, 1972.

Reed, John Shelton. *Minding the South.* Columbia: University of Missouri Press, 2003; rpt. Piscataway, NJ: Transaction Publishers, 2014.

Reed, John Shelton. *One South: An Ethnic Approach to Regional Culture.* Baton Rouge: Louisiana State University Press, 1982.

Rickels, Milton, and Patricia Rickels. *Richard Wright.* Austin: Steck-Vaughn Co., 1970.

Rowell, Charles Henry, ed. *Angles of Ascent: A Norton Anthology of Contemporary African American Poetry.* New York: Norton, 2013

Rubin, Louis D., Jr., et al. *The History of Southern Literature.* Baton Rouge: Louisiana State University Press, 1985.

Ryor, Colleen Marie. Interview with D. C. Berry. *Adirondack Review* (Summer 2003). http://www.theadirondackreview.com/interviewberry.html.

Sanderson, Jordan. "Life in Other Words: The Poetry of Angela Ball." *Valley Voices* 18, no. 1 (Spring 2018).

Schaefer, Ward. "Fletcher Cox Negotiates with Nature." *Jackson Free Press,* September 8, 2010. http://www.jacksonfreepress.com/news/2010/sep/08/fletcher-cox-negotiates-with-nature/.

Seaman, Donna. "*It Seems Like a Mighty Long Time* by Angela Jackson." February 1, 2015. March 5, 2019. www.booklistonline.com.

Shaw, David. "Etheridge Knight." https://web.wpi.edu/Pubs/E-project/Available/E-project -052609-224700/unrestricted/Etheridge_Knight_biography.pdf.

Shaw, Luci. "The Extraordinary Ordinary: Philip Kolin's *Reaching Forever.*" *The Cresset* 83, no. 1 (2019), 31–32.

"Simon Armitage Named Britain's New Poet Laureate." *Independent,* May 10, 2019. https://www.independent.co.uk/.

Simpson, Lewis P. *The Fable of the Southern Writer*. Baton Rouge: Louisiana State University Press, 1994.

Skei, Hans H. "William Faulkner." *Dictionary of Literary Biography*. Vol. 330, *Nobel Prize Laureates in Literature, Part 2: Faulkner-Kipling*, 3–19. Ann Arbor, MI: Gale Research Company, 2007.

Smith, D. L. "Angela Jackson." *Dictionary of Literary Biography*. Vol. 41, *Afro-American Poets since 1955*, 176–83. Ann Arbor, MI: Gale Research Company, 1985.

Solomon, Janera. "'There's So Much More to Explore': A Conversation with Poet Angela Jackson." Sampsonia Way. August 3, 2012. https://www.sampsoniaway.org/literary-voices /2012/08/03/theres-so-much-to-explore-a-conversation-with-poet-angela-jackson/.

Stanford, Donald. "A Backward Glance at the New *Southern Review*," *Explorations* 7 (1993).

St. Clair, Jane "A First Book of Poems." *Chattahoochee Review* 20, no. 2 (Winter 2000), 91–96.

Stokesbury, Leon, ed. *The Made Thing: An Anthology of Contemporary Southern Poetry*. 2nd ed. Fayetteville: University of Arkansas Press, 1999.

Taylor, Corey M. "An Interview with Sterling D. Plumpp." *Southern Quarterly* 55, no. 1 (Fall 2017): 136–58.

Thomas, Larry D. Review of *Reaching Forever*, by Philip C. Kolin. *Louisiana Literature* 36, no. 2 (2019): 152-54.

Thompson, Julius E. *The Anthology of Black Mississippi Poets*. Rochester, NY: Frederick Douglass Institute, 1988.

Thompson, Julius E. *Black Life in Mississippi: Essays on Political, Social, and Cultural Studies in a Deep South State*. Lanham, MD: University Press of America, 2001.

Thompson, Julius E. *Dudley Randall, Broadside Press, and the Black Arts Movement in Detroit, 1960–1995*. Jefferson City, NC: McFarland, 1999.

Tracy, Katherine, ed. *In the Eye*. Alamogordo, NM: Thunder-Rain Publishing, 2007.

Tuma, Keith. "Turner Cassity." *Dictionary of Literary Biography*. Vol. 105, 19–25, *American Poets Since World War II, Second Series*. Ann Arbor, MI: Gale Research Company, 1991.

"Turner Cassity. *New Georgia Encyclopedia*. georgiaencyclopedia.org.

Turner, Daniel Cross, and William Wright. *Hard Lines: Rough South Poetry*. Columbia: University of South Carolina Press, 2016.

Turner, Daniel Cross. "Southern Crossings: An Interview with Natasha Trethewey." *Waccamaw* 6 (Fall 2010).

Walker, Sue Brannan. Review of *Reading God's Handwriting*, by Philip C. Kolin. *Louisiana Literature*, 30, no. 1–2 (2013): 202–6.

Ward, Jerry W., Jr., and John Oliver Killens, eds. *Black Southern Voices: An Anthology of Fiction, Poetry, Drama, Nonfiction, and Critical Essays*. New York: Meridian, 1992.

Ward, Nancy. "Biography of Angela Jackson." Mississippi Writers and Musicians. mswritersandmusicians.com.

Warren, Nagueyalti. "History, Memory, and Nostalgia in the Works of Natasha Trethewey." *Southern Quarterly* 50, no. 4 (Summer 2013): 75–98.

Watkins, Lorie, ed. *A Literary History of Mississippi*. Jackson: University Press of Mississippi, 2017.

Watson, James G. *William Faulkner: Letters and Fictions*. Austin: University of Texas Press, 1987.

Weiland, Shanti. Review of *Talking Pillow*, by Angela Ball. *Valley Voices* 18, no. 1 (Spring 2018).

Welty, Eudora. *The Eye of the Story: Selected Essays and Reviews*. New York: Random House, 1978.

Wilson, Edmund. *The Wound and the Bow: Seven Studies in Literature*. New York: Oxford University Press, 1947.

Wilson, James Matthew. *The Fortunes of Poetry in an Age of Unmaking*. Oregon: Wiseblood Books, 2015.

Winchell, Mark Royden. "Making the Southern Canon." *Southern Partisan*, Fall 1987–Winter 1988.

Winters, Yvor. *Forms of Discovery: Critical and Historical Essays on the Forms of the Short Poem in English*. Denver, CO: Alan Swallow, 1967.

Winters, Yvor. *In Defense of Reason*. 3 vols. New York: Swallow Press and William Morrow, 1947.

Wise, Benjamin E. *William Alexander Percy: The Curious Life of a Mississippi Planter and Sexual Freethinker*. Chapel Hill: University of North Carolina Press, 2012.

Wyatt-Brown, Bertram. *The House of Percy: Honor, Melancholy, and Imagination in a Southern Family*. New York: Oxford University Press, 1992.

Wyman, Hastings. "Robert Sargent: Remembering a Friend and Poet." *Beltway Poetry Quarterly* 7, no. 4 (Winter 2008). http://washingtonart.com/beltway/sargent2.html.

Yates, Gayle Graham. *Mississippi Mind: A Personal Cultural History of an American State*. Knoxville: University of Tennessee Press, 1990.

Zheng, John [Jianiqng Zheng], ed. *African American Haiku: Cultural Visions*. Jackson: University Press of Mississippi, 2016.

Zheng, John, ed. *Conversations with Sterling Plumpp*. Jackson: University Press of Mississippi, 2016.

Zheng, John. "*Emmett Till in Different States: Poems*: An Interview with Philip C. Kolin." *Arkansas Review* 48, no. 3 (December 2017): 189–96. Includes two Kolin poems.

Zheng, John. Interview with Angela Ball. *Poetry South*, no. 1 (2009). Includes Ball poems.

Zheng, John. Introduction to poems by Angela Ball. *Valley Voices* 18, no. 1 (Spring 2018).

Zheng, John. *The Other World of Richard Wright: Perspectives on His Haiku*. Jackson: University Press of Mississippi, 2011.

INDEX

This index gives broad and representative coverage to Mississippi figures, places, and other topics pertinent to state literature and its context. Persons and places from outside Mississippi are included when deemed significant for the poets' careers or of importance to literary history. Universities, especially those within the region, are listed often in connection with poets' degrees and professional careers. The index includes likewise major awards, prizes, and certain important or historically significant periodicals. Recurrent themes, motifs, and aspects of versification appear as appropriate, as do the names of authors quoted, including those in the preface.

Williams, Miller, 151, 217, 218
Williams, Tennessee, x, 84, 111, 117
Williams, William Carlos, 24, 27, 29, 30, 83,
     89, 90, 91–92, 165, 195
Wilson, Edmund, 181
Wilson, James Matthew, 109
Winchell, Mark Royden, 4
Winters, Yvor, 5, 6, 49, 55, 67, 160
Women and women's interests, 29, 32,
     46, 71–72, 79, 80, 83, 84, 131, 210, 213,
     219. *See also* Abortion; Domesticity;
     Embodiment; Eroticism; Feminism and
     feminists; Misogyny; Stillbirth
Wood, 60
Wood, John, 131
Wordsworth, William, 111, 120
World War I, 77, 158, 162, 189, 220, 221
World War II, 62, 64, 82, 123, 174, 177, 183, 184,
     217, 226
Wright, C. D., 41, 48
Wright, Ellen, 211, 228
Wright, Julia, 230
Wright, Richard, ix, 98, 136, 209–10, 211, 214,
     215, 227–31
Wright, William, 48
Writers' conferences, 3. *See also* Furious
     Flower Conference and journal
Wyatt-Brown, Bertram, 158
Wyman, Hastings, 174

Yale Review, 159
Yale University Press, 62, 210
Yazoo River, 6
Yeats, William Butler, 26, 32, 46, 120, 192
Yerby, Frank, 209
Yoga, 46, 79, 83, 87
Yoknapatawpha, 8
Yoknapatawpha Press, 6, 14
Young, Al, 232–39
Young, Stark, x, 117

Zen Buddhism. *See* Buddhism
Zimbabwe, 167

Zion National Park, 47
Zukovsky, Louis, 89

ABOUT THE AUTHOR

Catharine Savage Brosman, professor emerita at Tulane University, specializes in both French and American literature, particularly poetry. Among her scholarly books are *Louisiana Creole Literature: A Historical Study*; *Southwestern Women Writers and the Vision of Goodness*; and *Louisiana Poets: A Literary Guide*, the latter published by University Press of Mississippi. A poet herself, she has published eleven collections of verse, and the twelfth collection is forthcoming in 2020.

ABOUT THE CONTRIBUTOR

Olivia McNeely Pass, who is retired from Nicholls State University, specializes in American literature and the teaching of composition. She served as editor of the *Louisiana English Journal* (1992–2000) and for three years was on the staff of the Louisiana Endowment for the Humanities. Her scholarly interests include Hawthorne, Welty, and Louisiana writers as well as poetry. She is coauthor of *Louisiana Poets: A Literary Guide*.

CPSIA information can be obtained
at www.ICGtesting.com
Printed in the USA
BVHW072152190720
583890BV00001B/1/J